The Iconography
of Preface and Miniature
in the Byzantine Gospel Book

The publication of this monograph has
been aided by a grant from the Samuel
H. Kress Foundation.

Frontispiece. Parma. Bibl. Palatina, MS gr. 5, f.5r, Prefaces of Irenaeus.

ROBERT S. NELSON

〃

The Iconography
of Preface and Miniature
in the Byzantine Gospel Book

PUBLISHED BY

NEW YORK UNIVERSITY PRESS

for the College Art Association of America

NEW YORK 1980

Monographs on Archaeology and the Fine Arts
sponsored by
THE ARCHAEOLOGICAL INSTITUTE OF AMERICA
and
THE COLLEGE ART ASSOCIATION OF AMERICA
XXXVI
Editor:
Isabelle Hyman

Library of Congress Cataloging in Publication Data

Nelson, Robert S   1947–
    The Iconography of Preface and Miniature in the
Byzantine Gospel Book.

    (Monographs on archaeology and the fine arts; 36)
    Based on the author's thesis.
    Includes bibliographical references and index.
    1. Illumination of books and manuscripts,
Byzantine.   2.   Evangeliaries.   I.   Title.
II.   Series: Monographs on archaeology and fine
arts; 36.
ND2930.N44   745.6'7487   80–15335
ISBN 0–8147–5756–1

In Memory of L. K. N. and R. R. N.

Contents

Acknowledgments

The following study began as part of my doctoral dissertation on a Byzantine illuminated manuscript in the Patriarchal collections in Istanbul (cod. 3) and was prompted by the epigrams accompanying the full-page evangelist symbols in that book. As one thing led to another, I gradually saw that the Istanbul miniatures and their verses were part of a much larger issue, namely the relation of evangelist symbols to various texts found in Greek Gospel books. My original plans were to treat the subject in a monograph on the Patriarchate manuscript, but as the research developed it became apparent that a more extended analysis of the affiliation of text and image would be necessary and that the presentation of this work would no longer be possible within the confines of a study on one particular manuscript. Thus, only a portion of the material collected was ever included in the dissertation. However, the basic thesis of Chapters II–V was described in a paper read at the annual meeting of the College Art Association in January 1976.

Many organizations aided my graduate studies, and I want to cite here the generous support from the American Research Institute in Turkey and the Samuel H. Kress Foundation and its director, Miss Mary K. Davis. With their help I was able to make the necessary tour of European collections of Greek manuscripts. Much of the actual research and writing was undertaken in that most ideal of surroundings, the impressive library and gardens of the Dumbarton Oaks Center for Byzantine Studies in Washington, D.C. For their hospitality I wish to thank the then Director, Mr. William R. Tyler, and Director of Studies, Professor William C. Loerke. The librarian, Ms. Irene Vaslev, and her staff made a very good situation even better by their constant attention to the needs of the resident fellows, and from my colleagues at Dumbarton Oaks I learned a great deal about Byzantine studies. Elsewhere I owe thanks to the many institutions that allowed me access to their materials, and the list of manuscripts cited in the Index documents in detail my debt. Readers of the final chapter will perceive how much those findings were based on research done at the Institut für Neutestamentliche Textforschung in Münster, West Germany, and there I wish to acknowledge the generosity of the Director, Professor Kurt Aland, and his associate, Dr. Klaus Junack. Profitable work was also undertaken in another major archive of microfilms, the Patriarchal Institute for Patristic Studies in Thessaloniki.

Many people have aided and abetted the present project, and the top of the list must be accorded to my doctoral adviser, Professor Hugo Buchthal, whose excellent courses on Byzantine art I will always remember. At the beginning of my manuscript explorations, I had the good fortune to participate in a seminar on Greek palaeography taught by Professor Linos Politis and sponsored by the Medieval Academy of America, and that experience has proved most useful. Several scholars have reviewed portions of my study, and their comments have definitely improved the final product. These include Professors John Duffy, Michael Jacoff, Herbert Kessler, Thomas Mathews, Linda Seidel, Dr. Temily Mark-Weiner, and an anonymous reader. In addition, many specific points were clarified by discussions with Professors Hans Belting, Harry Bober, Anthony Bryer, James Carder, Annemarie Weyl Carr, Vassilios Christides, Anthony Cutler, Ms. Robin Darling, Professors Ioli Kalavrezou-Maxeiner, Robert Kaster, Charles McClendon, Henry and Eunice McGuire, Paul and Ruth Magdalino, Ira Mark, John Nesbitt, Nicolas Oikonomides, Jean Owens Schaefer, Ihor Ševčenko, Kathleen Shelton, Ioannis Spatharakis, Cecil Striker, Warren Treadgold, and David Wright. Also I wish to thank Mr. Rolf Achilles, Dr. Robert Allison, Dr. Charlotte Lacaze, Ms. Laura Nelke, Ms. Judith O'Neill, Dr. Maria Panayotidi, and Dr. Bohumila Zásterová for aid in securing photographs. For some especially difficult to obtain images Professor Kurt Weitzmann most generously offered me his original prints. The University of Chicago through the efforts of Dean Karl Weintraub and Professor Charles Cohen provided financial assistance in preparing the final manuscript, and Ms. Diane Ignashev and Ms. Carolyn McCue did much of the typing. The University's art librarian, Mr. Scott Stapleton, as a matter of course solved problems large and small in securing needed books, and my colleagues in the Department of Art routinely furnished appropriate dosages of balm and coffee to promote the completion of the project. Finally, my editor, Professor Isabelle Hyman, has employed her considerable talents in transforming my manuscript into a College Art Association Monograph. To all the above as well as those that I have neglected to name I express my appreciation and gratitude.

Chicago
April 1979

Two events that have transpired since the above was written deserve comment. As this manuscript was about to be printed, all the photographs collected for the plates were stolen. I want to thank Ms. Despina Papazoglou of New York University Press and Mr. Stephen Stinehour of Meriden Gravure for working diligently and efficiently to replace the lost material. Those people who helped before to secure photographs have once more been called upon, and thus my debt to them has now doubled. Second, I wish to draw the reader's attention to the publication in recent months of George Galavaris' study, *The Illustrations of the Prefaces in Byzantine Gospels* (Vienna, 1979), which has appeared too late to be considered in my study. Although Professor Galavaris and I have treated similar problems, our discussions of various manuscripts and our conclusions about the general phenomenon of illustrated prefaces differ.

May 1980

Abbreviations

ActaArch Acta Archaeologica
AJA American Journal of Archaeology
AnalBoll Analecta Bollandiana
ArtB Art Bulletin
BGrottaf Bollettino della Badia greca di Gottaferrata
ByzF Byzantinische Forschungen
BZ Byzantinische Zeitschrift
CahArch Cahiers Archéologiques
CahCM Cahiers de Civilisation Médiévale, Xe–XIIe siècles
Δελτ. Χριστ. 'Αρχ. 'Ετ. Δελτίον τῆς Χριστιανικῆς 'Αρχαιολογικῆς 'Εταιρείας
DOP Dumbarton Oaks Papers
EO Echos d'Orient. Revue d'histoire, de géographie et de liturgie orientales
'Επ. 'Ετ. Βυζ. Σπ. 'Επετηρὶς 'Εταιρείας Βυζαντινῶν Σπουδῶν
GBA Gazette des Beaux-Arts
HThR Harvard Theological Review
JHS Journal of Hellenic Studies
JÖB Jahrbuch der Österreichischen Byzantinistik
JTS Journal of Theological Studies
JWalt Journal of the Walters Art Gallery
JWarb Journal of the Warburg and Courtauld Institutes

MémAcInscr Mémoires de l'Institut national de France, Académie des Inscriptions et Belles-Lettres
MünchJb Münchner Jahrbuch der bildenden Kunst
OrChr Oriens Christianus
PAPS Proceedings of the American Philosophical Society
PG Patrologiae cursus completus, Series Graeca, ed. J.-P. Migne
PL Patrologiae cursus completus, Series Latina, ed. J.-P. Migne
RBK Reallexikon zur Byzantinischen Kunst, ed. K. Wessel (Stuttgart, 1963–)
REB Revue des Études Byzantines
REG Revue des Études Grecques
RepKunstw Repertorium für Kunstwissenschaft
RIASA Rivista dell'Istituto Nazionale di Archeologia e Storia dell'Arte
RQ Römische Quartalschrift für christliche Altertumskunde und Kirchengeschichte
RSBN Rivista di Studi Bizantini e Neoellenici
TU Texte und Untersuchungen zur Geschichte der altchristlichen Literatur (Leipzig-Berlin, 1882–)
VizVrem Vizantijskij Vremennik
ZKunstg Zeitschrift für Kunstgeschichte

List of Illustrations

I   Introduction

The distinct majority of all the Greek manuscripts written during the Middle Ages were religious, comprising service books for the liturgy, biographies of saints, collections of sermons, theological treatises, and of course the Bible. The latter was seldom written in a single codex but would be divided into appropriate units of the Old and New Testaments. Although the Old Testament in Greek, known as the Septuagint, is a prime document of Jewish-Hellenistic literature, it is not as important for biblical scholars as the New Testament, which represents the original, untranslated version of the basic tenets of Christianity. Today approximately five thousand copies of some portion of the Greek New Testament are extant, and since the sixteenth century textual critics have been engaged in identifying, describing, and analyzing this large body of material with the goal of ascertaining the original form of the text.[1] Their slow, methodical collation of manuscripts now found in hundreds of diverse and often quite remote locations is not without consequence, for they are in effect probing the foundations of the Christian religion. Emendations of Greek texts made during the nineteenth and twentieth centuries have sometimes created controversies that call to mind the disputes with the Old Believers occasioned by the alteration of as much as a single letter of the Russian Bible.[2] The research into the text of the Greek New Testament continues to the present day, the most recent development being the new edition published under the auspices of the United Bible Societies in 1975, one of over one thousand editions that have been printed since the first in 1514.[3]

A portion of these thousands of manuscripts contain decoration of varying types, and the study of this illumination also has a long and distinguished history. Because Byzantine art frequently preserves forms that are centuries old, the illustrations in Greek biblical manuscripts have been analyzed with increasing frequency for the last century. Within the category of Byzantine art, manuscript illumination historically has received perhaps the greatest attention, and among the components of this subspecialty certainly illustrations in copies of the four Gospels have played an important role.[4] Kondakoff, the principal early investigator of Byzantine illumination and in some sense the founder of Byzantine art history, treated the subject in his *Histoire de l'art byzantin considéré principalement dans les miniatures,* translated from the Russian edition of 1876.[5] Another Russian, Pokrovskiĭ, discussed the iconographic traditions of Gospel illustration in his book of 1892.[6] German scholars of the late nineteenth century took up the subject of the sixth-century illustrated codex in Rossano with the resulting studies of von Gebhardt and Harnack of 1880 [7] and Haseloff of 1889.[8] The French in the early years of the present century also made substantial contributions in the facsimile publication by Omont of the extensively illustrated eleventh-century Gospels in Paris (Bibl. Nat. gr. 74) [9] and in the vast study of Byzantine Gospel iconography by Millet of 1916.[10] Between the two world wars there appeared various papers such as the one by Der Nersessian on the later Slavonic copies of Paris, gr. 74,[11] and the multivolume collaborative studies on the Rockefeller McCormick New Testament and the Gospels from Karahissar by scholars at the University of Chicago.[12] In the latter, both the biblical text and the pictorial cycles were investigated with a resulting synthesis that remains exceptional.

In the years after World War II a number of new publications have appeared on manuscripts from as early as the sixth-century Sinope Gospels,[13] to the tenth-century Paris, Bibl. Nat. gr. 115; [14] the extensively illustrated Gospel Book in Florence, Bibl. Laur. Plut. VI, 23, of the twelfth century; [15] or an early-thirteenth-century Gospels in Berlin.[16] Der Nersessian and others have continued to publish on Paris, gr. 74; [17] and studies have been made of illuminated Gospels written in Armenian [18] and Syriac,[19] although much more could be learned by analysis of related material in Georgian,[20] Arabic,[21] and Coptic.[22] The problems have been extended also to include the evidence of monumental painting; for example, in the recently published survey of the mosaics and frescoes at the fourteenth-century Constantinopolitan Church of the Chora.[23] Finally, mention must certainly be made of the significant researches of

Weitzmann on Byzantine Gospel lectionaries, the service book of the liturgy with readings arranged in the order of the church calendar. He has shown the mutual interaction of the Gospel and lectionary illustration in the tenth and succeeding centuries and thereby has contributed to the increased understanding of both types of illuminated manuscripts.[24]

The consequence of over two centuries of textual criticism and about one century of art-historical investigation is a reasonably clear understanding of the canonical text of the Greek Gospels and their accompanying illustrations. Yet there is more to be found in a typical manuscript of the four Gospels than just the accounts of Matthew, Mark, Luke, and John, and similarly one also encounters illustrations that do not pertain to the narrative of the four evangelists. In the category of supplemental elements practically ubiquitous are the useful chapter divisions (κεφαλαία) and their accompanying titles (τίτλοι), and often before each Gospel there is appended a list of these chapter titles that functions then as a table of contents.[25] Another series of divisions of the Gospels belongs to the system of concordance devised by Eusebius of Caesarea in the fourth century. By means of his preliminary tabulations, known as canon tables, the reader can determine which passages in one Gospel find parallels in the others.[26] The letter of Eusebius written to Carpianus explains the use of the tables and is frequently included along with them.[27] Finally, various other texts, to be presented shortly, often function as prefaces or postfaces to the four Gospels as a whole or to the individual books separately.[28]

Corresponding to the supplementary texts, there are categories of illustration that have no connection with the text of the Gospels per se. Chief among these are the portraits of the four evangelists, the most common subjects for illustration in medieval Gospel manuscripts. Their inclusion derives from the ancient custom of depicting the author before the beginning of his treatise, and no doubt such portraits, because of their widespread use, were the easiest figurative illustration for an artist to execute. In addition, the Eusebian canon tables often are given a highly ornamental form through the use of framing columns and arches with birds and fountains above. The accompanying epistle of Eusebius may be set within similar arches or may be written to fit into a decorated frame in the shape of a rectangle or a quatrefoil. Both the representations of the evangelists and the canon tables have been the subject of extensive study, and one should cite in this regard the efforts of Friend, Weitzmann, and Buchthal for the former [29] and the fundamental monograph by Nordenfalk on the latter.[30]

The basic development of these themes, therefore, is well known by now, but if one looks further into other varieties of illumination in Byzantine Gospel books, the situation is by no means so clear. It is not easy even to characterize the range of subject matter encountered, and thus explanations for the use of certain subjects are less forthcoming. One is reduced to citing examples of studies of particular themes, such as the recent note by Meredith [31] and the further comments of Weitzmann [32] on the practice of pairing certain biblical or extrabiblical scenes with a particular Gospel, and the analyses of Tsuji and Der Nersessian of the figural headpieces of Paris, gr. 74.[33] Also, lately there have been the discussions of the iconography of the Deesis,[34] the general subject of portraits in Byzantine manuscripts,[35] a peculiar miniature of the Ancient of Days set before the Gospel of Luke in a Cambridge manuscript,[36] and cycles of labors of the months and the virtues or series of prophets or apostles decorating the canon tables.[37] The literature, as one can see, is diverse and sporadic, and there have been few systematic treatments of nonnarrative illustrations in Greek Gospel books.

The goal of the present inquiry is to investigate precisely this latter category of illumination in conjunction with a particular body of textual material found in Greek Gospel manuscripts, namely the prologues introducing the various books. The discussion will focus on three themes: evangelist symbols, the *Maiestas Domini,* and portraits of evangelists accompanied by certain figures. These topics will be juxtaposed with prefaces in order to explore the relation of text and image and to define the genesis, evolution, and dissolution of that association. Not all questions related to these three iconographic themes will be broached, nor will the wealth of associations and contexts of the texts themselves be analyzed in full. The task of the present inquiry is more contained and is confined to the areas of conjunction of text and image; or, in mathematical terms, to the convergence of the set of known images of these themes with the set of all prologues.

Two of the three topics are well known to art historians. Evangelist symbols, of course, refer to those apocalyptic beasts found in the visions of the Old Testament and specifically to the four faces of the cherubim, those of the man, the calf, the lion, and the eagle. Their precise connection with the authors of the four Gospels and their appearance in Byzantine illumination are developed in Chapter II. The *Maiestas Domini,* the representation of the Lord God surrounded by these four beasts and possibly the cherubim and seraphim as well, is found throughout medieval art, especially in illuminated manuscripts, and its analysis is the topic of the following chapter. The third subject involves representations of the divine or apostolic inspiration of the evangelists, and the further explanation of this phenomenon in Greek manuscripts is reserved for Chapter IV.

If the visual subjects of the following pages are reasonably familiar to those trained in that field, the various texts presented are undoubtedly more foreign. Indeed, they have even remained outside the interests of centuries of New Testament scholars, perhaps because these prefatory tracts in prose and verse do not belong to the biblical canon and thus have no direct relevance for the establishment of the proper version of the Greek Gospels. Another factor contributing to their neglect could also be the pattern of their appearance. As will be discussed in Chapter V, prologues are characteristic of manuscripts from the ninth and succeeding centuries and thus are to be found in examples of the "Byzantine text" of the Gospels, a later recension and one not as crucial as some for the pursuit of the Urtext.[38]

However, fortunately for the present purposes, that indefatigable compiler of material, Hermann Freiherr von Soden, published a number of prologues and verses in his *Die Schriften des Neuen Testaments* of 1902.[39] Von Soden, who was in fact born in the United States, made a prolonged survey of Greek manuscripts for his edition of the New Testament. Although his work has been criticized subsequently, he is to be credited in the present context for recording the supplementary material he encountered in manuscripts. Yet at the same time he should be faulted for frequently failing to indicate the sources of his texts. Because he at best listed only one or two manuscripts for a particular prologue, von Soden's readings often cannot even be verified, and one is left with no sense of the comparative popularity of particular introductions and with the nagging perception that von Soden may have omitted many texts. Consequently, new editions of the prologues are much desired and would be of interest to all students of Greek manuscripts.

What will make this task both difficult and frustrating is the common tendency among cataloguers of manuscripts to omit notices of prefaces in their published descriptions. Only a small portion of the catalogues of the past ten to twenty years actually take note of the texts in question. Older catalogues of this century, much less those of the nineteenth and eighteenth centuries—frequently the sole sources—completely ignore prologues. As a result, one is obliged to examine personally most manuscripts to determine their precise contents.

Thus, it is not yet possible to make definite conclusions about all the prefaces found in the thousands of manuscripts; but for the present purposes this is not necessary; and it is sufficient here to note the parameters of the material and to comment on the more common texts. Von Soden has already divided the prologues into several categories, and for convenience the numbers he assigns to each passage will be used throughout the following pages. Basically there are two classes of prefaces, those introducing the four Gospels as a whole and those preceding the individual books. In the first group one finds the brief definitions of the onetime bishop of Constantinople, John Chrysostomos (d. 407), on the nature of the Gospels (von Soden, nos. 76, 80, 81) and a longer statement about the Gospels by Irenaeus, a second-century Greek writer, who became a bishop in Gaul (von Soden, no. 82).

The former are brief and offer no incentive to imagery in contrast to the Irenaean piece, which is the more significant for the present art-historical concerns and, probably not coincidentally, is one of the most common prologues. The text, taken from von Soden,[40] is as follows:

Περὶ τῶν τεσσάρων εὐαγγελίων καὶ τῶν δ' εἰκόνων. Ἰστέον, ὅτι τέσσαρά ἐστιν τὰ εὐαγγέλια καὶ οὔτε πλείονα οὔτε ἐλάττονα, ἐπείπερ τέσσαρα τὰ καθολικὰ πνεύματα καὶ τέσσαρα τὰ εὐαγγέλια, πανταχόθεν πνέοντα τὴν ἀφθαρσίαν καὶ ἀναζωπυροῦντα τοὺς ἀνθρώπους. Ἐξ ὧν φανερόν, ὅτι ὁ καθήμενος ἐπὶ τῶν χερουβὶμ φανερωθεὶς τοῖς ἀνθρώποις ἔδωκεν ἡμῖν τετράμορφον τὸ εὐαγγέλιον, καθὼς ὁ Δαυὶδ αἰτούμενος τὴν παρουσίαν αὐτοῦ φησιν <ὁ καθήμενος ἐπὶ τῶν χερουβὶμ ἐμφάνηθι>. Καὶ γὰρ τὰ χερουβὶμ τετραπρόσωπα καὶ τὰ πρόσωπα αὐτῶν εἰκόνες τῆς πραγματείας τοῦ υἱοῦ τοῦ θεοῦ. Τὸ γὰρ ὅμοιον λέοντι τὸ ἔμπρακτον καὶ βασιλικὸν καὶ ἡγεμονικὸν χαρακτηρίζει, τὸ δὲ ὅμοιον μόσχῳ τὴν ἱερουργικὴν καὶ ἱερατικὴν ἐμφαίνει, τὸ δὲ ἀνθρωποειδὲς τὴν σάρκωσιν διαγράφει, τὸ δὲ ὅμοιον ἀετῷ τὴν ἐπιφοίτησιν τοῦ ἁγίου πνεύματος ἐμφανίζει.

On the four Gospels and the four symbols. One must know that there are four Gospels, no more, no less. Since there are four universal winds, there are also four Gospels, blowing immortality from all of them and regenerating men. From these Gospels it is evident that he, who was shown to men sitting on the cherubim, gave us the four-part Gospel, just as David, praying for his advent said, "You who sit on the cherubim show yourself." For the cherubim have four faces, and their faces are the images of the dispensation of the Son of God. The one like the lion indicates the efficacious, royal, and authoritative nature. The one like the calf presents the sacerdotal and priestly nature. The manlike form depicts the incarnation, and the one like the eagle represents the visitation of the Holy Spirit.

The prologue is an abridgment of a portion of his principal work, Ἔλεγκος καὶ ἀνατροπὴ τῆς ψευδονόμου γνώσεως, often known as Adversus Haereses.[41] In it Irenaeus is concerned with refuting various heretical tenets.

Often his is the only surviving witness of small heterodox sects, and thus his text is an important source for the history of early Christianity. In the particular passage that has been adapted for a preface, Irenaeus is stating the orthodox position that there are "four Gospels, no more, no less," in opposition to those that recognized a different canon, or official set of Gospels.[42] He first employs a kind of Pythagorean number symbolism to make parallels to the fourfold nature of the Gospels, saying that the winds are four in number as are the faces of the cherubim. The cherubim are associated with the divine order and with the Lord who dwells among them. David's quote here is from Psalm 79:2, although the phrase used, ὁ καθήμενος ἐπὶ τῶν χερουβίμ, is common to a number of descriptions of the Lord of Hosts in the Septuagint.[43] Irenaeus concludes with his interpretation of the theological significance of each of these four faces, and it is his general argument for a divine rationale for the four-part Gospels that makes the whole passage a suitable introduction to that section of the New Testament.

The third prologue of this type to be mentioned here is one that also deals with the faces of the cherubim and their association with the Gospels. It reads as follows:

Παρασημείωσις τοῦ ἁγίου Ἐπιφανίου περὶ τῶν τεσσάρων εὐαγγελιστῶν. Εἰπέ μοι τὰ τέσσαρα εὐαγγέλια ποῦ ἐγράφησαν καὶ τίς γράψας καὶ εἰς τίνα ἀντίτυπα ἐγένοντο. Τὸ κατὰ Ματθαῖον ἐγράφη ἐν τῇ ἀνατολῇ ὑπὸ Ματθαίου ἑβραικοῖς γράμμασι καὶ διαλέκτῳ ἀντίτυπον ἐν ὁμοιώματι ἀνθρώπου τῶν χερουβίμ. Τὸ κατὰ

Μάρκον ἐγράφη ἐν τῇ Ῥώμῃ ὑπὸ Μάρκου ἐν ὁμοιώματι μόσχου. Τὸ κατὰ Λουκᾶν ἐπιτρέψαντος τοῦ ἁγίου Πέτρου ἐγράφη εἰς ὁμοίωμα λέοντος. Τὸ κατὰ Ἰωάννην ἐγράφη ὑπὸ Ἰωάννου ἐν τῇ Πάτμῳ τῆς Κύπρου[44] εἰς ὁμοίωμα ἀετοῦ ἐπὶ Τραιανοῦ τοῦ βασιλέως, ἐπανελθόντος δὲ αὐτοῦ ἐν τῇ Ἀσίᾳ ἔγραψε τὴν δεκάγολον.[45]

Note of St. Epiphanios on the four evangelists. Tell me where the four Gospels were written and who wrote them and by what antitype they were associated. The Gospel according to Matthew was written in the East by Matthew in Hebraic letters and language. Its antitype is the symbol of the man of the cherubim. The Gospel according to Mark was written in

Rome by Mark under the symbol of the calf. The Gospel according to Luke, bequeathed by St. Paul, was written under the symbol of the lion. The Gospel according to John was written by John on Patmos of Cyprus [sic] under the symbol of the eagle in the time of the emperor Trajan. Returning to Asia, he wrote the decalogue.

The prologue is attributed to St. Epiphanios. In the fourth century there was an Epiphanios of Salamis, who wrote a treatise entitled "On Weights and Measures," preserved today only in Syriac.[46] He discussed the four faces of the cherubim in terms patterned on the doctrines of the second-century author, Irenaeus, but the order that he assigned to the four animals (Matthew, man; Mark, lion; Luke, calf; and John, eagle) is not that of Irenaeus or the above preface. It is rather the scheme used later by St. Jerome.[47] Hence, the preface is unlikely to be the work of Epiphanios, and its origin remains unknown.[48]

Another category of prologues in von Soden's book is the group of biographical notices about the four evangelists. These verbal sketches, naturally, are set before the separate Gospels and function much like the pictorial representations of the authors found in many manuscripts. Von Soden lists a number of texts, of which some are published with only the beginning and ending lines.[49] The more significant prefaces in this class are those attributed to Dorotheus (von Soden, no. 106), termed a martyr and bishop of Tyre, but otherwise unknown,[50] and to Sophronius (von Soden, no. 107), who is given no further designation. The latter might be the seventh-century bishop of Jerusalem, but it should be mentioned that other texts were sometimes falsely assigned to this person.[51] Further research is needed on both sets of biographies.

Prologues pertaining to the Gospels and not merely to the evangelists form another class of prefaces. In terms of content, these texts are not necessarily so distinct from the preceding passages, but in frequency of appearance they are decidedly more common. One popular set is based again upon Irenaeus' *Adversus Haereses* (von Soden, no. 108). Each provides information about the writing of a Gospel, and since they will be referred to later it might be best to present them now: [52]

Ἰστέον ὅτι τὸ κατὰ Ματθαῖον εὐαγγέλιον ἑβραΐδι διαλέκτῳ γραφὲν ὑπ' αὐτοῦ ἐν Ἰερουσαλήμ ἐξεδόθη, ἑρμηνεύθη δὲ ὑπὸ Ἰωάννου· ἐξηγεῖται δὲ τὴν κατὰ ἄνθρωπον τοῦ Χριστοῦ γέννησιν καὶ ἐστιν ἀνθρωπόμορφον τὸ εὐαγγέλιον.

Ἰστέον ὅτι τὸ κατὰ Μάρκον εὐαγγέλιον ὑπηγορεύθη ὑπὸ Πέτρου ἐν Ῥώμῃ· ἐποιήσατο δὲ τὴν ἀρχὴν ἀπὸ τοῦ προφητικοῦ λόγου τοῦ ἐξ ὕψους ἐπιόντος τοῦ Ἠσαΐου τὴν πτερωτικὴν

εἰκόνα τοῦ εὐαγγελίου δεικνύς.

Ἰστέον ὅτι τὸ κατὰ Λουκᾶν εὐαγγέλιον ὑπηγορεύθη ὑπὸ Παύλου ἐν Ῥώμῃ· ἅτε δὲ ἱερατικοῦ χαρακτῆρος ὑπάρχον, ἀπὸ Ζαχαρίου τοῦ ἱερέως θυμιῶντος ἤρξατο.

Ἰστέον ὅτι τὸ κατὰ Ἰωάννην εὐαγγέλιον ἐν τοῖς χρόνοις Τραιανοῦ ὑπηγορεύθη ὑπὸ Ἰωάννου ἐν Πάτμῳ τῇ νήσῳ· διηγεῖται δὲ τὴν ἐπὶ τοῦ πατρὸς ἡγεμονικὴν καὶ πρακτικὴν καὶ ἔνδοξον τοῦ Χριστοῦ γενεάν.

Know that the Gospel according to Matthew, written in the Hebrew language, was published by him in Jerusalem, and was translated by John. The Gospel tells about the birth of Christ as a man, and it is anthropomorphic.

Know that the Gospel according to Mark was dictated by Peter in Rome. It began with the prophetic word of Isaiah, which proceeds from on high,

showing the winged image of the Gospel.

Know that the Gospel according to Luke was dictated by Paul in Rome. Since it is of a priestly character, it began with Zacharias the priest burning incense.

Know that the Gospel of John was dictated in the time of Trajan by John on the island of Patmos. It describes the lordly, real, and glorious generation of Christ from the Father.

Occasionally the preface to Matthew is followed immediately by the general Irenaean introduction to the Gospels,[53] forming one prologue at the beginning of a Gospel book.

Other prefaces to the Gospels are somewhat longer than the few sentences of the above. Though the passages would be separated by many folios in a manuscript, their distinctive character is maintained by the use of parallel language. Thus, one group (von Soden, no. 120) always begins in the following manner: Ὑπόθεσις τοῦ κατὰ Ματθαῖον [or Μάρκον, etc.] εὐαγγελίου. Κατὰ Ματθαῖον εὐαγγέλιον ἐπιγέγραπται ἐπειδὴ αὐτὸς ὁ Ματθαῖος. . . .[54] In manuscripts these prologues are usually found without any attribution, although von Soden says that sometimes Eusebius is mentioned as the author.[55]

In comparison, more is known about two other popular series of prefaces. One is taken from the *Christian Topography* of the sixth-century Alexandrian, Cosmas Indicopleustes (von Soden, no. 122), and these too begin similarly: Ματθαῖος [or Μάρκος, etc.] ὁ εὐαγγελιστής. Οὗτος πρῶτος [or δεύτερος, etc.] . . . .[56] The second set is based on Theophylact of Bulgaria (d. 1108) and is thus later in date.[57] Finally, to complete the discussion of prefaces to the individual Gospels, two forewords to Luke (von Soden, no. 125) and John (von Soden, no. 124) should be cited. The former is said to be by the ninth-century patriarch of Constantinople, Methodius.[58] It will be discussed further in chapter V. According to manuscripts, the prologue to John is by the Antiochene theologian, Theodore of Mopsuestia, and for once the validity of this attribution is not to be doubted, for the passage is taken from Theodore's commentary on the Gospel of St. John, the complete version of which was recently discovered in a Syriac translation.[59]

All the above introductions are written in prose, but there are in addition numerous poems that serve as prefaces to the four Gospels as a whole or to the books individually. These again were collected by von Soden,[60] and when possible his numbering of these texts will be used. They have been studied more recently by A. Komines, who properly printed his sources for the verses and included some that von Soden missed, but unfortunately he did not seem to have known of von Soden's work and consequently ignored other texts found in that compilation.[61] One four-line poem published by both scholars belongs to the category of forewords to the four Gospels and begins appropriately, Ἡ τετρὰς ὧδε τῶν μαθητῶν τοῦ λόγου. . . (von Soden, no. 1). It is the most common of the verses in this category and is occasionally illustrated, as for example in a Gospel book in Istanbul to be discussed later.[62] The poems pertaining to the evangelists were usually written as sets of four, although in any given manuscript verses from one series might be mixed with those from another. Further discussion of the transmission of the poems and their sometime association with evangelist portraits may be found in Chapter IV.

These varied texts in prose and verse are the material that will be juxtaposed on the following pages with the three iconographical themes. Those manuscripts that illustrate the prefaces most directly are treated first. Then follow other miniatures in which the relationship of text and image has become more casual. Scribes and illuminators did not always use the same model for their work, so that their contributions might not always be in accord with each other. Sometimes it is possible to reconstruct an earlier stage of the transmission of miniature and text in which the two were in agreement, but in other cases any trace of that relationship has entirely disappeared. One factor to consider in the latter instances is the effect of various external influences on the iconography. For some subjects the full history of a theme will be followed in order to chart the changing textual affiliations, but in general the discussion will be confined to those instances in which the knowledge of the contents of a Greek Gospel book will contribute to a better understanding of its decoration.

NOTES

1. A recent historiographical discussion may be found in B. M. Metzger, *The Text of the New Testament, Its Transmission, Corruption, and Restoration*, 2d ed. (Oxford, 1968), 95–146 (hereafter, *Text of the New Testament*).
2. Cf. the interesting case of J. W. Burgon, dean of Chichester in the late nineteenth century:

Metzger, *Text of the New Testament*, 135–36.
3. Ibid., 145–46.
4. Considering the differing textual value of the Greek Old and New Testaments, it is curious that Gospel iconography has not been as popular a subject of investigation as the illustration of the Old Testament, where most not-

ably K. Weitzmann has made significant contributions. As an indication of this difference, one may note the relative numbers of Old Testament and New Testament themes chosen for discussion in his review article, "The Study of Byzantine Book Illumination, Past, Present, and Future," *The Place of Book Illumination in Byzantine Art* (Princeton, 1975), 1–60.

5. *Istoriiă vizantiĭskago iskusstva i ikonografii po miniatiŭram grecheskikh rukopiseĭ* (Odessa, 1876). On the Russian contribution see the preface by C. Mango to D. V. Ainalov, the *Hellenistic Origins of Byzantine Art* (New Brunswick, 1961), viii–ix.

6. N. Pokrovskiĭ *Evangelie v pamiătnikakh ikonografii preimushchestvenno vizantiĭskikh i russkikh* (St. Petersburg, 1892).

7. O. von Gebhardt and A. Harnack, *Evangeliorum Codex graecus purpureus Rossanensis* (Berlin, 1880).

8. A Haseloff, *Codex purpureus Rossanensis* (Berlin, 1889).

9. H. Omont, *Évangiles avec peintures byzantines du XIe siècle*, 2 vols. (Paris, 1908).

10. G. Millet, *Recherches sur l'iconographie de l'évangile* (Paris, 1916).

11. S. Der Nersessian, "Two Slavonic Parallels of the Greek *Tetraevangelia:* Paris 74," *ArtB,* 9 (1927), 223–74. Also useful from the same period are the illustrations of Gospel miniatures, most notably those of Paris, Bibl. Nat. gr. 54, in H. Omont, *Miniatures des plus anciens manuscrits de la Bibliothèque Nationale du VIe au XIVe siècle* (Paris, 1929) (hereafter, *Miniatures des plus anciens manuscrits*).

12. E. J. Goodspeed, D. W. Riddle, and H. R. Willoughby, *The Rockefeller McCormick New Testament,* 3 vols. (Chicago, 1932); E. C. Colwell and H. R. Willoughby, *The Four Gospels of Karahissar,* 2 vols. (Chicago, 1936).

13. A. Grabar, *Les peintures de l'évangélaire de Sinope* (Paris, 1948).

14. C. Paschou, "Les peintures dans un tétraévangile de la Bibliothèque Nationale de Paris: le Grec 115 (Xe siècle)," *CahArch,* 22 (1972), 61–86.

15. T. Velmans, *Le tétraévangile de la Laurentienne, Florence, Laur. VI. 23* (Paris, 1971).

16. R. Hamann-MacLean with O. Rössler, "Der Berliner Codex Graecus Quarto 66 und seine nächsten Verwandten als Beispiele des Stilwandels in frühen 13. Jahrhundert," *Studien zur Buchmalerei und Goldschmiedekunst des Mittelalters, Festschrift für Karl Hermann Usener* (Marburg, 1967), 225–50 (hereafter, "Der Berliner Codex"). Mention must be made of the very useful corpora projects by S. M. Pelekanides et al., *The Treasures of Mount Athos,* I (Athens, 1973), II (Athens, 1975; hereafter, *Treasures*), and I. Hutter, *Corpus der byzantinischen Miniaturenhandschriften, I–II, Oxford Bodleian Library,* 1–2 (Stuttgart, 1977–78, hereafter, *Corpus,* I–II).

17. S. Der Nersessian, "Recherches sur les miniatures du Parisinus Graecus 74," *JÖB,* 21 (1972), 109–17; S. Tsuji, "The Headpiece Miniatures and Genealogy Pictures in Paris. Gr. 74," *DOP,* 29 (1975), 165–204 (hereafter, "Paris. Gr. 74").

18. S. Der Nersessian, "Armenian Gospel Illustration as Seen in Manuscripts in American Collections," *New Testament Manuscript Studies,* ed. M. M. Parvis and A. P. Wikgren (Chicago, 1950), 137–50; idem, *Armenian Manuscripts in the Freer Gallery of Art* (Washington, D.C., 1963); idem, *Armenian Manuscripts in the Walters Art Gallery* (Baltimore, 1973; hereafter, *MSS in the Walters Art Gallery*); H. and H. Buschhausen, *Die illuminierten armenischen Handschriften der Mechitharisten—Congregation in Wien* (Vienna, 1976). Most recently see T. F. Mathews, "The Gladzor Gospel Book of U.C.L.A.," *II International Symposium on Armenian Art* (Yerevan, 1978), for a preliminary survey of an important manuscript of 1307 now in Los Angeles.

19. J. Leroy, *Les manuscrits syriaques à peintures conservés dans les bibliothèques d'Europe et d'Orient* (Paris, 1964); C. Cecchelli, J. Furlani, and M. Salmi, *The Rabbula Gospels* (Olten, 1959).

20. The following are general introductions to this subject: H. Machavariani, *Georgian Manuscripts* (Tbilisi, 1970); S. Amiranashvili, *Gruzinskaiă miniatiŭra* (Moscow, 1966).

21. The prime example is an illustrated apocryphal Gospels in Arabic now in Florence. See A. Baumstark, "Ein apokryphes Herrenleben in mesopotamischen Federzeichnungen von Jahre 1299," *OrChr,* N.S., 1 (1911), 249ff.; K. Weitzmann, "The Selection of Texts for Cyclic Illustration in Byzantine Manuscripts," *Byzantine Books and Bookmen* (Washington, D.C., 1975), 78–79 (hereafter, "Selection of Texts"). For an interesting combination of Islamic and Byzantine illumination see J. Leroy, "Un évangéliaire arabe de la

bibliothèque de Topqapi Sarayi à décor byzantin et islamique," *Syria,* 44 (1967), 119–30.

22. The principal manuscripts are Paris, Bibl. Nat. Copte 13, and Paris, Institut Catholique, Copte 1. See J. Leroy, *Les manuscrits coptes-arabes illustrés* (Paris, 1974); M. Cramer, *Koptische Buchmalerei* (Recklinghausen, 1964).

23. Cf the articles of J. Lafontaine-Dosogne, P. A. Underwood, and S. Der Nersessian in *The Kariye Djami,* ed. P. A. Underwood, IV (Princeton, 1975), 195–350. Also, there is the survey article of the surviving evidence in manuscripts and wall painting by K. Wessel, "Evangelienzyklen," *RBK,* cols. 433–51, and another recent review by R. Deshman, "The Illustrated Gospels," *Illuminated Greek Manuscripts from American Collections,* ed. G. Vikan (Princeton, 1973), 40–43 (hereafter, *Illuminated Greek MSS*).

24. His numerous studies on this subject are summarized in Weitzmann, "Selection of Texts," 98–101.

25. Metzger, *Text of the New Testament,* 21–23; Hermann Freiher von Soden, *Die Schriften des Neuen Testaments,* I, 1 (Berlin, 1902), 402–32 (hereafter, von Soden, I, 1).

26. Metzger, *Text of the New Testament,* 24–25; von Soden, I, 1, 387–402.

27. Von Soden I, 1, 387–88.

28. Ibid., 300–327; Metzger, *Text of the New Testament,* 25–26.

29. A. M. Friend, Jr., "The Portraits of the Evangelists in Greek and Latin Manuscripts," *Art Studies,* 5 (1927), 115–50; 7 (1929), 3–29; K. Weitzmann, "The Constantinopolitan Lectionary, Morgan 639," *Studies in Art and Literature for Belle da Costa Greene,* ed. D. Miner (Princeton, 1954), 373; H. Buchthal, "A Byzantine Miniature of the Fourth Evangelist and Its Relatives," *DOP,* 15 (1961), 127–40. See also the fine survey by H. Hunger and K. Wessel, "Evangelisten," *RBK,* cols. 452–507.

30. C. Nordenfalk, *Die spätantiken Kanontafeln,* 2 vols. (Göteborg, 1938); idem, "The Apostolic Canon Tables," *GBA,* 6th ser., 62 (1963), 17–34 (hereafter, "Apostolic Canon Tables"); J. Leroy, "Nouveaux témoins des canons d'Eusèbe illustrés selon la tradition syrique," *CahArch,* 9 (1957), 117–45.

31. C. Meredith, "The Illustration of Codex Ebnerianus. A Study in Liturgical Illustration of

the Comnenian Period," *JWarb,* 29 (1966), 419–24 (hereafter, "Codex Ebnerianus").

32. K. Weitzmann, "An Illustrated Greek New Testament of the Tenth Century in the Walters Art Gallery," *Gatherings in Honor of Dorothy E. Miner,* ed. U. E. McCracken et al. (Baltimore, 1974), 26–30 (hereafter, "An Illustrated Greek New Testament").

33. See note 17 above.

34. C. Walter, "Two Notes on the Deesis," *REB,* 26 (1968), 311–38; idem, "Further Notes on the Deesis," *REB,* 28 (1970), 161–87.

35. I. Spatharakis, *The Portrait in Byzantine Illuminated Manuscripts* (Leiden, 1976).

36. H. Belting, "Stilzwang und Stilwahl in einem byzantinischen Evangeliar in Cambridge," *ZKunstg,* 38 (1975), 225–31 (hereafter, "Stilzwang").

37. On the former: H. Buchthal, "An Illuminated Byzantine Gospel Book of about 1100 A.D.," *Special Bulletin of the National Gallery of Victoria* (Melbourne, 1961), 1–12. On the latter: C. Nordenfalk, "The Apostolic Canon Tables," 17–34. The problem of the association of prophets with the canon tables in East Christian manuscripts is discussed by Der Nersessian, *MSS in the Walters Art Gallery,* 27–28. In addition, one might cite the inclusion of scenes of the life of Christ in the canon tables of a fragmentary manuscript in Berlin, Staatsbibl. Ham. 246. See K. Weitzmann, *Die byzantinische Buchmalerei des 9. und 10. Jahrhunderts* (Berlin, 1935), 68 (hereafter, *Byzantinische Buchmalerei*).

38. On the "Byzantine" text see most recently J. N. Birdsall, "The New Testament Text," *The Cambridge History of the Bible,* I (Cambridge, 1970), 318–23.

39. Von Soden, I, 1, 295–327, 361–84, 388–89.

40. Ibid., 303. Unless otherwise noted, all translations are the author's.

41. *PG,* 7, col. 886. The complete text of Irenaeus is now the Latin translation, but fragments of the original Greek are found in later authors, such as Anastasius Sinaites. See J. Quasten, *Patrology,* III (Utrecht, 1950), 290–329 (hereafter, *Patrology*); F. Sagnard, *Irénée de Lyon, Contre les hérésies. livre III* (Paris, 1952), 80–83 (hereafter, *Irénée*).

42. J. Lawson, *The Biblical Theology of Saint Irenaeus* (London, 1948), 44; A. Benoit, *Saint Irénée, Introduction à l'étude de sa théologie*

(Paris, 1960), 112–35; F. R. Hitchcock, *Irenaeus of Lugdunum, A Study of His Teaching* (Cambridge, 1914), 216–17; W. Neuss, *Das Buch Ezechiel in Theologie und Kunst bis zum Ende des XII. Jahrhunderts* (Münster, 1912), 27–28 (hereafter, *Ezechiel*). On the orthodox contents of the New Testament see the recent discussion by R. M. Grant, "The New Testament Canon," *The Cambridge History of the Bible*, I (Cambridge, 1970), 284–308.

43. I Kings 4:4; II Kings 6:2; IV Kings 19:15; I Chronicles 13:6; Isaiah 37:16.

44. This probably is a corruption. In Athens, Nat. Lib. cod. 57, f. 336r, it says ἐν πάτμῳ τῆς νῆσου, which is slightly better. Best is ἐν τῇ νήσῳ πάτμῳ in another preface—von Soden, I, 1, 307.

45. Von Soden, I, 1, 303–4.

46. On Epiphanios see Quasten, *Patrology*, III, 384–96. For the text about the cherubim: Neuss, *Ezechiel*, 46–47; P. de Lagarde, *Symmicta*, 2 (Göttingen, 1877–80), 190–91. The Syriac text has been translated into English by J. Dean, *Epiphanius' Treatise on Weights and Measures, The Syriac Version* (Chicago, 1935), 52. The most recent discussion of the treatise is E. D. Moutsoulas, "L'oeuvre d'Epiphane de Salamine 'De mensuris et ponderibus' et son unité littéraire," *TU*, 115 (1975), 119–22.

47. The agreement between Epiphanios and Jerome in the matter of the cherubim may be more than mere coincidence, since Jerome respected him highly and was his friend. See Quasten, *Patrology*, III, 385.

48. It may be only a later compilation of the fairly common information about the origins of the Gospels together with descriptions of the forms of the cherubim. For similar short biographies of the evangelists see von Soden, I, 1, 305 (nos. 90–91), 311 (no. 108). The name Epiphanios may have been attached to all this in order to give the preface a Patristic origin comparable to the more common prologue of Irenaeus (ibid., 303 [no. 82]). This pairing of the symbols is found in a treatise by the Pseudo-Athanasius (*PG*, 28, col. 432), another example of what probably is a later text assigned to a prominent early writer. See Quasten, *Patrology*, III, 39.

49. Von Soden, I, 1, 305–10.

50. Ibid., 307–8. Dorotheus is unknown to W. H. P. Hatch, *Facsimiles and Descriptions of Minuscule Manuscripts of the New Testament* (Cambridge, Mass., 1951), 29 (hereafter, *Facsimiles*), and to Metzger, *Text of the New Testament*, 25. The texts are also printed in the *PG*, 123, cols. 489, 685, 1129. It is perhaps relevant here to note that Eusebius in his *Ecclesiastical History* mentions a Dorotheus presbyter of Antioch. He became a good friend of the emperor, who put him in charge of the "purple-dye works at Tyre." Dorotheus knew Hebrew well, and Eusebius says that he "heard him giving a measured exposition of the Scriptures in Church." *Ecclesiastical History* 7, 32, 2–4. No writings are assigned to him by Eusebius, nor does Quasten mention any modern attributions. See Quasten, *Patrology*, II, 144.

51. Von Soden, I, 1, 308–10; *PG*, 123, cols. 140, 488, 684, 1128–29. The attribution is accepted by Hatch and Metzger in the references cited in the preceding note. On Sophronius see H.-G. Beck, *Kirche und theologische Literatur im byzantinischen Reich* (Munich, 1959), 434–36 (hereafter, *Kirche*). For a liturgical commentary falsely assigned to Sophronius see R. Bornert, *Les commentaires byzantins de la divine liturgie du VIIe au XVe siècle* (Paris, 1966), 210–11 (hereafter, *Commentaires*).

52. Von Soden, I, 1, 311.

53. Ibid.

54. Ibid., 314–16.

55. Ibid., 314.

56. Ibid., 316–21.

57. Ibid., 321–26.

58. Ibid., 327.

59. Ibid., 326. See also Quasten, *Patrology*, III, 406–7; R. Devreesse, *Essai sur Theodore de Mopsueste* (Vatican, 1948), 305–6.

60. Von Soden, I, 1, 377–84.

61. A. Th. Kominis, "Συναγωγὴ ἐπιγραμμάτων εἰς τοὺς τέσσαρας εὐαγγελιστάς," Ἐπ. Ἐτ. Βυζ. Σπ. (hereafter, "Συναγωγὴ ἐπιγραμμάτων"), 21 (1951), 254–79. On the epigrams see also E. Follieri, "Epigrammi sugli Evangelisti dai codici Barberiniani greci 352 e 520," *BGrottaf*, N.S., 10 (1956), 60–80, 135–56.

62. R. S. Nelson, "Text and Image in a Byzantine Gospel Book in Istanbul (Ecumenical Patriarchate, cod. 3)," Ph.D. dissertation, New York University, New York, 1978, 187–97 (hereafter, "Text and Image"). For a brief summary of these arguments see idem,

"Michael the Monk and His Gospel Book," *Actes du XVe Congrès international d'études byzantines,* in press (hereafter, "Michael the Monk"). The full text in translation is as follows:

Here the quaternity of the disciples of the Word pours forth as a stream of ever flowing words. Therefore he who thirsts does not shrink from imbibing, watering his soul and giving drink to his mind.

II The Symbols of the Evangelists

The principal subject of two of the general Gospel prologues quoted in the preceding discussion is the four faces of the cherubim and their affiliation with the Gospels or the evangelists; for this reason it is appropriate to begin with an analysis of these symbols. Concentrating on the evidence of illuminated manuscripts, the history of the theme will be traced into the Post-Byzantine era in order to observe its full development. For Western Europe, the consideration of such a time span from the early medieval to the Baroque periods would be rather difficult owing to the myriads of surviving examples of the subject. Yet the effort is more manageable for Byzantium, for here symbols are never as common as in the West, nor do they appear as early in illuminated manuscripts. Perhaps because of this comparative rarity, problems do arise in the iconography of the Byzantine symbols, since their association with a particular evangelist varies considerably, making it necessary to study the theme over an extended period. In contrast, after the early Middle Ages the pairing of symbol and evangelist proposed by St. Jerome becomes firmly established in Europe, so that this particular issue ceases to be of much scholarly interest; [1] and today students of Christian iconography would readily take Jerome's ordering of Matthew—man, Mark—lion, Luke—calf, and John—eagle to be the standard, correct interpretation.

The iconography of Byzantine evangelist symbols has been discussed frequently since the late nineteenth century, but usually only in passing, and partly as a result, the opinion of one of the first Byzantine art historians, Kondakoff, has often been repeated to the present day. Kondakoff thought that the appearance of symbols in Byzantine art was due to Western influence,[2] a position followed by Gerstinger, Wulff, Dölger, Neuss, Nordenfalk, and most recently, Nilgen and Frolow.[3] Against this dominant view, Lazarev and Boeckler argued for early pre-Iconoclastic Eastern models for the Middle Byzantine manuscripts,[4] and Buchthal, Rosenbaum, and Bruce-Mitford doubted the existence of such early examples.[5] Kitzinger stressed that in contrast to Western medieval art the connection between the apocalyptic beasts and the symbols was "little known" in the East.[6] A brief survey of the literature on the problem has recently been given by Alexander concerning an Oxford manuscript,[7] and a somewhat more extended discussion is presented by Vikan in a catalogue entry on a Gospel book in the Harvard College Library. Vikan's succinct analysis is the most useful study of Byzantine symbols yet to appear. Concerning the matter of Western influence, he cautiously refrains from giving an opinion,[8] and that issue is best postponed until the evidence presented by the various manuscripts themselves is analyzed.

The evangelist symbols under discussion may be divided into three chronological categories: (1) the tenth to the early thirteenth century, or approximately the Middle Byzantine period; (2) the Palaeologan era, 1261–1453; and (3) the Post-Byzantine period after 1453. Of the three, the first category is the most significant for the relation of prefaces to miniatures, but the later epochs are of interest in and for themselves and for the subsequent history of the earlier developments. The material to be studied is tabulated in Appendix I. Tables A and B present all the monuments of the first group that are known to this writer. Table C, devoted to the time of the Palaeologan dynasty, concentrates more on the evidence from illuminated manuscripts without pretension for completeness; Tables D and E represent only a sampling of works of art after 1453 with identified symbols of the evangelists. These monuments, then, are the visual evidence that will be juxtaposed with various prologues in order to assess the character, extent, and chronological range of the influence of such introductions on the patterns of iconographic usage. As will become clear, that impact is by no means uniform or consistent, and for once it is the art of Byzantium, not Western Europe, that has the more complex iconographic history.

MIDDLE BYZANTINE PERIOD

All but two of the examples listed in Tables A and B are from manuscripts. The exceptions are a twelfth-century enameled pendant with an image of the *Maiestas Domini* in which symbols are inscribed with the names of the evangelists [9] and a fragmentary fresco of the same subject at Corfu from the years 1074 to 1075. [10]

The earliest works include a Gospel book written in Capua in 991 with symbols in the initials [11] and two other Gospel manuscripts from the second half of the eleventh century, Athens, Nat. Lib. cod. 57 (fig. 2), [12] and Moscow, Hist. Mus. gr. 13. [13] In the latter two books the symbols are placed above the headpieces at the beginning of the Gospels. This enumeration of early manuscripts with symbols intentionally omits what has heretofore been considered to be the first example of symbols in a Greek manuscript, namely those framed by medallions and set in the margins of the renowned tenth-century Gospels in the Stavronikita Monastery at Mt. Athos, cod. 43 (figs. 73–74). Closer scrutiny has shown that these symbols are later additions, and the argument is advanced in Appendix II that the alteration may have occurred in the Palaeologan era for reasons, however, that are still puzzling.

The Preface of Epiphanios

Six different ways of pairing evangelists and symbols are listed in Table B. Greek prologues account for two of these systems and suggest an explanation for the unparalleled iconographic diversity of Byzantine symbols. The interaction between text and image is best seen in the first group in which the man is matched with Matthew, the calf with Mark, the lion with Luke, and the eagle with John. The scheme is found in two prologues. One is a brief passage on the association of the four heads of the cherubim with the evangelists. The text has been noted in manuscripts in Milan (Bibl. Ambros. H. 13 of the eleventh century) [14] and Rome (Vatican gr. 1548 of the eleventh century [15] and gr. 1254 of the tenth or eleventh century [16]); it reads as follows:

Τάδε τὰ τέσσαρα χερουβίμ.
Τὸ κατὰ Ματθαῖον ὅμοιον ἀν(θρώπ)ου.
Τὸ κατὰ Μάρκον ὅμοιον μόσχου.

Τὸ κατὰ Λουκᾶν ὅμοιον λέοντος.
Τὸ κατὰ Ἰω(άννην) ὅμοιον ἀετῷ.
Αὐτὴ ἡ διδαχὴ τοῦ χερουβίμ. Ἀμήν.

These are the four cherubim:

The Gospel according to Matthew is like the man.

The Gospel according to Mark is like the calf.

The Gospel according to Luke is like the lion.

The Gospel according to John is like the eagle.

This is the doctrine of the cherubim. Amen.

The passage is little known, since von Soden did not publish it. Although it could scarcely be more explicit about the evangelist symbols, in none of the three manuscripts is this subject illustrated, nor has any influence of the text been detected in other manuscripts.

For this reason, the second preface is the more important for the present discussion. It is the prologue attributed in manuscripts to Epiphanios and the one introduced in the preceding chapter. It gives a brief biography of each of the evangelists and in the process notes which face of the cherubim is to be associated with each man. This text is without a doubt more common than the preceding passage; therefore the arrangement of symbols found in both will be termed, for convenience, the order of Epiphanios. But it must be remembered that the appellation denotes this particular prologue, not the writings of the fourth-century author of that name, for, as mentioned above, Epiphanios of Salamis actually gave a different interpretation to the symbols.

The earliest of the six manuscripts with the arrangement of symbols found in the preface is a Gospels in the National Library in Athens, cod. 57, from the third quarter of the eleventh century.[17] Besides canon tables and evangelist portraits, the book is decorated with headpieces above which are medallions containing the evangelist symbols (fig. 2). A cross and the identifying name of the evangelist indicate that these images are not merely decorative like most animals atop such panels. The evangelist portraits appear on the facing versos in their standard position before the opening of the Gospel (fig. 1).

The book contains several prologues mentioning the evangelist symbols. On f. 104v at the conclusion of the Gospel of Matthew the following appears:

Τὸ κατὰ Ματθαῖον εὐαγγέλιον ἐγράφη ὑπ' αὐτοῦ ἐν τῇ ἀνατολῇ ἑβραΐδι διαλέκτῳ καὶ γράμμασιν ἑβραϊκοῖς καὶ ἐξεδόθη ἐν Ἰ(ερουσα)λήμ· ἑρμηνεύθη δὲ ὑπὸ Ἰωάννου καί ἐστι ἀνθρωπόμορφον.[18]

The Gospel according to Matthew was written by him in the East in Hebraic language and letters and was published in Jerusalem and translated by John. It has the human form [as symbol].

This is a version of the part of the Epiphanios text pertaining to Matthew. Such variations are commonly encountered, because the prologues were seldom standardized. The passage about Mark is found on f. 106v (fig. 3) at the end of the chapter lists for that Gospel:

Τὸ κατὰ Μάρκον εὐα(γγέλιον) ἐγράφη ἐν τῇ Ῥώμῃ ὑπ' αὐτοῦ ἐν ὁμοιώματι μόσχου.

The Gospel according to Mark was written by him in Rome under the symbol of the calf.

The calf follows on f. 108r (fig. 2) after the evangelist portrait (fig. 1), and as a result the text is closer to the image in this case. Finally, the notes about Luke and John, like the one for Matthew, come at the end of the Gospels:

Τὸ δὲ κατὰ Λουκᾶν εὐαγγέλιον ἐπιτρέψαντος τοῦ ἁγίου πέτρου ἐγράφη εἰς ὁμοίωμα λέοντος.

The Gospel according to Luke, bequeathed by St. Peter, was written under the symbol of the lion.

Τὸ κατὰ Ἰωάννην εὐαγγέλιον ἐγράφη ἐν Πάτμῳ τῆς νήσου ὑπ' αὐτοῦ ὡς ὁμοίωμα ἀετοῦ.

The Gospel according to John was written by him on the island of Patmos under the symbol of the eagle.

The latter three prefaces also are much like the prologue of Epiphanios, although the statement that Luke's Gospel was derived from St. Peter is a corruption and agrees neither with the basic prologues nor with the established tradition on this matter.[19] The arrangement of the symbols corresponds exactly to these prefaces in the manuscript, and the scribe's decision to subdivide the preface made the association of text and image even clearer. That the scribe or the book's patron was interested in the symbols of the evangelists is further demonstrated by the subsequent notes at the end of the book; here there is written the second half of the general prologue of Irenaeus (von Soden, no. 82) in which he defines the spiritual significance of each animal ("the lion indicates the efficacious, royal, and authoritative nature," etc.).[20] Thus, Athens 57 has a logical and consistent program of symbols and prologues.

Often, however, this careful coordination of text and image was disrupted, as scribes and illuminators followed separate traditions. Such is the case with most of the other manuscripts in the first category of Table B. The second book, Athens, Nat. Lib. cod. 163, is a lectionary of the late eleventh or early twelfth century and at present is decorated with the portraits of Matthew, Luke, and John, each accompanied by symbols.[21] Although the pairing used is that of Athens 57, the manuscript contains no prologue, nor, as a rule, do other Greek lectionaries.[22] It would seem, then, that the illuminator was either copying the portraits of a *tetraevangelium* or adhering to some iconographic tradition originating in such a manuscript. Two Gospel books, Vienna, Nat. Lib. Suppl. Gr. 164, dated 1109,[23] and Holkham Hall cod. 4 of the twelfth century (fig. 4) [24] also employ the order of symbols found in the prologue of Epiphanios, but again neither has the actual text. Then too the opposite situation may be encountered. Thus, although a portion of this preface is present in Manchester, John Rylands Lib. ms. gr. 13, the symbols are arranged in a different manner (Category III). In fact, the contents of the entire manuscript are rather confused; only the Gospel of Mark is introduced by a prologue, and hence the book lacks a complete series of prefatory texts.[25]

The last two Gospels with the system of Epiphanios are, strictly speaking, not Byzantine. One is a Georgian manuscript, and the other, though Greek, was written in Seljuk Anatolia, but both seem to depend upon Byzantine models. The former book is known as the Ghelati Gospels and is now in Tbilisi (MSS Institute of the Academy of Sciences, MS No. A 908, fig. 5). Its evangelist portraits are fine examples of the manneristic style of late Comnenian art, and a cursory study of its narrative scenes suggests that the iconography is, in the main, Byzantine. This probably is due both to the models used and to the place of execution, the Iviron Monastery on Mount Athos, according to Lazarev and Amiranashvili.[26] Its evangelist portraits are inscribed in Greek and show the author seated before his desk. In the sky above, an animal flies down to him. Like Byzantine portraits, such as those in Vienna, Suppl. Gr. 164, or in Athens, cod. 163, the symbol is placed in the upper right corner of the frame. Luke here (fig. 5) is paired with the lion, and the rest of the symbols are arranged in the manner of Epiphanios. Unfortunately, however, there has been some confusion in this matter, because engravings of 1900 made after the manuscript by Prince Gagarine show the symbols of Mark and Luke reversed. The result is to change the order to that of St. Jerome and of European art in general.[27] These reproductions have achieved a certain prominence because they were included in the Index of Christian Art, and the error has thus been perpetuated. This and other publications by Gagarine, one of the earliest to reproduce Byzantine works of art extensively, are noticeably inaccurate,[28] and one wonders if he might not have even "corrected" the miniatures to align the symbols with the then more common and to him more proper scheme of St. Jerome. If so, the situation would have precedents as early as the Palaeologan period, as noted below.

The other example of the Epiphanios order is found in a curious little Gospel book in the Gennadeion Library in Athens, MS 1.5, with scribal colophons in Greek and Armenian, saying that it was written by Basil *protonotarius* in

Caesarea in 1226 under the Seljuk sultan Kayqubād.[29] The style of the miniatures is provincial, but the iconography follows perfectly the tradition first seen
in Athens 57. The Epiphanios preface is written on f. 1v inside an ornamental
frame (fig. 6), and subsequently the symbols are placed in the exterior margins
of the initial page of each Gospel (fig. 7). They face to the left and toward the
evangelist portrait on the opposing page. Unfortunately, only two of the symbols are well preserved—the lion of Luke and eagle of John. However, there is a
faint trace of the hoof and book of the symbol for Mark, so this must be the calf,
and hence Matthew had originally the angel, which is now entirely effaced.
After MS 1.5 the peculiar pairing of symbol and evangelist described in the
prologue of Epiphanios simply disappears. Thus, to judge from the evidence
known to this writer, the system was in use only during the comparatively short
interval separating the two Athens manuscripts, Nat. Lib. cod. 57 of the third
quarter of the eleventh century and the Gennadeion Gospels of 1226.

The Preface of Irenaeus

The Epiphanios prologue has been analyzed first, because it is an especially
clear example of the impact of such texts on the iconography of evangelist
symbols. The preface, however, is not nearly as common as the other principal
introduction to the four Gospels, the prologue of Irenaeus that was also quoted
in the Introduction. As mentioned above, the passage is an excerpt from
Irenaeus' treatise on heresies, and it is of some interest in the present context to
compare the prologue with its source.[30] In doing so, it is apparent that the
wording of both the section about the four winds, the four Gospels, and the
four faces of the cherubim and the part describing the nature of the faces follow
Irenaeus closely. What is important is not the small deviations from the Greek
version of Irenaeus, as transmitted by Anastasius Sinaites, but the prologue's
omission of Irenaeus' subsequent discussion of the nature of the Gospels. There
he identifies each evangelist with one of the animals of the cherubim,[31] and
because that portion was not chosen for the prologue, this preface, unlike the
one attributed to Epiphanios, contains no specific pairing of symbols.

The consequences of this omission are twofold. First, the text cannot be an
obvious source for the ordering of evangelist symbols. This is significant, because the Irenaean preface is the most common introduction to the Gospels as a
whole and thus may be considered to be the Greek equivalent of the prologue of
St. Jerome found in many Latin Gospel books (*Plures fuisse . . .*).[32] Jerome also
discusses the four symbols, but in this case the symbols are identified with
specific evangelists according to the scheme almost universally followed in

Western medieval art. Although the lack of this detail may not necessarily be the cause of the great variance in the iconography of evangelist symbols in the Middle Byzantine period, it in no way discourages that multiplicity. Second, this failure to include some specific arrangement of symbols may have paradoxically engendered a new system, for it is only natural to suppose that an iconographer or illuminator in the absence of explicit guidelines might at times be influenced by the order in which the symbols are discussed in the preface and simply match this list with the sequence of Gospels in the Bible. Looking back at the preface, the lion is the first mentioned, followed by the calf, the man, and the eagle. This is precisely the arrangement of the symbols in one class of Middle Byzantine manuscripts grouped under no. II in Table B.

As far as is known to this writer, there is no source that expressly orders the symbols in this manner. Since the system appears in several manuscripts, it is unlikely to be a random aberration repeated in subsequent books. The monuments in this category are too diverse in date, style, and format for this explanation and include four or five Gospel books as well as the enamel pendant mentioned above. The earliest manuscript is Moscow, Hist. Mus. gr. 13 (518) from the late eleventh century,[33] and it, like Athens 57, represents the symbols atop the headpieces at the beginning of the Gospels. The second Moscow manuscript, Hist. Mus. gr. 14 (519), may be assigned to the late twelfth century.[34] In it the symbol is combined with the representation of the evangelist and a scene appropriate for the particular Gospel. Here, one sees Matthew seated at his desk and above a lion with a book and a small vignette of the Nativity, the usual event pictured at the beginning of Matthew (fig. 8). In another twelfth-century Gospel book in Geneva, Bibl. publ. et univ. cod. gr. 13 (fig. 9), the same three elements are composed differently.[35] Instead of having the various units float incongruously on a gold ground, the illuminator has placed the evangelist in a rectangle flanked by two columns, and above in the gable there is a medallion enclosing the symbol. For example, the eagle, from the portrait of John (fig. 9) faces to the right and toward the beginning of the Gospel on the opposite recto, where the initial headpiece incorporates the feast scene.

The third twelfth-century manuscript with this particular ordering of the symbols is a Gospel book in Bratislava. It has recently been published by Benda and Myslivec, who illustrated details of the four evangelist portraits (figs. 10–13).[36] They considered the book to be dated to the year 1183 because of a note by a priest, Michael Pepagomenos, stating that he bought the manuscript in that year.[37] The Greek is partly ambiguous; and a later owner, Michael Kantakouzenos, or perhaps his librarian, states in a subscription of 1560 that the manuscript was written 377 years ago, or in 1183 (fig. 14).[38] Yet this person apparently was not too sure of himself. He drew a box at the end of his sentence and left the number of years blank. Another hand, similar to the signature of Michael Kantakouzenos, then filled in the number 377.[39] His was not, however, the correct interpretation of the entry, and the position taken by the present writer is that the note of 1183 merely constitutes a *terminus ante quem* for the book. The manuscript was indeed purchased in 1183 but was not necessarily written in that year.

Like the Geneva Gospels, the depiction of the evangelist at work in the Bratislava manuscript occupies a rectangular space between two columns, and the feast scene is above in an oversized lintel. Framing the Nativity (fig. 10) and the Baptism (fig. 11) is a chevron design and a pediment, respectively, and these are drawn so that they appear to lie either over or behind the border of the rectangular field. In comparison, the portraits of Luke (fig. 12) and John (fig. 13) are simpler because they lack this added frame. In all four miniatures, the symbol of the evangelist shares the author's domain; in the first three it perches on the lectern before the evangelist; and in the fourth the eagle rests on a hill at the right.

The particular placement of the symbols in the manuscript in Bratislava is one found in other manuscripts as well,[40] and perhaps closest in this respect is another twelfth-century Gospel book, Megaspelaion, cod. 8.[41] Three of its symbols sit on the lecterns, and the fourth, the eagle of John, stands on a mountaintop; the feast scenes are to be found in medallions set inside the gables of the lintels. The Megaspelaion and Bratislava Gospels also compare well in terms of style, especially in the treatment of ornamental details, such as the arches, columns, and peculiar corner finials, and in turn both may be connected with dated manuscripts of 1101 (Paris, Bibl. Nat. suppl. gr. 1262) and 1105 (Cambridge, Mass., Harvard College Lib. MS gr. 3).[42] The evangelist symbols of the Megaspelaion miniatures, as well as other portions of the compositions, have been damaged by later repainting, and consequently it is difficult now even to identify the order of the symbols.[43] At the present time, it appears that both Matthew and Mark are matched with the lion, which surely is not correct; but since Luke has the man and John the eagle, a configuration found only in the system under discussion, it may be proposed that originally the symbols of Megaspelaion cod. 8 were arranged like those of the other twelfth-century Gospels in Moscow, Geneva, and Bratislava.

These four, or most likely five, Gospel books together with the enamel now at the Vatopedi Monastery are witnesses, then, of the same iconographic convention, one that can be documented as extending only from the beginning to the end of the twelfth century. It thus is relatively short-lived and in this respect can be compared with the history of the Epiphanian order, for neither seems to continue into the Palaeologan era and remains generally restricted to the Middle Byzantine period. The textual source for the second system in Table B is most likely the general introduction to the Gospels of Irenaeus, in spite of the fact that the preface is not explicit about a pairing. Of the above five Gospel books only Moscow gr. 14 actually contains the preface of Irenaeus,[44] but this need not disprove the theory. As stated before, the Gospel text and the supplementary material are not always coordinated with various nonnarrative illustrations like the symbols, because scribes and artists could rely on their own individual and differing traditions or models.

The Order of Irenaeus

With the remaining categories presented in Appendix I the evidence for the influence of prefaces becomes increasingly weaker. For example, the third system, originating ultimately in the *Adversus Haereses* of Irenaeus,[45] is not mentioned, as explained above, in the principal Greek prologue to the four Gospels (von Soden, no. 82) and to date has been encountered only in passages found in two books in the Bibliothèque Nationale in Paris, gr. 93 and suppl. gr. 612 of 1164. On ff. 5v–7v of the latter there is an unpublished version of Irenaeus' comments on the four Gospels, the four faces of the cherubim, and their association with the individual Gospels. Because of the additional information, the text must ultimately be based upon Irenaeus' treatise, not on the derivative prologue (von Soden, no. 82). In Paris gr. 93 another series of prefaces has been emended to include pairings for the symbols.[46] Such disparate, miscellaneous texts, however, are not likely to be the source of the iconography listed under no. III in Table B, and it is more reasonable to suspect the impact of the original statements of Irenaeus.

The number of later repetitions and paraphrases of his comments on the symbols is proof of his continued influence throughout the period under discussion.[47] For instance, a section of the Ἐρωτήσεις καὶ ἀποκρίσεις (*Questions and Answers*) of Anastasius Sinaites, who died soon after 700, is sufficiently close to the Latin translation of Irenaeus to be printed in the *Patrologia graeca* and in other editions as the equivalent of the missing Greek.[48] The doctrine about the cherubim reappears in a more abbreviated form in the liturgical commentary most likely written by the patriarch Germanos (d. 733) and is best preserved in a Latin translation of 869–70.[49] Andrew of Caesarea of the late sixth or early seventh century wrote on the same subject in his commentary on the

Apocalypse and matches symbol with evangelist, "as Irenaeus says" to do.[50] The pairing, however, is different in a text by the Pseudo-Athanasius that is based loosely on Irenaeus.[51] The commentary to *Mark* by Theophylact of Ochrid of the eleventh century relies on Irenaeus for the evangelical identity and symbolism of each animal.[52] Still later is the liturgical commentary by the Pseudo-Sophronius, which again is an accurate restatement of Irenaeus.[53] Although there was a Sophronius, who was a seventh-century patriarch of Jerusalem, Bornert in his recent book on liturgical commentaries considers the treatise to have been written in the twelfth century.[54]

In addition to the prologues in the two Paris Gospels there is additional manuscript evidence concerning the impact of Irenaeus' ideas about the significance of each animal. That doctrine, to recapitulate, said the faces of the cherubim were symbols of "the dispensation of the Son of God." His royal, priestly, and human natures were represented by the lion, calf, and man, respectively, and the eagle stood for the "gift of the Spirit" flying down to the church. One example of such characterizations is an epigram in a twelfth-century New Testament in Basel, Universitätsbibl. MS A.N. IV. 2. There the lion is described in the following Irenaean terms (fig. 15):

Ἀλκῆς φέρων μίμημα καὶ κράτους   The lion, who is the model of
   λέων   strength and courage, prefigures
Ἄνακτα Χριστὸν πανσθενῆ προ-   Christ the King, as all-powerful.
   δεικνύει.[55]

The poem written below the portrait of John and Prochoros in the manuscript probably was added later, since the script is certainly more cursive than the rest of the book. Because the Basel New Testament now has only this one evangelist portrait, it is impossible to know if there were epigrams for the other Gospels.

That this is at least a possibility is suggested by a second twelfth-century Gospel book, Oxford, Bodl. Lib. Auct. T. inf. 1.3. Fragmentary epigrams have been written at the bottom of the initial page to each Gospel, and these refer to the symbols in the headpieces above.[56] The poem for Mark is completely erased, and a number of words in the other three are difficult to read, although their basic meaning is reasonably clear. The angel of Matthew is the "human image of God," and the calf of Luke is identified with the priestly or sacrificial function. Finally, the verses about the lion of John (fig. 16) are identical to the above inscription in the Basel manuscript, indicating that all these epigrams may be a part of a standard set, heretofore unknown. Once again the ultimate origin for the texts is the passage of Irenaeus.

There is no way to be certain about the immediate source of the poems; they could just as easily have been based upon the Irenaean prologue (von Soden, no. 82) as the *Adversus Haereses* itself. Such is not the case, however, with four poems found in three Gospel books—Istanbul, Ecumenical Patriarchate cod. 3 [57] of the late twelfth century; London, Brit. Lib. Egerton 2783; [58] and Mt. Athos, Vatopedi 937, [59] the latter two from the fourteenth century. The verses are presented here in the order of their appearance in the earliest manuscript, the Istanbul Gospels.

Lion

Τὴν ἀρχικήν τε καὶ βασιλικωτάτην
Ἰσχὺν παριστᾷ τοῦ θ(εο)ῦ καί δεσπό-
του.

He presents the royal and most imperial power of God and the Lord.

Man (fig. 18)

Τὴν ὡς καθ' ἡμᾶς τοῦ θ(εο)ῦ παρουσίαν
Ἀνθρωπόμορφος ἀγγέλου πάλ(αι) φύσις
Καὶ φανέρωσιν ἐμφανῶς διαγράφει.

The anthropomorphic nature of the angel depicts clearly the appearance and manifestation of God to us.

Calf

Ἐνταῦθα μόσχος ἱερουργίας τύπον
Ἐξεικονίζει καὶ καλῶς παρεισάγει.

Here the calf represents and introduces beautifully the symbol of priestly service.

Eagle (fig. 19)

Τὴν δό[σιν?] ὄντως πν(εύματο)ς παναγίου
Ἱπταμένην ἄνωθεν ἐμφανίζει τοῖς κάτω.

He shows to those below the gift [?] of the all-holy Spirit flying from above.

Again, the basic characterizations of the symbols are those of Irenaeus, and the appreciation of this fact allows one to complete the abbreviation δο in the first line of the poem on the eagle (fig. 19). This should be δόσιν (gift), for that was the word used by Irenaeus in the passage quoted previously.[60] Soteriou hypothesized that the word was δότιν (gift).[61] The latter is a theoretical possibility, given the requirements of the syntax and meter for a two-syllable feminine noun beginning with δο; the word δόξαν (glory) might be another choice if it were not for the source of the text in the *Adversus Haereses.* The word does not appear in the preface (von Soden, no. 82), which has an entirely different term, ἐπιφοίτησιν. The author of the poems in the Istanbul Gospels, then, has ignored that prologue found in many manuscripts including the three in Istanbul, London, and Mount Athos and has turned directly to Irenaeus or one of the later writers quoting him. The example of these books thus suggests an explanation for the appearance of the Irenaean system of ordering the symbols. The latter, like the epigrams, probably had its origin in the various theological tracts and not in Gospel prologues.

The surviving visual evidence for the order of Irenaeus comprises only the three manuscripts presented in Table B, and none of these contradicts the above hypothesis. The twelfth-century Gospels in Oxford, Bodl. Lib. Auct. T. inf. 1.3, is decorated with preliminary canon tables and headpieces that enclose a symbol set within a roundel.[62] Each animal, such as the lion of John (fig. 16), carries a book and looks to the right. The manuscript has no Gospel prologues whatsoever, and even the aforementioned verses written at the bottom of the page do not seem to be by the original scribe. Thus, initially no connection of the symbols with any text was envisioned. In his arrangement of the symbols the illuminator probably was following an iconographical tradition learned somewhere else.

The same is likely to be true for the Gospels in Manchester, John Rylands Lib. gr. 13, and in Cambridge, Mass., Harvard College Lib. cod. TYP215H, a portion of which is now in the possession of the Dumbarton Oaks Collection in Washington, D.C., acc. no. 58.105. The Manchester Gospels was mentioned before, because it contains on f. 52r a prologue for the Gospel of Mark that specifies that it has the form of the calf, the pairing used in the preface of Epiphanios.[63] Yet the symbol of Mark that decorates the preceding page, f. 51v, is the eagle, not the calf, and the other two extant portraits of Luke and John also conform to the system of Irenaeus. The Gospels at Harvard has been the subject of a recent study by G. Vikan, who discusses how its two sets of evangelist portraits are additions perhaps of the second half of the twelfth and of the early thirteenth centuries respectively, made to a basic text of the eleventh century.[64] The evangelist symbols, then, are not part of the original decorative program of the manuscript, and again the inspiration for the matching of symbol and evangelist probably is due to an artistic convention, not a Gospel preface. Thus, for the particular iconography of evangelist symbols in these three books other influences external to the contexts of manuscripts themselves seem to be at work.

The Order of St. Jerome

Prefaces also do not appear to be the primary source for the fourth method of arranging evangelist symbols (Table B) or in that scheme employed by St. Jerome and widely followed in Western Europe. Again, the surviving textual evidence is rather meager. The first example that can be associated with some date is a passage on the four evangelists that Schermann published long ago. Basically, it is an adaptation of Irenaeus' comments on the symbols and the evangelists combined with an entirely different pairing, that of St. Jerome, all of which points to the derivative nature of the piece. Schermann based his work on three manuscripts—Vat. gr. 1506, Vat. gr. 1974, and Vat. Ottob. gr. 268—the earliest of which is Vat. gr. 1506 of 1024.[65] The latter came from Grottaferrata, and because of the provincial quality of the script and ornament it may be south Italian in origin, though Devreesse was doubtful of this.[66] Vat. gr. 1974 has been assigned to the tenth or eleventh century,[67] and Ottob. gr. 268 to the sixteenth century.[68]

One important early witness to the Hieronymian order is a single poem written at the end of an uncial lectionary in the Vatican, gr. 1522.[69] Wholly explicit, the verses associate the man with Matthew; the lion with Mark; the calf with Luke; and the eagle with the son of Zebedee, meaning John. The text is written in gold letters (fig. 17) and is framed by two arches, probably in imitation of the format of Eusebian canon tables or the letter to Carpianus. The poem, then, was considered to be an important part of the manuscript, and hence it is significant for assessing the impact of its particular pairing of symbols. Unfortunately, there has been some confusion in recent literature about the date of the Vatican lectionary, and since the matter has a direct bearing upon whether the poem should be presented here or later on in this chapter in the section on the Palaeologan period, the issues have to be confronted.

Since the eighteenth century the manuscript had been dated to the ninth or tenth century,[70] but both the 1950 Vatican catalogue description by Giannelli [71] and the detailed article of Bonicatti from 1959 argued differently.[72] Giannelli suggested that the book was written in the fourteenth century by a scribe imitating a script of the ninth or tenth century. Indeed there is an uneven, ragged appearance to the uncial letters, indicating that each was made with several strokes of the pen, perhaps because the scribe was not proficient in the normal fluid penmanship seen in other uncial texts. Bonicatti supported this idea of a late date for most of the manuscript but noted that the four evangelist portraits; a miniature of Moses receiving the law; and other pages, such as the ones with the verses in question, were not integral to the basic text and dated instead to the late ninth century. In his stylistic analysis he followed Weitzmann's perceptive comments of 1935 on the five miniatures. To Bonicatti, then, parts of an early manuscript, possibly a *tetraevangelium,* were reused for the later lectionary.[73]

Another piece of evidence to be included in the discussion is the script and decoration of a second lectionary now in Paris, Bibl. Nat. gr. 278. Omont long ago had recognized that its palaeography was peculiar and attributed it on one occasion to the fourteenth century.[74] His observation is relevant here, because it has been recognized that the Paris manuscript was written by the same scribe as was Vat. gr. 1522.[75] The scripts, initials, and ruling pattern compare closely, and each has a preliminary poem about Moses, a passage that in the Vatican codex accompanies the illustration of Moses receiving the law. Weitzmann thought both books were painted by the same artist and compared the style with that of the famous Paris, Bibl. Nat. gr. 510 from 880–83.[76] Certainly the soft painterly technique, the enlivening touches of red on the cheeks and lips, the gentle gradations of color, and the delicate white surface highlighting in the Vatican miniatures are hallmarks of the late ninth century. Since these miniatures, however, are not integral to the manuscript, they do not constitute conclusive evidence for dating, but such is not the case with the only figural representation surviving in Paris gr. 278. The bust of an angel decorating its f. 220r [77] is rendered in the same facial tones with the identical illusionism of Vat. gr. 1522, and therefore it provides the desired documentation for both manuscripts, since the angel is painted on a text page. If the Paris lectionary is from the late ninth century, so too is the basic text of the Vatican codex; hence, there is every reason to believe that the contemporary poems and miniatures of gr. 1522 were designed for the book. Its verses on the symbols, then, become an early example of yet another manner of associating evangelist and symbol in the Middle Byzantine period.

Other isolated examples of this pairing are occasionally encountered. For instance, it occurs in a note at the end of a manuscript in Venice, Bibl. Marc. Z539. According to Mioni, this *tetraevangelium,* written in Greek and Arabic, is from Italy or Sicily and dates to the twelfth century.[78] A second case is an eleventh-century Gospels in Moscow, State Lenin Lib. gr. 10, with the words ἀν(θρωπ)ος, λέων, and so on, written on the first pages of the Gospels. The order is that of Jerome.[79]

The final example is a set of poems appearing in two Gospel books, Florence, Bibl. Laur. Plut. VI. 36, and Mt. Athos, Stavronikita 56. Both have evangelist portraits in the style of the so-called Nicaea manuscripts and perhaps date to the early thirteenth century.[80] The Florence Gospels has the more complete version of these four-line epigrams on the symbols,[81] whereas the verses in the Mt. Athos manuscript lack the last two lines of the Matthew and Mark poems.[82] In a much later example from the fifteenth century, Moscow, Hist. Mus. gr. 17, only the first lines of the poems to each Gospel remain.[83] The matching of animal to evangelist is according to the system of St. Jerome, but the spiritual significance attributed to each beast is generally similar to that of Irenaeus and suggests that these poems are a compilation of two different doctrines.

The textual evidence for the Hieronymian order in the period under study is, therefore, disparate, isolated, and derivative and cannot compare in this respect with the other traditions already discussed. Likewise, no distinctive pattern emerges from the two illustrated manuscripts adhering to the iconography. The earlier in date is a lectionary in the Vatican, gr. 2138, written in 991 in Capua by the monk Cyriacus,[84] and not surprisingly it is wholly Western in style and iconography (fig. 20). The symbols are depicted in initials, a Latin practice, as Grabar noted;[85] and related examples appear, for example, in a missal in the Vatican, Barb. lat. 560, which has been assigned to the end of the tenth century.[86] Because of these Italian characteristics, the Vatican lectionary stands apart from the Byzantine developments under discussion.

In contrast the second manuscript, a Gospels in the National Library in Athens, Nat. Lib. cod. 2251, shows no evidence of being from such a provincial area of cultural interchange.[87] Certainly its fine full-page symbols are traditional in format (fig. 21), for the animals also occupy entire pages in the aforementioned Gospels in Istanbul (figs. 18–19) and in several other manuscripts.[88] Usually the symbols of this sort precede the evangelist portraits, but one Gospels, Mt. Athos, Dochiariou 52 (fig. 22), has the same layout of the animal framed by a square and facing the evangelist on the adjacent verso.[89] The precise date of the Athens manuscript is not easily determinable. Its evangelist portraits display elements of the dynamic style of the late twelfth or early thirteenth century, but the subsequent history of this style of illumination is little known.[90] The palaeography also is confusing; the number of enlarged letters points to the twelfth century, but the strong uniformity of the other characters suggests a somewhat later date. Furthermore, the iconography of the evangelist symbols is more typical of the Palaeologan era, so that the inclusion of the Athens Gospels within the chronological limits of Appendix I remains problematical.

The two illuminated manuscripts and the handful of texts so far found indicate that this system was not widely used in the Middle Byzantine era, and this impression is supported by the absence of any texts with this pairing in von Soden's book. Thus, no long-term tradition seems to be at work here, and in these circumstances, the likelihood of sporadic influence from the Latin West is strong. Manuscripts like the Vatican lectionary, gr. 2138, serve as clear cases in point. In addition, the contrived nature of some of the texts, combining the Irenaean theological significance of the animals with the different pairing, gives these passages an artificial quality and implies that one tradition has been grafted onto another. In sum, during the period in question the order commonly associated with St. Jerome is one of minor importance.

Miscellaneous Pairings

The final category in Table B is labeled "Miscellaneous" largely because it comprises three manuscripts that still continue to puzzle this writer. The first listed is the aforementioned Istanbul Gospels, whose full-page miniatures of the evangelist symbols and their accompanying epigrams attest to the importance given to this subject (figs. 18–19).[91] As one can see, no other monument subscribes to the arrangement of symbols found in the manuscript, and it has no supplementary texts that match animal and evangelist in this manner. On the contrary, the poems inscribed around the miniatures, as noted above, are based upon the treatise of Irenaeus or one of its close copies. Two theologians, however, have paired symbols and evangelists in the manner of the Patriarchate Gospels. One is the Latin writer, Augustine,[92] and the other is the third-century Roman author, Hippolytus, who was one of the last of that school to write in Greek. Hippolytus reportedly called himself a pupil of Irenaeus,[93] and this relationship may be observed in his commentary on Ezekiel's apocalyptic vision. The spiritual significance of each face of the cherubim recalls that of Irenaeus, whereas the order of the symbols is Hippolytus' own contribution. Today the commentary is only partly preserved in a Syriac translation,[94] and whether the Greek original of the third century had any direct influence on the iconographer of the twelfth-century Gospel book or its model is simply not known.

The second manuscript in this group is a recently rediscovered Gospel book of 1156 A.D. now in the collection of Mr. H. P. Kraus in New York. Two or perhaps three of the evangelist portraits have symbols. Mark is paired with a lion; Luke, with a bird that little resembles an eagle. There is no symbol with John, and the only possible one in the Matthew portrait is a human bust used as the support for the lectern, although the latter element is more likely decorative.[95] Comparison with Table B will show that the ordering of the symbols in the portraits of Mark and Luke is without precedent. This fact plus the haphazard use of symbols in the manuscript does not inspire confidence in the abilities of the painter, and it may be suggested that the disposition of symbols here is the result of an arbitrary decision by the illuminator rather than the only surviving witness of a sixth manner of arranging symbols in the Middle Byzantine period. In any event, it can be stated that the pairing chosen was not inspired by any supplementary text in the Gospel book.

The final manuscript scarcely warrants the use of that term, for the object now in the Freer Gallery of Art in Washington, D.C., consists of only five badly flaked parchment leaves that were published in 1914 by C. R. Morey. Many of his comments, including his attribution of the manuscript to the second half of the twelfth century,[96] are still valid, and he correctly perceived the importance of the two surviving portraits of Mark and John. Each contains an evangelist symbol, a rare feature, he noted, in a Byzantine manuscript.[97] In each portrait the symbol carrying the codex perches on the bookstand in front of the evangelist. Before Mark there is a bird (fig. 23); and before John, a human figure, according to Morey,[98] although the latter symbol is almost impossible to identify today. The position of the symbols recalls other twelfth-century Gospel books, such as those in Bratislava (figs. 10–13) and Megaspelaion (cod. 8), but to judge from only the two portraits, the pairing used is unique. Since the Freer miniatures are fragments from an unknown book, there is no way of knowing if the original Gospels contained prefaces, but no texts with such an ordering of symbols have been encountered to date. In general, the rationale for the iconography of evangelist symbols in the three books in Istanbul; New York; and Washington, D.C., continues to be perplexing, but whatever answers may eventually be offered, it is unlikely that the solution will involve Gospel prologues.

Such texts, however, did prove to be the source for the first two categories in Table B. In all, twenty-two examples of evangelist symbols are listed in Table A. Two of that number, Mt. Athos, Dochiariou, cod. 52,[99] and Istanbul, Ecumenical Patriarchate, cod. 5, cannot be really judged, since only one miniature survives in the former and only one is published from the latter.[100] One other manuscript, the Ghelati Gospels in Tbilisi, can be included in the total, because, as discussed before, its evangelist portraits seem to follow Byzantine models. This leaves twenty-one monuments prior to the early thirteenth century that can be evaluated for their ordering of the symbols, and of this number thirteen fall into Categories I and II, or the ones dependent upon Gospel prologues. Thus, these texts do prove to be important for understanding the majority of surviving examples so far uncovered. The other schemes are more independent of such sources and are also less common. The system of Irenaeus probably is derived either directly from his theological writings or indirectly from some of their later reflections. The so-called Hieronymian order has considerably less documentary support in the Greek world and may reflect Western influence. The fifth group of manuscripts in Table B have so far defied interpretation, but they serve to emphasize the general lack of iconographic consistency in the treatment of evangelist symbols in Byzantine art prior to the early thirteenth century.

THE ORDER OF ST. JEROME IN THE PALAEOLOGAN AND POST-BYZANTINE PERIODS

When one turns to Palaeologan art, the situation is suddenly quite different. Instead of multiplicity, there is uniformity. Now both texts and images (with only one exception, a passage in Sinai, gr. 176 of 1286 A.D.[101]) conform to either the Hieronymian or the Irenaean systems. Furthermore, the former clearly prevails. Among the nineteen pictorial and eight textual examples from this period presented in Table C, the order of St. Jerome is used in twenty cases, versus five for the pairing of Irenaeus. This too is a change from the earlier era, covered by Tables A and B. The Hieronymian arrangement, relatively rare earlier, has suddenly become the most common in the Palaeologan period.

In this last phase of Byzantine art, just as in the preceding era, there is only sporadic textual evidence for the system of Jerome. A Gospel book in Paris, Bibl. Nat. gr. 106, of the fourteenth century has a set of epigrams on the evangelists in which the symbols are paired in this manner,[102] and the same is true for some poems on the evangelist symbols written by Manuel Philes (c. 1275–1345).[103] In the latter case Philes may well have been acquainted with the by then almost standard iconography of Palaeologan art. Certainly it has been shown several times by others that his descriptions of objects are detailed and accurate.[104] These poems could well have been written for a manuscript, for it is known that he composed dedications for books.[105] In any case, it is not likely that either of these series of poems served as the textual models for the new Palaeologan iconography.

The dominance of the order of St. Jerome in the monuments presented in Table C is not some fluke of survival but represents a conscious, deliberate change in the iconography of evangelist symbols. At this time there was an awareness that the older orderings of symbols were wrong, and frequently they were corrected. This process can be observed in several texts and works of art, providing insights into the new Palaeologan attitude toward the symbols.

One of the best examples of a deliberate alteration of an iconographic model occurs in a late-fourteenth-century icon in the National Museum of Sofia from the Bulgarian Monastery of Poganovo (fig. 24).[106] One side represents a vision of Christ with the four apocalyptic beasts. Leaving no doubt about the pictorial source for the scene, an inscription on the icon states that it is a copy of the famous early Christian mosaic in the apse of the Church of Hosios David at Thessaloniki (fig. 25).[107] There are several differences between the icon and mosaic, but one detail, concerning the symbols, has not really been commented on by earlier scholars.[108] Beside each animal on the icon abbreviated names of the evangelists are written, according to the sequence of Jerome. There are no such inscriptions on the mosaic or on any other Eastern *Maiestas Domini* of the Early Byzantine period.[109] Apparently at the end of the fourteenth century the artist felt a need to identify each animal specifically.

Similarly, the symbols are again labeled according to the Hieronymian system in other Palaeologan examples of the theme, such as a miniature in a Gospels in Leningrad (Publ. Lib. gr. 101) of the late thirteenth century (fig. 40); another in Cambridge (Univ. Lib. MS Dd. 9. 69), probably of the third quarter of the fourteenth century;[110] or a New Testament-Psalter in Rome (Vat. gr. 1210), possibly of 1447 A.D. (fig. 43).[111] Very few Middle Byzantine examples of the theme are so identified.[112] In fact, one case, which at first sight seems to be an exception to the rule, proves it instead. The *Maiestas* in a Gospels in Florence, Bibl. Laur. Plut. VI. 32, f. 8, has symbols inscribed with the names of the evangelists (fig. 47). The miniatures in the book are in the style of the "Nicaea" manuscripts and may be assigned to the late twelfth or early thirteenth century. However, the labels on the symbols are by a later hand,[113] so that this miniature becomes one more example of the Palaeologan or Post-Byzantine preference for identifying the symbols, albeit in the system of Irenaeus.

The Bratislava Gospels and Related Manuscripts

One of the more interesting instances of this "modernization" of the iconography of evangelist symbols in the Palaeologan era involves the previously mentioned Gospel book in Bratislava and its subsequent influence. To recapitulate, the manuscript appears to have been produced in the early twelfth century and bought by the priest Michael Pepagomenos in 1183. Its evangelist portraits (figs. 10–13) are framed by columns that support a superstructure containing a feast scene. The symbols arranged in the order of category II in Table B are perched on the lecterns in front of the evangelists with the exception of John's eagle, which stands on a small hill (fig. 13). The portraits in two other manuscripts, it is maintained, are based on a source that is very similar if not identical to this Bratislava manuscript.

The first is another Gospels in the Megaspelaion Monastery in Greece, cod. 1. The basic text was written and decorated during the tenth century, and Weitzmann has shown how its headpieces and canon tables are closely related to the group with "gold ciboria," especially Paris, Bibl. Nat. gr. 70. As he notes, the evangelist portraits in Megaspelaion, cod. 1, do not belong to the original text (figs. 26–29),[114] and it has been proposed that these miniatures were from the twelfth century.[115] The latter is an interesting if untenable hypothesis in view of the affiliations of the set of evangelist portraits with those in the Bratislava Gospels. If the corresponding portraits in each book are compared, the nature of this relationship may be more precisely defined. Consider first the two Matthews (figs. 10, 26). In the Bratislava codex the distinctive lintel with its chevron frame for the Nativity has been noted previously, and it appears in precisely the same form in Megaspelaion 1, so that even the way in which the chevron overlaps the lintel is identical. The ornamental patterns of that upper rectangular area generally agree, as do the marginal palmettes. Inside the arches the architecture, furniture, and position of the evangelist are the same in both.

The two miniatures are so similar, in fact, that it is less cumbersome to describe their differences than to enumerate the features they have in common. The portraits differ in three elements: the feast scenes, the iconography of John dictating to his disciple Prochoros, and the evangelist symbols. Although both manuscripts represent the Nativity with Matthew, as is standard, the precise iconography of that scene in cod. 1 is more involved and includes in addition the three Magi on horseback at the right. The Virgin does not lie horizontally and thus bisect the composition, as she does in the Bratislava roundel; instead, she is shown in a half-seated position. Other figures are shifted around, and in general the conception of space is different. Whereas the components of the Bratislava scene are arranged for symmetrical and hierarchical purposes, the painter of the other miniature evokes a comparatively more naturalistic sense of a deeper and more spatially coherent setting in which the drama is performed.

It is especially this last characteristic that serves to date the Megaspelaion miniature, for such a rendition of space is a principal development of Palaeologan painting in the thirteenth and fourteenth centuries.[116] Although Byzantine art never went as far as the one-point perspective of the Quattrocento, in the thirteenth century it did evolve a more spacious stagelike setting for its religious art; thus, between the twelfth and fourteenth centuries there are significant differences in the treatment of space. This is evident, for example, in a comparison of the Nativity landscape of Daphni of the late eleventh century,[117] or shortly before the Bratislava Gospels, with that in the Kariye Djami in Constantinople of c. 1315–21.[118] The unified or continuous landscape of the latter suggests depth, and the effect is often repeated in other works of the period, including to a lesser degree perhaps the Megaspelaion Nativity.

Other details of the miniature also find parallels in the Palaeologan period. For example, the Magi galloping toward the Holy Family are not commonly represented in the formal feast scene of the Nativity during the Middle Byzantine period, but they appear in a manner similar to the miniature in the early-fourteenth-century mosaic at the Church of the Holy Apostles in Thessaloniki.[119] Furthermore, the position of the Virgin and the general character of the rocky landscape may be compared with the Nativity panel in a fourteenth-century miniature mosaic in Florence.[120]

A similar analysis could be made of the other feast scenes in Megaspelaion 1 to the same end. The relation of the various participants in the Baptism to the surrounding hills differs in the two books (figs. 11, 27), and the effect of the higher crags in cod. 1 (fig. 27) is to envelop the figures in a more earthly setting.[121] The two Annunciations also vary in a similarly small but significant detail. In the Bratislava version (fig. 12), the low wall in the background appears only between Gabriel and Mary, and on either side there is merely the gold ground. In the Megaspelaion scene (fig. 28) that same wall continues across the entire roundel, thus creating an enclosed garden that has noticeable vegetation.[122] Finally, the medallion of the Anastasis demonstrates more overtly the same difference between landscapes of the Middle and Late Byzantine period (figs. 14, 29).[123]

All the feast scenes in the Megaspelaion miniature, therefore, fall into a similar pattern, one that allows these added pages to be dated to the fourteenth century. For the most part, the portrayals of Matthew, Mark, and Luke follow their counterparts in the Bratislava codex, but this is not the case with the group of John and Prochoros (fig. 29). The new elements added by the Palaeologan illuminator are the furniture and the building at the left, the emphasis on the spiritual fervor of John through his more energetic stance, and the placement of the evangelist symbol on a lectern in the center of the scene.

Considering the fidelity of the other portraits to the earlier types, the immediate problem here is how to interpret these alterations in the representation of the fourth evangelist. Did the artist merely want formal unity among all four portraits and thus has included a desk and a background pavilion that are similar to those in the earlier illustration of Mark (fig. 11)? Or is there another source involved that differs in this one miniature from the Bratislava Gospels? These questions must remain open, but the possibility should be considered that these deviations in the portrait of John are merely due to the preferences of the later painter. Palaeologan artists, as is becoming increasingly apparent, were capable of reproducing earlier styles so closely at times that only in the last few years have manuscripts been properly attributed to the later period.[124] Conversely, on other occasions these illuminators could depart significantly from their model to modernize both style and iconography.[125]

One example of the second trend is conveniently furnished by the four portraits in the Megaspelaion Gospels, for the third major difference between it and the Bratislava codex is the pairing of symbol and evangelist. The actual form of the symbols in cod. 1 is relatively close to the earlier book, as seen in the symbols of the man (figs. 12, 26) or the calf (figs. 11, 28), and in view of this relationship it is all the more significant that the order of the Irenaean prologue is no longer followed. The illuminator has disregarded his Middle Byzantine source and instead has arranged the symbols in the manner of St. Jerome. This feature, like the spacious landscapes of the feast scenes, also speaks for the Palaeologan date of the Megaspelaion illustrations.

The second manuscript to be introduced into the discussion is one that heretofore has been unknown to art historians and is presently in the Chester Beatty Library in Dublin, cod. W135.[126] If its set of four evangelist portraits (figs. 30–33) are juxtaposed with those of the Bratislava Gospels (figs. 10–13), the resemblances are striking. Almost every feature of one series finds its counterpart in the other. The evangelists are all in the same poses, even including John, and the feast scenes follow the Middle Byzantine iconography. In the Annunciation, for example, the background wall in the Dublin version (fig. 32) conforms to the limits of this motif in the Bratislava scene (fig. 12) and does not follow the Palaeologan fashion of the Megaspelaion Gospels. Even the plants growing next to the portraits are identical, so that those beside Luke in the Dublin miniature (fig. 32) have five petals sprouting from a central trefoil just as in the twelfth-century illustration (fig. 12).

The evangelist portraits of the Gospel book in Dublin may be insertions into an earlier text, possibly of the eleventh century. The style of the miniatures is not easily datable because of the close adherence to the model, but the portraits may be tentatively placed in the fifteenth or sixteenth century [127] and hence after the Megaspelaion illustrations. In spite of the later date of the Dublin evangelist portraits, they are the more faithful copies of the Bratislava series. Historically it is plausible that the latter served as the model, since both manuscripts may have been in Constantinople at the same time. The Bratislava Gospels was owned by the famous bibliophile, Michael Kantakouzenos, and he signed it in 1560 (fig. 14). Since Michael was a prominent official at the Ottoman court, his library was no doubt in Constantinople. The Dublin Gospel book can be traced back to 1668, when it was the property of a Frankish church in that city.[128] Thus, both books may have been in Constantinople in the centuries after the fall of the Byzantine capital.

Yet even though the manuscripts are intimately related, there is one detail in which they differ, and this once again is the arrangement of the evangelist symbols. The Post-Byzantine artist follows the order of St. Jerome, the one that is almost universally subscribed to in the Orthodox lands outside Russia (cf. Table D). In the latter there is still a continuation of the Irenaean system of the Palaeologan era, but the Hieronymian scheme clearly dominates (cf. Table E). Though a full-scale discussion of evangelist symbols in Post-Byzantine art is outside the scope of the present inquiry, the preliminary evidence collected and presented in Table D indicates that the disposition of the symbols in the Chester Beatty Gospels is following the by then standard Orthodox iconography. Since the miniatures show no sign of having been influenced by the innovations of the portraits in Megaspelaion 1, it must be the Dublin illuminator himself who has independently made a conscious alteration of the Middle Byzantine iconography, a change that in the case of the particular Palaeologan and the Post-Byzantine painters was not inspired by Gospel prologues. Neither of the two later manuscripts contains any texts specifying the Hieronymian order.

Textual Alterations

The art-historical evidence can be supplemented by various literary witnesses to this change in the ordering of evangelist symbols in the Palaeologan period. An interesting case is the brief text about the symbols found in Milan, Bibl. Ambros. H. 13; Vat. gr. 1548; and Vat. gr. 1254. The simple passage, as discussed earlier, arranges the symbols in the order of Epiphanios, the system that seems to disappear entirely after the early thirteenth century. Not only has it not been found in the Palaeologan era, but there is textual evidence that it was actually considered to be erroneous. For example, in one of the three manuscripts, Vat. gr. 1254 of the tenth or eleventh century, there is written beside μόσχῳ and λέοντος the words λεόντη (sic) and μόσχῳ by a later, not very well educated scribe.[129] The alteration has the effect of matching the lion with Mark and the calf with Luke, so that the order becomes that of Jerome. Another example occurs in Venice, Bibl. Marc. gr. I, 14, the basic text of which probably is from the twelfth century.[130] At the conclusion on f. 261v the passage about the animals appears, but now someone, again at a later date, has erased the names of the three animals and has rewritten them in accordance with the Hieronymian scheme.

Yet another case of the switch to this system is a Gospel book in Patmos, cod. 81 of 1335. At the beginning it has the Irenaean preface to the Gospels (von Soden, no. 82) like many Middle Byzantine Gospel books, but here in the margin the scribe has written the names of the evangelists beside the sentences about the symbols, so that the pairing becomes that of Jerome, and hence contrary to the original passage of Irenaeus, the basis for the prologue.[131] Finally, one finds this Palaeologan doctrine present in a set of four verses on the symbols that were added to a tenth-century Gospels in Paris, Bibl. Nat. Coislin 20. According to Devreesse, these are in "a hand of the thirteenth century," and the order used, as usual, is that of Jerome.[132]

The last example of this phenomenon of the change to the Hieronymian pairing is to be found in the complicated textual history of the *Historia ecclesiastica,* one of the texts that repeats the definition of the Gospels of Irenaeus, discussed earlier. In order fully to understand this passage as printed in the *Patrologia graeca,* it is necessary to examine the development or the progressive corruption of the text after its probable author, Germanos, wrote it, and here the problems fortunately have been studied recently by Bornert.[133] The version of the *Historia* published by Migne is based on an edition of 1779 by Galland [134] and has been shown to be substantially corrupt, for at the end of the nineteenth century there was discovered a Latin translation of Germanos' treatise made by Anastasius Bibliothecarius on a visit to Constantinople in 869–70.[135] Brightman and Borgia have reconstructed the original text from the Latin, a task made possible by the later Greek versions.[136] The resulting treatise is shorter and less elaborate than the one in Migne, so that it is clear that additions have been made over the centuries, and Bornert has analyzed these developments.[137]

The particular section on the four Gospels and the four symbols is an interesting example of the accretions that occurred. In the following the passages from the reconstructed version of Brightman are compared with the text in the *Patrologia graeca* by means of printing in boldface those sections of the latter not found in the former, the earlier version of the commentary: [138]

Ματθαῖος, ἑρμηνεύεται, μέλι· Μάρκος, οἶνος· Λουκᾶς, γάλα· Ἰωάννης, ἔλαιον. Τὰ τέσσαρα εὐαγγέλιά εἰσι, κατὰ τὰ τέσσαρα πνεύματα καθολικά, ἀπηλιώτην, ζέφυρον, νότον καὶ βορρᾶν. Αὐτὰ γάρ εἰσι πρὸς σύστασιν τοῦ παντός. Καθολικὰ δὲ λέγονται, διὰ τὰ ἀντιπνέοντα ὀκτώ. Καὶ ἄλλως· Τέσσαρά εἰσιν εὐαγγέλια, καὶ τέσσαρα καθολικὰ πνεύματα, κατὰ τὰ τετράμορφα ζῷα, λέγω δὴ τὰ χερουβίμ, ἐν οἷς κάθηται ὁ τῶν ὅλων θεός· ἐξ ὧν φαίνεται, ὅτι ὁ καθήμενος ἐπὶ τῶν χερουβὶμ θεός. Καὶ συνέχων τὸ πᾶν, φανερωθεὶς ἔδωκεν ἡμῖν τετράμορφον τὸ εὐαγγέλιον, ἑνὶ δὲ πνεύματι συνεχόμενον· καὶ γὰρ τετραπρόσωπά εἰσι· καὶ τὰ πρόσωπα αὐτῶν εἰκονίζουσι τὴν πραγματείαν τοῦ υἱοῦ τοῦ θεοῦ. Τὸ μὲν γὰρ πρῶτον ζῷον, φησίν, ὅμοιον λέοντι, τὸ ἔμπρακτον αὐτοῦ καὶ ἡγεμονικὸν καὶ βασιλικὸν χαρακτηρίζον. Τὸ δὲ δεύτερον, ὅμοιον μόσχῳ, τὴν ἱερουργικὴν καὶ ἱερατικὴν τάξιν ἐμφαῖνον. Τὸ δὲ τρίτον ἔχον πρόσωπον ἀνθρώπου, τὴν κατὰ ἄνθρωπον αὐτοῦ παρουσίαν φανερῶς διαγράφον. Τὸ τέταρτον ὅμοιον ἀετῷ πετομένῳ, τὴν τοῦ ἁγίου πνεύματος ἐφιπταμένην δόσιν σαφηνίζον. Τοίνυν καὶ τὰ εὐαγγέλια τούτοις σύμμορφά εἰσιν, ἐν οἷς ἐπικάθηται ὁ Χριστός. Τὸ μὲν γὰρ, ἀετόσ, κατὰ Ἰωάννην εὐαγγέλιον, τὴν ἀπὸ τοῦ πατρὸς ἡγεμονικὴν αὐτοῦ καὶ ἔνδοξον γέννησιν διηγεῖται λέγων· "Ἐν ἀρχῇ ἦν ὁ λόγος." Καὶ, "Πάντα δι'

αὐτοῦ ἐγένετο· καὶ χωρὶς αὐτοῦ ἐγένετο οὐδὲ ἓν ὃ γέγονεν." Τὸ δὲ, ταῦρος, κατὰ Λουκᾶν, ἅτε ἱερατικοῦ χαρακτῆρος ὑπάρχον, ἀπὸ Ζαχαρίου ἱερέως θυμιῶντος ἄρχεται λέγων· " Ἐπειδήπερ πολλοὶ ἐπεχείρησαν ἀνατάξασθαι διήγησιν," καὶ τὰ ἑξῆς. "Ἤδη γὰρ ὁ σιτευτὸς μόσχος ὑπὲρ τῆς εὑρέσεως τοῦ νεωτέρου παιδὸς ἔμελλε θύεσθαι. Βοῦς τὸ ὀρεκτικὸν ἧπαρ σημαίνει. Ποικίλος δὲ ἵππος, Λουκᾶς, ὡς εὐγλωττότερον καὶ ποικιλώτερον τὸ κατὰ τὸν κύριον ἐκθέμενος. Ματθαῖος δὲ, τὴν κατὰ ἄνθρωπον αὐτοῦ γέννησιν κηρύττει, λέγων· "Βίβλος γενέσεως Ἰησοῦ Χριστοῦ," καὶ τὰ ἑξῆς· "Τοῦ δὲ Ἰησοῦ Χριστοῦ ἡ γέννησις οὕτως ἦν." Ἀνθρωπόμορφον οὖν τὸ εὐαγγέλιον τοῦτο. Ἄνθρωπος, τὸ λογικόν. Ἄνθρωπος μὲν, τὸ ἐγκέφαλον· Λατῖνοι δὲ λέγουσι, ρατζιωνάβιλε, Ἕλληνες δὲ λέγουσι φρόνησιν καὶ λογιότητα· οἱ δὲ Ἄραβες ἤτοι Σαρακηνοὶ, ἐλαφάκαρ, ἐλακὶλ, ἐλτζινοῦν. Πυρρὸς οὖν ἵππος. Ματθαῖος, ὡς τὰ τῆς ἐνανθρωπήσεως τοῦ κυρίου τρανῶς ἐκθέμενος. Λέοντος δὲ Μάρκος ἀπὸ τοῦ προφητικοῦ πνεύματος, τοῦ ἐξ ὕψους ἐπιόντος τοῖς ἀνθρώποις, τὴν ἀρχὴν ἐποιήσατο λέγων· " Ἀρχὴ τοῦ εὐαγγελίου Ἰησοῦ Χριστοῦ, ὡς γέγραπται ἐν τοῖς προφήταις· Ἰδοὺ ἐγὼ ἀποστέλλω τὸν ἄγγελόν μου πρὸ προσώπου σου," τὴν πτερωτικὴν εἰκόνα τοῦ εὐαγγελίου διὰ τούτων δεικνὺς· λέων θυμικόν·

Λατῖνοι λέγουσιν, ἰρασκίβιλε. Καὶ ἄλλως· Τὸ θυμικὸν, ἀνδρίαν καὶ δειλίαν· Λατῖνοι ἰρασκίβιλε, Σαρακηνοὶ ἐλγαδὰβ, ἔνιγδε, οὐελγίβην. Καὶ ἄλλως· ψαρὸς ἵππος, Μάρκος, ὡς διανθέστερον τὸ εὐαγγέλιον γράψας· Ἰωάννης, ἀετὸς, τὸ πνευματικόν. Καὶ ἄλλως· Ἀετὸς δὲ ἡ ψυχή. Καὶ ἄλλως· Λευκὸς ἵππος Ἰωάννης, ὡς λευκότερον πᾶσαν αἴνεσιν στη λιτεύσας.[139]

In the first section on the four Gospels and the four faces of the tetramorph the differences are not important for the present discussion. However, in the following part concerning each of the evangelists there are significant variations. At the beginning of the first sentence devoted to each author, except Matthew, the word ἀετὸς or ταῦρος or λέοντος has been inserted, making the symbols and evangelists follow the system of Jerome. As before, Matthew is unchanged, because his symbol is the man in both pairings. The conflated text about Mark is contradictory. Mark is matched with the lion, but at the same time he is said to be the "winged picture." The latter is from Irenaeus and refers to his pairing of Mark with the eagle. This confusion is a further indication of the corruption of the text.

All that can be said definitely about the date of these interpolations is that they were made after 869–70. However, in view of the above evidence concerning the popularity of the system of Jerome in the Palaeologan and Post-Byzantine periods, one would expect the alterations to have been made fairly late, and the textual history supports this hypothesis. Brightman in his 1908 study of the text mentions these additions and says that they are due to further reference to Irenaeus and to "a new and curious application of his method." [140] The interpolations are found in a group of manuscripts he calls B[ii]. Bornert, the more recent investigator of the matter, notes them in a version that he labels D[a], the penultimate stage of the text's history. [141] Of the manuscripts with the additions in question, the earliest cited by either scholar is Milan, Bibl. Ambros. G 8 sup. of 1286, the others being mostly from the fourteenth or fifteenth century. [142] Given the aforementioned data on the Hieronymian pairing of symbols, it seems likely that these additions to Germanos' text were composed not long before the Milan codex.

Although the fact of the dominance of the order of St. Jerome in the Palaeologan era seems clear, the reasons behind the change are not easy to discover. Certainly there is no strong rationale for this order in the Byzantine manuscripts themselves, for there is no "Jerome" preface. The revisions made to the liturgical commentary of St. Germanos suggest a theological change, but more work is necessary on this point to ascertain its importance. The pairing of symbols in the other miscellaneous texts in manuscripts or the epigrams of Manuel Philes might be derived from some theological tract, or they might just as well follow actual works of art. The latter explanation seems to apply especially well to the poems of Manuel.

The possibility of Western artistic influence at this time is not to be discounted. The opportunities for contacts with the West were numerous both in the Palaeologan period and before, during the Latin domination of much of the Byzantine Empire. One pertinent case is the frescoes of the life of St. Francis recently discovered at the Kalenderhane Djami in Constantinople. They are painted in the style of a crusader manuscript, the Arsenal Bible, of c. 1250.[143] The mixture of a basically Eastern painting style with Latin iconography suggests the types of artistic interchange that took place in the thirteenth century.

Evidence of Latin influence in Palaeologan painting, sculpture, and architecture has been cited by a number of scholars, and the state of the problem concerning painting has been reviewed by O. Demus in his basic study of 1958 on the origin of Palaeologan painting.[144] But, as he noted later,[145] this period in the succeeding years has become one of the most active fields of research in Byzantine art, and consequentially to his summary one may add some additional material. For instance, with respect to manuscript illumination, two iconographic motifs of Late Byzantine evangelist portraiture, the author erasing a page or sharpening a pen, have been noted first in Latin miniatures.[146] Further, certain bilingual Greek and Latin illustrated manuscripts from the period demonstrate that interrelations between Greek artists and Latin scribes at times were close.

One example, a Gospel book in Paris, Bibl. Nat. gr. 54, is painted in what appears to be a thoroughly Byzantine manner,[147] but the several different colors of ink used in both the Latin and Greek text remind one of a Gothic manuscript. Hence, in this case the Greek scribe has adapted to a Western convention. Yet this is not the only feature that is peculiar for a Byzantine book. The quire structure of Paris gr. 54 is not based upon the normal Byzantine quaternion, or eight folios to a gathering; instead, its maker has grouped ten folios together, forming a quinion.[148] This seemingly small feature is a telling detail because it indicates that the non-Byzantine character of the book is not merely superficial. More research is necessary on the Gospel book, especially with regard to its Latin script, before all of its secrets are revealed, but it may be of interest to note that ten sheets to a quire is characteristic of Italian manuscripts during this period [149] and that the folios are also so arranged in a second dual language manuscript, a Psalter in Berlin, Staatl. Mus. MS 78 A.9, known as the

Hamilton Psalter.[150] According to Buchthal, its marginal illustrations of the late thirteenth century are the work of a Western artist copying a Byzantine model, and its French calendar and litany point to Cyprus as a place of origin.[151]

In the fourteenth century certain manuscripts also show Western traits. For example, others have cited the illustrations of a Book of Job in Paris, Bibl. Nat. gr. 135, and those of a Romance of Alexander the Great at the Hellenic Institute of Byzantine and Post-Byzantine Studies in Venice.[152] Also, Belting pointed to the Italianate style of a typicon, written in 1346 for a monastery in Trebizond.[153] Grabar saw Western influence in family portraits in the Palaeologan period, and it is true that Byzantine families adopted coats of arms in imitation of medieval Europe.[154] Finally, various Western elements have been noted in Serbian and Bulgarian frescoes of the thirteenth and fourteenth centuries, as well as in Palaeologan architecture of the period.[155]

While an enumeration of varied examples of Western artistic influence in the Palaeologan era does not of course prove anything about the matter of the evangelist symbols themselves, it does show that the adoption of Western iconography was widespread at this time. In the absence of any other explanation, inspiration from Western Europe is also the most likely cause for the sudden change in the Byzantine iconography of symbols in the thirteenth and fourteenth centuries. Once the Hieronymian system was established in this period, it became the standard for Post-Byzantine art in the Orthodox lands outside Russia (cf. Table D). No doubt contacts with European powers, such as Venice, strengthened the acceptance of the scheme, and the older conventions came to be considered erroneous, as has been seen in the above examples. Possibly Prince Gagarine's alteration of the evangelist symbols of the Ghelati Gospels for his 1900 publication is a very late instance of the same phenomenon.

In sum, Gospel prologues serve to explain several problems with the Middle Byzantine iconography, and the preceding discussion has revealed the existence of both carefully planned programs of texts and images, as in Athens cod. 57, as well as the great confusion between the two in later manuscripts. Because the verbal and pictorial are so well chosen in the Athens Gospels, it is well to remember that it is one of the earliest surviving manuscripts with evangelist symbols, thus pointing to the formative importance of Gospel prologues. Yet other factors also played a role in the development of the iconography of Byzantine evangelist symbols throughout the many centuries surveyed in the foregoing pages. Similar patterns of iconographic transmission and alteration will be found in the following juxtaposition of prefaces with the theme of the *Maiestas Domini*.

NOTES

1. The system of St. Jerome is discussed below and in Appendix I, Table B. For a review of the literature on the problem of evangelist symbols in Western medieval art see U. Nilgen, "Evangelistensymbole," *Reallexikon zur deutschen Kunstgeschichte,* 6 (Munich, 1973), cols. 517–49 (hereafter, "Evangelistensymbole").

2. Kondakoff, *Histoire de l'art byzantin,* 252.

3. H. Gerstinger, *Die griechische Buchmalerei* (Vienna, 1926), 32; O. Wulff, *Altchristliche und byzantinische Kunst* (Berlin, 1918), 532; F. Dölger, *Mönchsland Athos* (Munich, 1943), 208; Neuss, *Ezechiel,* 167; C. Nordenfalk, "Review of Paul Buberl and Hans Gerstinger, *Die byzantinischen Handschriften (der Wiener Nationalbibliothek) . . . ,*" *ZKunstg,* 8 (1939), 74; U. Nilgen, "Evangelistensymbole," col. 519; A. Frolow, "Un bijou byzantin inédit," *Mélanges offerts à René Crozet,* I (Poitiers, 1966), 628 (hereafter, "Un bijou").

4. V. Lazarev, *Storia della pittura bizantina* (Turin, 1967), 193 (hereafter, *Storia*); A. Boeckler, "Die Evangelistenbilder der Adagruppe," *MünchJb,* 3–4 (1952–53), 134ff. M. Alpatov ("Les reliefs de la Sainte-Sophie de Trebizonde," *Byzantion,* 4 [1927–28], 416–17) at an early date said there was no Western influence but cited no evidence concerning illuminated manuscripts. Morey also very early disbelieved the thesis of Western influence (*East Christian Painting in the Freer Collection* [New York, 1914], 40). Nordenfalk ("Die Evangelistensymbole," *Das Einhardkreuz* [Göttingen, 1974], 55) now thinks that early Greek symbols were influential in the West in the Carolingian age.

5. H. Buchthal, "A Byzantine Miniature of the Fourth Evangelist and Its Relatives," *DOP,* 15 (1961), 138–39; E. Rosenbaum, "The Evangelist Portraits of the Ada School and Their Models," *ArtB,* 38 (1956), 89, n. 61; R. L. S. Bruce-Mitford, *Evangeliorum Quattuor Codex Lindisfarnensis* (Olten, 1960), 143 (hereafter, *Codex Lindisfarnensis*).

6. E. Kitzinger, "The Coffin-Reliquary," *The Relics of Saint Cuthbert* (Oxford, 1956), 229–30.

7. In Oxford, Bodleian Library, *Greek Manuscripts in the Bodleian Library* (Oxford, 1966), 42 (hereafter, Oxford, *Greek Manuscripts* [1966]).

8. Vikan, *Illuminated Greek MSS,* 144–45.

9. Frolow, "Un bijou," 627–32, pl. 1.

10. P. L. Vocotopoulos, "Fresques datées du XIᵉ siècle à Corfu," *CahArch,* 21 (1971), 153–54, figs. 4–5.

11. See below, page 30.

12. See below, page 18.

13. Lazarev, *Storia,* 250; Vikan, *Illuminated Greek MSS,* 145; K. Treu, *Die griechischen Handschriften des Neuen Testaments in der UdSSR* (Berlin, 1966), 238–39 (hereafter, *Griechische Handschriften*).

14. For the manuscript see A. Martini and D. Bassi, *Catalogus codicum graecorum Bibliothecae Ambrosianae* (Milan, 1906), 502–3. The colophon states that the book was finished on Sunday, September 1, of the third indiction. This information can be used to calculate possible dates for the manuscript by consulting the perpetual calendar in V. Grumel, *La chronologie* (Paris, 1958), 316–17. The list of years in which September 1 fell on a Sunday can be determined, and the choices reduced further, because only one fifteenth of these years were also the third indiction. The latter calculation is somewhat complicated by the fact that the indiction begins on September 1, not January 1 as the calendar year, so that one has in fact to search for indiction 2 in this case. The resulting computations yield the years 944, 989, 1034, and 1079, with none in the twelfth and thirteenth centuries. The style of the miniatures does not appear to belong in the tenth century, but it is not easy to choose between the years 1034 and 1079 without more study. On the miniatures see M. L. Gengaro et al., *Codici decorati e miniati dell'Ambrosiana, Ebraici e Greci* (Milan, n.d.), 132–35, pls. XLI–XLIX.

15. C. Giannelli, *Codices Vaticani graeci codices 1485–1683* (Vatican, 1950), 126, with the incipit and explicit (hereafter, *Codices Vaticani graeci*).

16. C. R. Gregory, *Textkritik des Neuen Testaments,* I (Leipzig, 1900), 158 (hereafter, *Textkritik*). No mention here is made of the text, and the manuscript has not yet been catalogued. I know it from the microfilm at

the Institut für Neutestamentliche Textforschung in Münster, Westfallen, West
Germany.

17. Athens, *Byzantine Art, An European Art*
(Athens, 1964), 313–14, 544 (hereafter, *Byzan-
tine Art, An European Art*); P. Buberl, *Die
Miniaturenhandschriften der Nationalbibliothek
in Athen* (Vienna, 1917), 9–12, pls. X–XIII
(hereafter, *Miniaturenhandschriften*); Vikan,
Illuminated Greek MSS, 145; A. Marava-
Chatzinicolaou and C. Toufexi-Paschou,
*Catalogue of the Illuminated Byzantine Manu-
scripts of the National Library of Greece*
(Athens, 1978), 108–17 (hereafter, *Catalogue*).

18. All these texts are unpublished.

19. For example, see von Soden, I, 1, 305, 307,
309, 311–13, 324, and Chapter IV below.

20. Καὶ γὰρ τὰ χερουβὶμ τετραπρόσωπ(α) καὶ τὰ
πρόσωπα αὐτῶν εἰκόνες τῆς πραγματ(είας)
τοῦ υἱοῦ τοῦ θ(εο)ῦ. Τὸ γὰρ ὁμοίωμα λέοντ(ι)
τὸ ἔμπρακτο(ν) καὶ βασιλικὸν καὶ
ἡγεμονικὸ(ν) χαρακτηρίζει. Τὸ δὲ ὅμοιον
μόσχου τὴν ἱερουργικὴν καὶ ἱερατικὴν
ἐμφαίνει. Τὸ δὲ ἀνθρωποειδὲς τὴν σάρκωσιν
διαγράφει. Τὸ δὲ ὅμοιον ἀετῷ τὴν
ἐπιφοίτησιν τοῦ ἁγίου πν(εύματο)ς ἐμφανίζει.
Cf. von Soden, I, 1, 303 (no. 82).

21. Buberl, *Miniaturenhandschriften*, 12–13, figs.
29–31; Vikan, *Illuminated Greek MSS*,
145; Marava-Chatzinicolaou and Toufexi-
Paschou, *Catalogue*, 189–97.

22. Two exceptions are Paris, Bibl. Nat. gr. 278,
and Rome, Vat. gr. 1522, which contain some
rare verses but no prose prefaces. On these
manuscripts see below, pages 28ff.

23. P. Buberl and H. Gerstinger, *Die byzantinischen Handschriften, 2, Beschreibendes Verzeichnis der illuminierten Handschriften in Österreich*, 4 (Leipzig, 1938), 4, 46–49, no. 10,
pls. XIX–XXI (hereafter, *Byzantinische Handschriften*); *Byzantine Art, An European Art*,
331; H. Hunger, *Katalog der griechischen
Handschriften der Österreichischen Nationalbibliothek. Supplementum Graecum* (Vienna,
1957), 101–2 (hereafter, *Katalog . . . Supplementum Graecum*); Belting, *ZKunstg* (1975),
225, n. 30.

24. C. W. James, "Some Notes upon the Manuscript Library at Holkham," *The Library*, 4th
ser., 2 (1922), 225; W. O. Hassal, "Byzantine
Illumination at Holkham," *The Connoisseur*,
133 (April 1954), 90. The latter cites No. 1b as
an illustration of an evangelist from MS 4,
but it is in fact from MS 3.

25. Unpublished. I owe my knowledge of this
manuscript to photographs of Professor
Buchthal and to the microfilm at the Institut
für Neutestamentliche Textforschung in
Münster.

26. Lazarev, *Storia*, 221, 264; S. I. Amiranashvili,
Gruzinskaĩa Miniatũra (Moscow, 1966),
23–24, 50, pls. 34–39, with additional bibliography; H. Machavariani, *Georgian Manuscripts* (Tbilisi, 1970), pls. 20–28. The style of
some of these scenes compares with Athens,
Nat. Lib. cod. 93, also of the late twelfth century. Cf. ibid., pl. 26, and Buberl,
Miniaturenhandschriften, figs. 53, 55. There is
a microfilm of the manuscript at the Dumbarton Oaks Center for Byzantine Studies in
Washington, D.C.

27. G. Gagarine, *Recueil d'ornaments et d'oeuvres
d'architecture byzantins, georgiens et russes*,
2ᵉ serie (St. Petersburg, 1900), pl. XXVIII.
Three symbols are correctly described in
N. V. Pokrovskiĩ, "Miniatũry evangeliĩa
gelatskogo monastyria," *Zapiski otdelenie
russkoi i slavianskoi arkheologii Imperatorskogo
russkogo arkheologicheskogo obshchestva*, 4
(1887), 13, 29, 36. He overlooks the symbol of
John (p. 45).

28. For one example of the inaccuracy of
Gagarine's work see D. T. Rice, ed., *The
Church of Hagia Sophia at Trebizond* (Edin-
burgh, 1968), 243–44.

29. E. Zomarides, *Die Dumba'sche Evangelien-
Handschrift vom Jahre 1226* (Leipzig, 1904).
The Greek colophon is given on p. 21 and the
Armenian one in a German translation on
pp. 21–22. Idem, "Eine neue griechische
Handschrift aus Caesarea vom J. 1226 mit
armenischer Beischrift," *Studien zur Palaeographie und Papyruskunde*, 2 (Leipzig, 1902),
3–6; P. G. Croquison, "Manuscrits," *Collection Hélène Stathatos, Les objets byzantins et
post-byzantins* (Limoges, 1957), 79, pls.
XIV–XV; S. Vyronis, Jr., *The Decline of
Medieval Hellenism in Asia Minor and the Process of Islamization from the Eleventh through
the Fifteen Century* (Berkeley, 1971), 233; B.
Atsalos, *La terminologie du livre-manuscrit à
l'époque byzantine, première partie, Termes dé-
signant le livre-manuscrit et l'écriture* (Thessaloniki, 1971), 252.

30. *PG*, 7, cols. 885–86.

31. Ibid., cols. 886–88. The specific equation of the eagle with John is missing in the now fragmentary text, but it is to be inferred from later sources and because of the pairing of the other three symbols.

32. *PL*, 26, cols. 15–22. The text is from his commentary on Matthew. On the standard contents of Latin Gospels see E. Rosenbaum, "Evangeliar," *Reallexikon zur deutschen Kunstgeschichte*, 6 (Munich, 1973), col. 439, and R. M. Walker, "Illustrations to the Priscillian Prologues in the Gospel Manuscripts of the Carolingian Ada School," *ArtB*, 30 (1948), 1. For prefaces in Latin manuscripts see P. McGurk, *Latin Gospel Books from A.D. 400 to A.D. 800* (Paris, 1961), 7–8; S. Berger, "Les Préfaces jointes aux livres de la Bible dans les manuscrits de la Vulgate" (1904), 1–78; J. Chapman, *Notes on the Early History of the Vulgate Gospels* (Oxford, 1908); J. Regul, *Die Antimarcionitischen Evangelienprologe* (Freiburg, 1969; hereafter, *Evangelienprologe*).

33. See note 13, p. 44.

34. Lazarev, *Storia*, 193, 252, fig. 265; *Iskusstvo vizantii v sobrianiïakh SSSR*, II (Moscow, 1977), 55 (hereafter, *Iskusstvo vizantii*); Treu, *Griechische Handschriften*, 239–42.

35. H. Omont, "Catalogue des manuscrits grecs des bibliothèques de Suisse," *Centralblatt für Bibliothekswesen*, 3 (1886), 46; C. Meredith, "The Illustration of the Codex Ebnerianus. A Study in Liturgical Illustration of the Comnenian Period," *JWarb*, 29 (1966), 420–21 (hereafter, "Codex Ebnerianus"). The manuscript was to have been included in the 1976 exhibition in Geneva, for which see B. Gagnebin, *L'enluminure de Charlemagne à François Ier. Manuscrits de la Bibliothèque publique et universitaire de Genève* (Geneva, 1976). The latter was not available to me.

36. K. Benda and J. Myslivec, "The Illuminations of the Codex Maurocordatianus," *Byzantinoslavica*, 38 (1977), 1–13 (hereafter, "Codex Maurocordatianus"); K. Aland, *Kurzgefasste Liste der griechischen Handschriften des Neuen Testaments* (Berlin, 1963), 65 (hereafter, Aland); K. Gábriš, "Codex Maurocordatianus I–II," *Communio Viatorum, A Theological Quarterly*, 1 (1958), 33–36, 169–83. The other two parts of the latter were not available to me. I am much indebted to Dr. Bohumila Zástěrová in Prague for sending me a set of photographs of the manuscript.

37. Benda and Myslivec, "Codex Maurocordatianus," 1–2.

38. Αὐτὴ ἡ βίβλος ἐγράφη μὲν ὅτε δεῖ καὶ ἐγράφη ἐξωνήθη δὲ παρὰ Μιχαὴλ ἱερέως τοῦ Πεπαγωμ(έν)ου ἐν αἴτι !=ἔτει] ϛχζα [1183] ἐπὶ τῆς βασιλείας τοῦ εὐσεβεστάτ(ου) πορφυρογεννήτ(ου) κῦρ Ἀλεξίου τοῦ Κομνηνοῦ κ(α)τ(ὰ) μῆνα αὔ(γουσ)το(ν) διδασκομένου αὐτοῦ τὰ ἱερὰ γράμματ(α) παρὰ Ἀντ(ω)ν(ίου) εὐτ(ε)λ(οῦς) (μον)αχ(οῦ) καὶ ἱερέ(ως) τοῦ Τζίρου καὶ κ(α)τ(ὰ) θ(εὸ)ν π(ατ)ρ(ὸ)ς αὐτοῦ.

Ἐν ἔτει ϛξη [1560] ἀριθμήσαμεν τὴν παροῦσαν βίβλον εἰς τὰς λα τοῦ μαρτίου ἀφ' οὗ ἐπροεγράφη ἔτη εἰσὶν 377. Μιχαὴλ Καντακουζηνός αφξ [1560].

This book was written whenever it was written [and] bought by Michael Pepagomenos, in the year 6691 [= 1183] under the reign of the most pious porphyrogennitos Lord Alexios Komnenos, in the month of August. Michael was taught the Holy Scriptures by Antonios Tziros, his father in God.

In the year 7068 [= 1560] we numbered the present book on the 31st of March. From the time it was written 377 years have passed. Michael Kantakouzenos 1560.

Professor Politis furnished me the above transcription of the text and a translation, and Professors Oikonomides and Ševčenko further advised me on the meaning of the first passage.

39. The writer of the subscription of 1560 might be someone employed by Michael, because he says "we numbered" the book, and then Michael himself signed the statement. There was a servant of his who owned a manuscript of readings from the prophets now in the Athens National Library, MS 24 of 1579. See Sakkelion, Κατάλογος, 4. Michael was a well-known and very wealthy Phanariote of the period. He possessed a large library that was dispersed after his execution by the sultan. See D. M. Nicol, *The Byzantine Family of the Kantakouzenos (Cantacuzenus) ca. 1100–1460, A Geneaological and Prosopographical Study* (Washington, D.C., 1968) (hereafter, *Byzantine Family*). V. R. Förster (*De antiquitatibus et libris manuscriptis Constantinopolitanis* [Rostochius, 1877], 27–29) published an inventory of his library taken from a list in a manuscript of the second half of the

sixteenth century in Vienna, Nat. Lib. Hist. gr. 98. There is no mention of a manuscript containing the Gospels. However, he certainly had some. Stephan Gerlach bought from him an illustrated New Testament with Psalter. See E. Legrand, "Notice bibliographique sur Jean et Théodose Zygomalas," *Recueil de textes et de traductions*, 2 (Paris, 1889), 122. Crusius, a contemporary observer, reports that after the death of Michael manuscripts of the Gospels were sold (M. Crusius, *Turcograecia* [Basil, 1584], 509). A Psalter in the Harvard College Library (MS gr. 3) has a note of 1589 written by a Michael Kantakouzenos. See L. Nees, "An Illuminated Byzantine Psalter at Harvard University," *DOP*, 29 (1975), 207 (hereafter, "Byzantine Psalter"). This cannot be the same person who owned the Bratislava Gospels, for that Michael was killed in 1578.

40. Washington, D.C., Freer Gallery of Art, No. 09.1685 (Morey, *East Christian Paintings*, 34–40, pls. III, V); Istanbul, Ecumenical Patriarchate, cod. 5 (G. Soteriou, Κειμή-λια τοῦ Οἰκουμενικοῦ Πατριαρχείου. Πατριαρχικὸς Ναὸς καὶ Σκευοφυλάκιον [Athens, 1937], 63; hereafter, Κειμήλια); Cambridge, Mass., Harvard College Library, cod. TYP 215 H and Washington, D.C., Dumbarton Oaks, cod. acc. No. 58.105 (Vikan, *Illuminated Greek MSS*, 142–47). Symbols on the evangelists' lecterns also appear in the frescoes of the Church of Hagia Sophia at Trebizond. See Rice, *Trebizond*, 108–11, pls. 37–39.

41. *Byzantine Art, An European Art*, 580, 590, with bibliography; Nees, "Byzantine Psalter," passim. For the portraits see E. Tsimas and S. Papachadjidakis, Χειρό-γραφα Εὐαγγέλια Μονῆς Μεγάλου Σπηλαίου (Athens, n.d.), pls. 49, 55, 57.

42. All but the Bratislava codex are discussed by Nees, "Byzantine Psalter," esp. 216–17. For the ornament cf. his figs. 1–2, 7, 10, with the evangelist portraits of the Bratislava Gospels. The sketchy quality of the floral forms in one headpiece of the Harvard Psalter (ibid., fig. 2) also resembles the Bratislava headpieces.

43. Perhaps it would be possible to obtain this information from a close examination of the manuscript, but unfortunately I know it only from a microfilm and a set of photographs.

44. Treu, *Griechischen Handschriften*, 241.

45. *PG*, 7, cols. 887–88.

46. The texts are von Soden, no. 108. The prefaces for Matthew and Mark already contain a reference to the appropriate symbol for these evangelists, the man and eagle, respectively. The scribe of Paris, gr. 93, has added the following sentences to the prologues for Luke and John: f. 124r (Luke) καὶ ἔστιν ὅμο-ιον μόσχ(ου), and f. 194r (John) καὶ ἔχ(ει) χαρακτῆρα λέοντ(ος) διὰ τὸ βασιλικὸν καὶ ἡγεμονικόν.

47. In general see F. van der Meer, *Maiestas Domini, Théophanies de l'Apocalypse dans l'art chrétien* (Rome, 1938), 228–29; G. Millet, *La Dalmatique du Vatican* (Paris, 1945), 47–48. Van der Meer underestimates the importance of Irenaeus.

48. *PG*, 89, cols. 797–800; H. G. Beck, *Kirche*, 442. On the text see Sagnard, *Irénée*, III, 80.

49. F. E. Brightman, "The *Historia Mystagogica* and Other Greek Commentaries on the Byzantine Liturgy," *JTS*, 9 (1908), 338–89 (hereafter, "Historia Mystagogica"). On the history of the text see Bornert, *Commentaires*, 127–42.

50. *PG*, 106, cols. 256–57.

51. *PG*, 28, col. 432; Quasten, *Patrology*, III, 39.

52. *PG*, 123, col. 493.

53. *PG*, 87c, col. 4000.

54. Bornert, *Commentaires*, 210–11; Beck, *Kirche*, 434–36.

55. These verses are printed in K. Lake, "Codex 1 of the Gospels and Its Allies," *Texts and Studies, Contributions to Biblical and Patristic Literature*, 7, no. 3 (Cambridge, 1902), xiii. On the manuscript see K. Escher, *Die Miniaturen in den Basler Bibliotheken, Museen und Archiven* (Basel, 1917), 20–21, pl. 1, 1; Meredith, "Codex Ebnerianus," 419, 421, 423–24; Hatch, *Facsimiles*, 192, pl. LX; Omont, "Catalogue des manuscrits grecs des bibliothèques de Suisse," 7. The manuscript is an important witness to one textual family of Byzantine Gospel books. Besides Lake, see Devreesse, *Introduction*, 157, and Metzger, *Text of the New Testament*, 61.

56. The passages are unpublished and are ignored in the Oxford catalogue: F. Madan, *A Summary Catalogue of Western Manuscripts in the Bodleian Library at Oxford*, 4 (Oxford, 1905), 592, no. 29236. On the manuscript see Hutter, *Corpus*, I, 75–76, figs. 279, 282–84, with the previous bibliography.

57. Soteriou, Κειμήλια, pls. 47–50; Vikan, *Illuminated Greek MSS*, 145; C. Walter, "Two

Notes on the Deesis," *REB*, 26 (1968), 315; idem, "Further Notes on the Deesis," *REB*, 28 (1970), 169; Nelson, "Michael the Monk."

58. M. Richard, *Inventaire des manuscrits grecs du British Museum* (Paris, 1952), 87; *Catalogue of Additions to the Manuscripts in the British Museum in the Years 1888–93* (London, 1894), 474. The miniatures are unpublished.

59. K. Weitzmann, *Aus den Bibliotheken des Athos* (Hamburg, 1963), 57–58, pl. 10; A. van Buren in *Illuminated Greek MSS*, 193; H. Belting, *Das illuminierte Buch in der spätbyzantinischen Gesellschaft* (Heidelberg, 1970), 14, 40 (hereafter, *Das illuminierte Buch*); S. Eustratiades and Arcadios, *Catalogue of the Greek Manuscripts in the Library of the Monastery of Vatopedi on Mt. Athos* (Cambridge, 1924), 173 (hereafter, *Catalogue*). On the confusion concerning the proper number of the manuscript see Nelson, "Michael the Monk," n. 16. G. Vikan first mentioned the similarity of the Vatopedi manuscript to the Patriarchate Gospels in his review of H. Belting, *Das illuminierte Buch . . .* in *Byzantine Studies*, 1 (1974), 198.

60. The Greek is that of Anastasius Sinaites. The Latin translation of Irenaeus has *gratiam* (Sagnard, *Irénée*, III, 196). Germanos, who paraphrases Irenaeus, also used δόσιν. See Brightman, "Historia Mystagogica," 389.

61. Soteriou, **Κειμήλια**, 75.

62. See note 56 above.

63. See above, page 20 and note 25.

64. *Illuminated Greek MSS*, 142–47.

65. T. Schermann, *Prophetarum vitae fabulosae indices apostolorum discipulorumque Domini Dorotheo, Epiphanio, Hippolyto aliisque vindicata* (Leipzig, 1907), 129–130.

66. R. Devreesse, *Les manuscrits grecs de l'Italie meridionale* (Vatican, 1955), 19 (hereafter, *Les manuscrits grecs*); Giannelli, *Codices Vaticani graeci*, 41–43; K. and S. Lake, *Dated Greek Minuscule Manuscripts to the Year 1200*, 7 (Boston, 1937) (hereafter, *Miniscule Manuscripts*).

67. A. Rahlfs, *Verzeichnis der griechischen Handschriften des Alten Testaments* (Göttingen, 1914), 269.

68. E. Peron and F. Battaglini, *Codices manuscripti graeci ottoboniani Bibliothecae Vaticanae* (Rome, 1893), 150.

69. Ὁ τετραμόρφοις Χερουβ(ὶμ) ἐφεδρεύων / τετράμορφον δέδωκε τὴν νέαν χάριν· / τὸι

Ματθαῖον μὲν ἀνθρώπου θεωρίαν· / τὸν Μάρκον δὲ λέοντος πάλιν εἰδέαν· / τὸν δ' αὖθις Λουκᾶν ὁμοιότιτα μόσχου· / αετοῦ δίκην τὸν υἱὸν Ζεβεδαίου· / παράσχου καμοὶ τὸν τούτοις προσφυγότα· Ἰγνάτιον οἴκτιστον πταισμάτων λύσιν.

70. The literature is compiled by M. Bonicatti, "L'Evangeliario Vaticano greco 1522: problemi di scrittura onciale liturgica," *La Bibliofilia*, 61 (1959), 130–34 (hereafter, "L'Evangeliario").

71. *Codices Vaticani graeci*, 68–69. Recently S. Der Nersessian followed Giannelli and considered the manuscript to be from the fourteenth century: "L'Illustration du sticheraire du monastère de Koutloumous No. 412," *CahArch*, 26 (1977), 139.

72. Bonicatti, "L'Evangeliario," 129–56.

73. Ibid., 144–56; Weitzmann, *Byzantinische Buchmalerei*, 6.

74. H. Omont, *Inventaire sommaire des manuscrits grecs de la Bibliothèque Nationale*, I (Paris, 1886), 30 (hereafter, *Inventaire Sommaire*). See also idem, *Fac-similés des plus anciens manuscrits grecs en onciale et en minuscule de la Bibliothèque Nationale du IVe au XIIe siècle* (Paris, 1892), 10, pl. XXI. In the latter his attribution is to the "X^e et XVe siècles(?)." H. Bordier (*Description des peintures et autres ornements contenus dans les manuscrits grecs de la Bibliothèque Nationale* [Paris, 1885], 94) assigned the book to the tenth to twelfth centuries but correctly noted the relation of the manuscript's initials to Paris, gr. 510.

75. Most recently see G. Cavallo, "Funzione e strutture della maiuscola greca tra i secoli VII–XI," *La paléographie grecque et byzantine* (Paris, 1977), 109, figs. 48–49. According to Cavallo, both manuscripts are products of the same Constantinopolitan scriptorium of the tenth or the fourteenth century. He thus remains undecided about the date.

76. Weitzmann, *Byzantinische Buchmalerei*, 6–7. On the date of the manuscript, see I. Spatharakis, "The Portraits and the Date of the codex Par. Gr. 510," *CahArch*, 23 (1974), 97–105; and most recently I. Kalavrezou-Maxeiner, "The Portraits of Basil I in Paris Gr. 510," *JÖB*, 27 (1978), 19–24.

77. Weitzmann, *Byzantinische Buchmalerei*, fig. 28. There is a color illustration published in C. Couderc, "La miniature au moyen âge," *L'Illustration*, 168 (December 4, 1926).

78. E. Mioni, in Venice, Palazzo Ducale, *Venezia e Bisanzio* (Venice, 1974), 213 (hereafter, *Venezia e Bisanzio*).

79. Treu, *Griechische Handschriften*, 315. It is entirely possible or even likely that such entries could have been added later, but without examining the manuscript their date cannot be determined. Since Treu did not say specifically that they were later, he presumably considers them to be from the eleventh century, the date of the execution of the book.

80. A. W. Carr, "The Rockefeller McCormick New Testament: Studies toward the Reattribution of Chicago University Library, Ms. 965," Ph.D. dissertation at the University of Michigan, Ann Arbor, 1973, 50–51 (hereafter, "Rockefeller McCormick New Testament"); A. Cutler and A. W. Carr, "The Psalter Benaki 34.3, an Unpublished Illuminated Manuscript from the Family 2400," *REB*, 34 (1976), 304. F = Florence MS. S = Stavronikita MS.

Ματθαῖος ἐστι μυστικὸς ¹ πρῶτος τύπος
Ἐξ εἰκονίζων ἰδέαν ἀνθρωπίνην
Ἐφ' ᾧ τὸν ἀνθρώπινον αὐξάνει πλέον ²
Τοῖς κατὰ Χριστὸν οἰκονομίας λόγον.

1. F = μυστικῶς   2. lines 3 and 4 in F only.

Ὁ ¹ Μάρκος ἐστι ² δεύτερος τύπος πάλιν
Λέοντος ἡμῖν μυστικῶς ᾐνιγμένος
Τὸ βασιλικὸν καὶ δυνατὸν τοῦ λόγου ³
Ὃν ἐξ ἰούδα ἰσραὴλ σκύμνον ἔφυ.

1. F only   2. S = ἐστὶν   3. lines 3 and 4 only in F.

Λουκᾶς δ' ὁ θεῖος τρίτος ὕπαρχος τύπος
Μόσχου νοητῶς εἰκονίζων ¹ ἰδέαν
Χριστοῦ διδαχαῖς ἀροτριοῦντος φρένας
Ὃν καὶ πατὴρ θύσειεν ἀσώτῳ γόνῳ.

This poem is found in S only. 1. S = εἰκονίζων.

Ἰωάννης τέταρτος αὖθις εἰκόνα
Τὴν ἀετοῦ δείκνυσιν ὕψει τῶν λόγων
Ὑψιπετὴς γάρ ἐστιν ὡς θεολόγος
Οὐ(ραν)ίοις δόγμασιν αἰθεροδρόμος.

81. E. Rostagno and N. Festa, "Indice dei Codici greci Laurenziani non compresi nel Catalogo del Bandini," *Studi italiani di filologia classica*, 1 (1893), 53. He gives only the first and last lines of the verses.

82. The texts are not mentioned by S. P. Lambros, *Catalogue of the Greek Manuscripts on Mount Athos*, I (Cambridge, 1895), 79 (hereafter, *Catalogue*).

83. Treu, *Griechische Handschriften*, 245–46. The verses according to him are added to this eleventh–twelfth century Gospels in the fifteenth century.

84. H. Follieri, *Codices graeci Bibliothecae Vaticanae selecti temporum locorumque ordine digesti commentariis et transcriptionibus instructi* (Vatican, 1969), 50–51, with bibliography, pl. 32; Weitzmann, *Byzantinische Buchmalerei*, 85–86, figs. 581–89; Devreesse, *Les manuscrits grecs*, 11, 30.

85. A. Grabar, *Les manuscrits grecs enluminés de provenance italienne* (Paris, 1972), 37–38.

86. *Quinto Centenario della Biblioteca Apostolica Vaticana* (Vatican, 1975), 94–95. In E. A. Loew, *The Beneventan Script, A History of the South Italian Minuscule* (Oxford, 1914), 261, it is dated to the eleventh–twelfth century and assigned to the province of Rome.

87. Athens, *Byzantine Art, An European Art*, 310–11, 543; Vikan, *Illuminated Greek MSS*, 106, 134, 145–46.

88. E.g., London, Brit. Lib. Egerton 2783 (see above, Chapter II, page 26); Mt. Athos, Vatopedi, cod. 937 (see above, Chapter II, page 26); Moscow, Hist. Mus. gr. 25 (407) (Belting, "Stilzwang," fig. 15); New York, General Theological Seminary, cod. DeRicci 3 (van Buren in *Greek Illuminated MSS*, 192–93). The format of a framed symbol on a separate page was used in the Khitrovo Gospels, a Russian manuscript of the 1390s done in the workshop of Theophanes the Greek. See V. N. Lazarev, *Theophanes der Grieche und seine Schule* (Vienna, 1968), 74–78, pls. 118–21 (hereafter, *Theophanes*); idem, *Storia*, 401, 437. The Khitrovo Gospels in turn was the model for the Gospels of the Cathedral of the Dormition in Moscow. See T. Ukhova and L. Pisarskaya, *Manuscript from the Dormition Cathedral* (Leningrad, 1969); Lazarev, *Theophanes*, 93–94.

89. Vikan, *Illuminated Greek MSS*, 145; Lambros, *Catalogue*, 238; Morey, *East Christian Paintings*, 39. The latter two authors say there are portraits of Matthew and Luke in the manuscript, and Morey further states that opposite Matthew there is a picture of a bird. However, I saw only the miniatures of Luke and

the calf on the microfilm of the manuscript at the Patriarchal Institute for Patristic Studies in Thessaloniki.

90. Matthew has a rippling drapery fold beneath his right arm and scattered highlighting on the drapery about his legs. The portraits are unpublished. The style of the manuscript is related to Patmos cod. 80, for which see Athens, *Byzantine Art, An European Art*, 321–22, and G. Jacopi, "Le miniature dei codici di Patmo," *Clara Rhodos*, 6–7 (1932–41), pls. VII–X.

91. See above, pages 26–27.

92. *PL*, 34, col. 1046.

93. This is mentioned by the ninth-century Byzantine intellectual Photius, who says that in one text Hippolytus called himself μαθη-τῆς δὲ Εἰρηναίου: Photius, *Bibliotheca*, cod. 121. See H. Achelis, *Hippolytstudien* (Leipzig, 1897), 27.

94. H. Achelis, *Hippolytus Werke*, I, 2 (Leipzig, 1897), 183, provides a German translation and refers to publications of the Syriac text. Also see Neuss, *Ezechiel*, 32–33. I wish to thank Ms. Robin Darling for translating the Syriac for me.

95. A bust appears in the same position in the portrait of Matthew in Mt. Athos, Vatopedi cod. 939, a manuscript related to the Kraus Gospels and to the general problem of the "Nicaea" group. See Carr, "Rockefeller McCormick New Testament," fig. 176. I wish to thank Mr. Kraus for kindly allowing me to examine the manuscript and Professor Carr for her observations on the subject. She presented a paper on the manuscript at the XVᵉ Congrès International d'Études Byzantines in Athens in 1976.

96. Morey, *East Christian Paintings*, 59–60.

97. Ibid., 34–40.

98. Ibid., 35.

99. See note 89 above.

100. Soteriou (Κειμήλια, 93, pl. 63) illustrates only the portrait of John. The portraits of Mark and Luke survive, but he does not describe them, and I was not given permission by the authorities in Istanbul to examine the manuscript.

101. Von Soden, I, 1, 312 (no. 114). The manuscript cited as 1314 is Sinai, gr. 176. See Gardthausen, *Catalogus*, 34.

102. Von Soden, I, 1, 382; Omont, *Inventaire sommaire*, I, 13.

103. E. Miller, *Manuelis Philae, Carmina* (Paris, 1860), I, 19–21, nos. XXII, XXV, XXXVIII. On Manuel Philes see K. Krumbacher, *Geschichte der Byzantinischen Litteratur* (Munich, 1897), 774–80 (hereafter, *Geschichte*). Some of his poems on art are translated by C. Mango, *The Art of the Byzantine Empire 312–1453* (Englewood Cliffs, N.J., 1972), 347-48 (hereafter, *Art*).

104. Krumbacher first pointed this out (*Geschichte*, 777). A. Xyngopoulos thought that Philes' poems on the life of St. Demetrios were based on a series of icons, because of the discovery of cycles that closely correspond to the epigrams. He suggests that the poems may have been inscribed on miniatures of a manuscript (Ὁ Εἰκονογραφικὸς Κύκλος τῆς Ζωῆς τοῦ Ἁγίου Δημητρίου [Thessaloniki, 1970], 47–49). He also cited the poem on an icon τοῦ Καλλιέργη, whom he identifies as a known painter of the period (ibid., 60). J. Strzygowski thought that Philes' descriptions of labors of the months also were based on pictorial sources ("Die Monatscyclen der Byzantinischen Kunst," *RepKunstw*, 11 [1888], 37). A. Frolow showed how very close a poem on an encolpion of the despot Demetrios was to a reliquary at the Vatopedi Monastery and thought that the text was written with a very similar object in mind ("Un nouveau reliquaire byzantin," *REG*, 66 [1953], 101–9). S. Der Nersessian compared an illustration of the story of Barlaam and Joasaph with another poem of Manuel (*L'Illustration du roman de Barlaam et Joasaph* [Paris, 1937], 67), cited by Mango, *Art*, 247, n. 17. Belting points to his poems for icons and suggests that some were also for miniatures (*Das illuminierte Buch*, 13–14). In particular, he notes the connection of some with Psalter iconography. See Belting, "Zum Palatina-Psalter des 13. Jahrhunderts," *JÖB*, 21 (1972), 31–32. Most recently C. Mango has studied Philes' poems for frescoes, icons, and books commissioned by Michael Glabas Tarchaneiotes in H. Belting et al., *The Mosaics and Frescoes of St. Mary Pammakaristos (Fethiye Camii) at Istanbul* (Washington, D.C., 1978), 12–16.

105. He wrote a dedication for a book donated to the Chora Monastery, and Ševčenko thinks that he may have composed another for an eleventh-century Gospels rebound by a δέ-

σπουνα Maria Comnene Palaeologina ("Theodore Metochites, the Chora, and the Intellectual Trends of His Time," *The Kariye Djami*, 4 [Princeton, 1975], 37, n. 141). Also, Xyngopoulos thinks it possible that the dedication in an illuminated Menologion at Oxford was written by Manuel Philes for the donor, Demetrius Palaeologus (Κύκλος, 60). Belting considers another of Manuel's poems to be a dedication inscription for a manuscript (*Das illuminierte Buch*, 49, n. 152).

106. Lazarev, *Storia*, 376, 418, n. 97, with bibliography, pl. 535. Most recently see *Icones bulgares IXe–XIXe siècle* (Paris, 1976), no. 20.

107. T. Gerasimov, "L'icone bilatérale de Poganovo au Musée Archéologique de Sofia," *CahArch*, 10 (1959), 279–80.

108. For other changes see A. Grabar, "À propos d'une icone byzantine du XIVe siècle au Musée de Sofia," *L'art de la fin de l'antiquité et du moyen âge*, II (Paris, 1968), 849.

109. The symbols are not identified in the much later description of the mosaic in the Διήγησις, ed. A. Papadopoulos-Kerameus, *Varia graeca sacra* (St. Petersburg, 1909), 107. On the early Eastern *Maiestas Domini* see C. Ihm, *Die Programme der Christlichen Apsismalerei von vierten Jahrhundert bis zur Mitte des achten Jahrhunderts* (Wiesbaden, 1960), 42–51, 190–91, 195–209.

110. Belting, "Stilzwang," fig. 6.

111. The manuscript is art historically unpublished and contains portraits of David (f. 1r), Moses (f. 64r), Matthew (f. 107r), Luke (f. 127r), Christ and apostles (f. 323r), and Christ in Majesty (f. 325r). The miniatures have been added to a manuscript of the eleventh century. Liturgical tables and chapter lists are also inserted later, and a colophon to these texts (f. 322v) gives a date of June 5, 1447. This date may apply to the miniatures, as the style is that of this period. The *Maiestas*, for example, can be compared with Russian manuscripts of the first half of the fifteenth century, a time when Byzantine influence was still strong. See below, Chapter III, page 64, and fig. 44. For a general discussion of the art of the period see S. Radojčić, "La pittura bizantina dal 1400 al 1453," *RSBN*, N.S., 5 (1968), 41–60.

112. Only two cases come to mind—the enameled pendant at the monastery of Vatopedi (see Frolow, "Un bijou," 626, pl. 1), and a Maie-

stas in Vienna, Nat. Lib. Suppl. gr. 164 of 1109 (Buberl and Gerstinger, *Byzantinischen Handschriften*, IV, 2, pl. XIX, 1). In neither is the pairing that of Jerome.

113. A. M. Bandini, *Catalogus codicum manuscriptorum Bibliothecae Mediceae Laurentiae*, I (Florence, 1764; reprinted, Leipzig, 1961), 158. He says that the names of the symbols are added by a more recent hand.

114. Weitzmann, *Byzantinische Buchmalerei*, 15.

115. Athens, *Byzantine Art, An European Art*, 579–80. The same opinion is expressed in M. Chatzidakis and A. Grabar, *Byzantine and Early Medieval Painting* (London, 1965), fig. 101 and its caption, although on p. 28 the miniatures are discussed as belonging to the fourteenth century.

116. This has been discussed in relation to architectural backgrounds by T. Velmans, "Le role du décor architectural et la représentation de l'espace dans la peinture des Paléologues," *CahArch*, 14 (1964), 183–216.

117. Lazarev, *Storia*, fig. 275.

118. Underwood, *Kariye Djami*, II, pl. 166.

119. A Xyngopoulos, Ἡ Ψηφιδωτή Διακόσμησις τοῦ Ναοῦ τῶν Ἁγίων Ἀποστόλων Θεσσαλονίκης (Thessaloniki, 1953), pl. 11.

120. Lazarev, *Storia*, fig. 489.

121. Cf. the fourteenth-century miniature of the Baptism in Oxford, Bodl. Lib. MS Gr. th. f.1. (Pächt, *Byzantine Illumination*, fig. 16).

122. The space created by the wall is more tangible in other Palaeologan versions of the theme. Cf. Lazarev, *Storia*, figs. 489, 492, 499, 500.

123. A comparable Anastasis is found in Oxford, Bodl. Lib. MS Gr. th. f.1 (Hutter, *Corpus*, II, fig. 7) and a triptych at Mt. Sinai (G. and M. Soteriou, *Icones du Mont Sinaï* [Athens, 1956], pl. 220).

124. Cf. the cases of a Psalter in the Walters Art Gallery and the Smyrna Physiologus. On the former: A. Cutler, "The Marginal Psalter in the Walters Art Gallery," *JWalt*, 35 (1977), 37–62. On the latter: O. Demus, "Bemerkungen zum Physiologus von Smyrna," *JÖB*, 25 (1976), 235–58. At a later date I hope to make a study of the influence of twelfth-century illumination during the Palaeologan period. A preliminary version, entitled "The Later Impact of a Group of Twelfth-Century Manuscripts," was presented to the

Byzantine Studies Conference in New York, December 1977.

125. Cf. also Mt. Athos, Vatopedi cod. 937, and London, Brit. Lib. Egerton 2783, both of which seem to be derived from a Middle Byzantine model very similar to the Gospels in Istanbul, Ecumenical Patriarchate, cod. 3. This material is also projected for future publication. In the meantime see Nelson, "Text and Image," 232–60.

126. P. Casey, "The 'Lost' Codex 106 of the Gospels," *HThR*, 16 (1923), 394–95 (hereafter, "Codex 106"); Aland, 66. In both, the manuscript is assigned to the tenth century. Since I know it only from the microfilm at the Institut für Neutestamentliche Textforschung in Münster and from photographs supplied by the library, it is difficult to date, but the text looks to be eleventh century.

127. The portrait of Luke (fig. 32) has radiating chrysography on the stool and the desk. This is a feature found from the fourteenth to at least the sixteenth century. Examples: H. Buchthal, "Toward a History of Palaeologan Illumination," *The Place of Book Illumination in Byzantine Art* (Princeton, 1975), fig. 40 (hereafter, "Toward a History"); M. Chatzidakis, V. Djurić, and M. Lazović, *Les icones dans les collections suisses* (Bern, 1968), pl. 13. The head of Prochoros (fig. 33) may be compared with that of a young apostle in an icon of the Pentecost, attributed to the sixteenth century. See ibid., pl. 16.

128. Casey, "Codex 106," 395.

129. Observed on the microfilm at Münster.

130. E. Mioni, *Bibliothecae Divi Marci Venetiarum Codices graeci manuscripti*, I, 1 (Rome, 1967), 19–20.

131. I. Sakkelion, **Πατμιακὴ Βιβλιοθήκη** (Athens, 1890), 52, a wholly inadequate description of the manuscript, which I know from the microfilm in Münster. For the miniatures that it contains see Belting, *Das illuminierte Buch*, 67, with further bibliography, and Buchthal, "Toward a History," 152–57.

132. R. Devreesse, *Les fonds Coislin* (Paris, 1945), 16–17. There are two poems of four lines each on f. 9v. The second one is devoted to the symbols. Devreesse only prints the first line of the first poem and the last line of the second. The latter reads as follows:

Ἀνθρωπικὸν πρόσωπον αὐγεῖ Ματθαῖος.
Λέοντος εἶδος εἰκονίζει τὸν Μάρκον.
Λουκᾶν ὁ μόσχος γνησίως ὑπογράφει.
Ὡς ἀετοῦ σκόπει γε τὸν Ἰωάννην.

Matthew illumines the human person.
The form of the lion portrays Mark.
The calf truly exemplifies Luke,
As the eagle looks to John.

133. Bornert, *Commentaires*, 125–80. It should be noted that the authorship of the text was disputed in the Middle Ages with some assigning it to St. Basil the Great. I follow the conclusions of Bornert that Germanos was the actual author: *Commentaires*, 142–60.

134. *PG*, 98, cols. 383–454; Bornert, *Commentaires*, 126.

135. Bornert, *Commentaires*, 127.

136. F. E. Brightman, "The *Historia Mystagogica*," 248–67, 387–97; D. N. Borgia, *Il Commentario Liturgico di S. Germano Patriarca Constantinopolitano e la versione latina di Anastasio Bibliotecario* (Grottaferrata, 1912).

137. Bornert, *Commentaires*, 128–42.

138. Brightman, "Historia Mystagogica," 388–89.

139. *PG*, 98, cols. 413–16.

140. Brightman, "Historia Mystagogica," 253.

141. Bornert, *Commentaires*, 138–40.

142. Ibid.; Brightman, "Historia Mystagogica," 253.

143. C. L. Striker and Y. Kuban, "Work at Kalenderhane Camii in Istanbul: Second Preliminary Report," *DOP*, 22 (1968), 191–92. Professor Striker discussed further the Western iconography of the frescoes in a lecture at the XVᵉ Congrès International d'Études Byzantines in Athens, September 1976.

144. "Die Entstehung des Paläologenstils in der Malerei," *Berichte zum XI. Internationalen Byzantinisten-Kongress* (Munich, 1958), 33–41.

145. O. Demus, "The Style of the Kariye Djami and Its Place in the Development of Palaeologan Art," *The Kariye Djami*, IV, 108. See ibid., 136–39, for further comments on Western influence.

146. For the first: H. Hunger, "Evangelisten," *RBK*, col. 462. For the second: Buchthal, "Toward a History," 146.

147. Omont, *Miniatures des plus anciens manuscrits*, pls. XC–XCVI; Lazarev, *Storia*, 280–81, 333, with older bibliography; Belting, *Das il-*

luminierte Buch, 40–41: S Papadaki-Oekland, "Οἱ μικρογραφίες ἑνὸς χαμένου χειρογράφου τοῦ 1298," Δελτ. Χριστ.'Αρχ.'Ετ., 8 (1975–76), 30, 37–48.

148. A detailed study of the gatherings of Byzantine manuscripts has not been made, but J. Irigoin has commented briefly on the matter. According to him, "le type normal pour les manuscrits byzantins est le quaternion" and "le quinion . . . est rare." Cf. "Pour une étude des centres de copie byzantins," *Scriptorium*, 12 (1958), 220–21.

149. I am much indebted to Professor Richard H. Rouse of the University of California at Los Angeles for kindly answering my inquiry on this matter. The matter of the quire size requires more attention, but it may be noted that Destrez, for one, has found that scribes working for the University of Bologna in the thirteenth and fourteenth centuries regularly formed gatherings of ten folios, a practice that differs from that of copiests at other European universities. See J. Destrez, *La Pecia dans les manuscrits universitaires du XIIIe et du XIVe siècle* (Paris, 1935), 47.

150. Not having personally studied the manuscript, I owe my knowledge of its codicology to a conversation with Dr. Christine Havice of the University of Kentucky. Dr. Havice has written her doctoral dissertation for Pennsylvania State University on the Psalter.

151. Buchthal, "Toward a History," 149, with bibliography.

152. On Paris, gr. 135, and this phenomenon see T. Velmans, "Le Parisinus Graecus 135 et quelques autres peintures de style gothique dans les manuscrits grecs à l'époque des Paléologues," *CahArch*, 17 (1967), 209–35. On the Alexander manuscript see A. Xyngopoulos, *Les Miniatures du roman d'Alexandre le Grand dans le codex de l'Institut Hellénique de Venise* (Athens, 1965). His is by no means the last word on the subject. See M. Garidis, "Review of A. Xyngopoulos, *Les miniatures du Roman d'Alexandre . . . ,*" *CahArch*, 18 (1968), 271–75.

153. Belting, *Das illuminierte Buch*, 32. Also Lazarev, *Storia*, 379.

154. A. Grabar, "Une pyxide en ivoire à Dumbarton Oaks," *L'art de la fin de l'antiquité et du moyen âge*, I (Paris, 1968), 233–34; Nicol, *The Byzantine Family*, xiv.

155. See the comments by A. Xyngopoulos, "Review of G. Millet, *La peinture du moyen âge en Yougloslavie*, III, présenté par A. Frolow," *Makedonika*, 5 (1961–63), 588; R. Krautheimer, *Early Christian and Byzantine Architecture* (Baltimore, 1965), 295–96, 299, 301–3, 309.

III   The *Maiestas Domini*

The theme of the *Maiestas Domini,* or Christ enthroned on a rainbow and surrounded by a mandorla and the four apocalyptic beasts, is a subject found throughout Byzantine art. In the Early Byzantine period the most celebrated example is the fifth-century mosaic decorating the apse of the small Church of Hosios David in Thessaloniki (fig. 25),[1] but apse decorations in other regions of the Eastern Mediterranean in the centuries before Iconoclasm also feature the theme. Because it is often associated with the liturgy, C. Ihm has called it the liturgical *Maiestas.*[2] At this time it appears too in other media, as K. Weitzmann has recently demonstrated in his publication of a seventh-century icon from the Monastery of St. Catherine on Mount Sinai.[3] Immediately after Iconoclasm, the *Maiestas Domini* and other theophanic imagery were especially favored, for these biblical visions of God related well to the doctrines of the supporters of images both during and after the controversy, as A. Grabar has so admirably explained.[4] The *Maiestas* is used occasionally thereafter in apse compositions of the Middle Byzantine period but is gradually superseded by the Deesis, a subject that again is closely related to the liturgy performed in the bema below the fresco.[5]

After Iconoclasm the representation of Christ in Majesty is also used to decorate Greek manuscripts, as the following pages will show, and in this respect it parallels to a degree the deployment of the composition in Western medieval miniatures. In the latter domain the subject has been analyzed in detail in recent years, and one might cite in particular the studies of C. Nordenfalk in conjunction with his monograph on an Ottonian Gospels from Echternach [6] and that of H. Kessler in his book on illustrated Bibles from Tours.[7] In view of the Byzantine developments to be presented shortly, it is interesting that Kessler calls attention to the use of the theme as a frontispiece to the Latin Gospel book and associates the illustration with St. Jerome's prologue to the four Gospels, the one that begins *Plures fuisse*.[8] But in contrast to Latin manuscripts, the *Maiestas* is not so common in Greek Gospel books, and other categories of illustration, such as those enumerated in Chapter I, play a larger role here. Nevertheless, the iconography is found in some of the finest manuscripts and thus deserves a more extended discussion than it has heretofore received.[9] As in the preceding chapter, the emphasis will be on the interaction of miniatures and prologues, but again certain additional factors will require attention as well, and chief among these is the impact of the liturgy.

GOSPEL BOOKS IN PARMA AND OXFORD

The only Byzantine miniature that heretofore has been linked with a Gospel prologue is the *Maiestas Domini* in a headpiece to a Gospel book in Parma, Bibl. Palatina, MS gr. 5, of the late eleventh century (frontispiece).[10] The image on f. 5r is a carefully composed hierarchy that proceeds outward from the central circle containing the enthroned Christ surrounded by the cherubim, seraphim, and the spinning wheels of Ezekiel's vision. Next are four smaller circles with the evangelist symbols; then in the corners of the rectangle the evangelists are shown seated at their desks. Mark at the top left and Matthew at the top right are clearly labeled, but no inscriptions are visible for the bottom two evangelists, although undoubtedly Luke is to the left and John to the right. Six figures, each inscribed, stand beside the miniature. To the left and right are David and Isaiah; below Peter, Paul, John the Evangelist, and the emperor Trajan flank the title written in uncial letters.[11] Belting and Tsuji have both mentioned in passing that the miniature was an illustration of the preface of Irenaeus (von Soden, no. 82),[12] but neither has analyzed in detail the components of the headpiece nor described in full the texts that follow it.

The prefaces written on this and subsequent pages originally consisted of a series of five prologues all based on Irenaeus. The first, a preface to the Gospel of Matthew, is part of a series of four prologues giving brief biographies of the evangelists (von Soden, no. 108).[13] The Matthew preface continues on f. 5v and is followed immediately by the Irenaean prologue to the entire Gospels (von

Soden, no. 82). The two were occasionally written together at the beginning of a Gospel book, as von Soden notes.[14] The second preface begins with an initial letter, as does each sentence about the faces of the cherubim, further emphasizing the four symbols and their spiritual significance. The second prologue undoubtedly continued on the next page, f. 6r, but about 72 mm of text have been cut from the top of this folio. After the lacuna come prefaces to the Gospels of Luke and John (von Soden, no. 108). Besides the conclusion of the general prologue to the Gospels, the missing lines most likely included the Irenaean introduction to Mark (von Soden, no. 108), thereby completing the set of prologues for each Gospel. The prefaces follow the letter of Eusebius to Carpianus (ff. 3r–4v) and precede the chapter lists to the Gospel of Matthew (ff. 6v–7v), the canon tables (ff. 8r–12r), illustrations of Eusebius and Carpianus writing and Ammonius addressing a group of people (f. 12v), the Nativity above and Constantine and Helena below (f. 13r), and the portrait of Matthew (f. 13v). The Gospel of Matthew then begins on f. 14r.[15]

The headpiece introducing the prologues is a detailed illustration of all five texts, especially the general preface to the Gospels (von Soden, no. 82) that inspired the central part of the headpiece. The main circle containing Christ in a mandorla with cherubim and seraphim clustered around illustrates the principal subject of the preface, "He who was shown to men seated on the cherubim." The four smaller roundels with the evangelist symbols depict the four faces of the cherubim, or the "images of the dispensation of the Son of God." The prophet David in the left margin is included, because according to the text, he foretold the theophany. The evangelists, whose accounts were given to us by him who is enthroned on the cherubim, anchor the corners of this image of the divine order, just as the four winds to which the evangelists are compared occupy the sides of medieval world maps.[16]

The evangelists also are shown, because they are the subjects of the prefaces to the individual Gospels (von Soden, no. 108): the series derived from Irenaeus and quoted above in Chapter I.[17] The remaining figures depicted on f. 5r refer to these four texts. The prophet Isaiah, standing at the right and holding his scroll of prophecy, is mentioned in the prologue to Mark.[18] Peter and Paul to the left of the title are said to be sources for the accounts of Mark and Luke, who, unlike Matthew and John, were not among the original disciples. The presence of the evangelist John and the emperor Trajan on the right side of the title is less profound, as the biography of John merely says that he wrote in the time of Trajan. Thus, all components, except the stock scene of the animals beside the fountain at the top, derive directly from the five prefaces that follow, making this headpiece one of the most complete and accurate prologue illustrations in Byzantine art.

The iconography of the *Maiestas Domini* is only one of a number of unusual miniatures in the Parma Gospels. One can cite as evidence of the originality of its iconographic program such illustrations as the portraits of Eusebius, Carpianus, and Ammonius (f. 12v), the Nativity with Constantine and Helena (f. 13r) shown below, the three pages of feast scenes between the Gospels of Matthew and Mark, or the peculiar choice of scenes for the headpieces to the beginnings of each Gospel.[19] The subject matter is not routine and traditional as in many Byzantine Gospel books and suggests that the illustrations were selected with some care, for reasons, however, that are not yet fully understood.

The headpiece to the Gospel prefaces is no different in this respect from the other miniatures, for everything about these few pages is uncommon. First of all, the grouping of the five prologues at the beginning is not normal and, to this writer's knowledge, occurs elsewhere only in a related Gospels in Oxford, Bodl. Lib. E. D. Clarke 10 (fig. 34).[20] The usual procedure in Greek manuscripts is to write the prologue to the four Gospels at the beginning by itself or sometimes joined to the Matthew preface. The prologues to the other Gospels then typically precede the individual books. Such a practice is followed in both the Parma and Oxford Gospels, even though the prefaces are also given initially. Thus, the decision to collect all five prefaces at the front of the Parma Gospels or its model was both novel and deliberate. A reason for the placement of the prefaces on the opening pages of the manuscript is suggested by the title: "the contents of the harmony of the evangelists" (ὑπόθεσις τῆς τῶν εὐαγγελιστῶν συμφωνίας). Just as the combination of the prefaces in this position is unusual, so too is their title. Again, the only other example of prefaces with such a designation occurs in the Oxford Gospels, suggesting that this feature is an innovation of the person who wrote or designed the layout of the manuscript or its model.

The source of the wording is most likely a similar title sometimes used with Eusebius' note to Carpianus on the canon tables. Published editions of the Eusebian letter do not mention any title for the text, but in several manuscripts from as early as the Rossano Gospels of the sixth century the following is found: "the contents of the canons of the harmony of the evangelists"(ὑπόθεσις κανόνος [or κανόνων] τῆς τῶν εὐαγγελιστῶν συμφωνίας).[21] For obvious reasons, κανόνος (canon) has been deleted from the Parma title, but otherwise the wording is the same as the heading of the letter, undoubtedly its original context.

The fact that the title of the preface is not traditional but most likely an innovation of the creator of the Parma Gospels or its model is important for interpreting the broader significance of both the texts and their illustration. The prefaces are said to be a demonstration of the harmony or unity of the four Gospels, and for this reason they are presented together at the beginning of the book. This harmony of the Gospels proceeds from "He who was shown to men sitting on the cherubim," for, according to the preface, "he gave us the four-part Gospels." Christ in the center of the miniature is the visual and the theological focus for the dependent satellite figures of the evangelists and their symbols. Therefore, in composition and iconography this *Maiestas Domini* is an illustration of the unity of the four Gospels in Christ.[22]

A second example appears in the Gospel book in Oxford, Bodl. Lib. E. D. Clarke 10 (fig. 34), from approximately the same period as the Parma manuscript.[23] It too has a complex headpiece preceding a series of prologues, and again there is a central roundel of Christ, smaller circles with the evangelist symbols, and square panels of the four evangelists. The latter are not identified, but their order seems to differ from that in the Parma Gospels. The two authors at the top have gray hair and beards and are thus John and Matthew; the younger dark-haired Mark and Luke are shown in the lower corners. A more significant variant from the Parma miniature, however, is the principal roundel with Jesus. In the Oxford version he stands alone without his heavenly entourage. In this position he twice contradicts the phrase of the preface, "He who was shown sitting on the cherubim." The prologues here are the same as those found in Parma 5 and begin with the note about Matthew (von Soden, no. 108), followed by the general introduction to the Gospels (von Soden, no. 82) and the short entries on Mark, Luke, and John (von Soden, no. 108). Finally, as mentioned above, the title to the prefaces, ὑπόθεσις τῆς τῶν εὐαγγελιστῶν συμφωνίας, is the same one used in Parma 5. Thus, the Oxford miniature is also meant to be a prologue illustration, but owing to iconographic abridgment it no longer is as accurate as the Parma headpiece.[24]

Still, both Gospel books are closely related pictorially and textually. As seen in Appendix II, the contents of each are virtually alike. They have the same unusual collections of prefaces following the letter of Eusebius to Carpianus and preceding the *kephalaia* of Matthew and the canon tables. In each book some of the prologues are repeated again before the individual Gospel. These redundant texts are placed after the *kephalaia* in each, and according to J. J. G. Alexander,[25] the menologia at the ends of the two books are identical. The only details not shared are the later entries in E. D. Clarke 10 and the preface before Mark (von Soden, no. 108).

A similar close relationship exists in the programs of illustrations with the following subjects appearing in both: headpiece with portraits of Eusebius and

Carpianus, the *Maiestas Domini*, headpiece to Matthew with the Flight to Egypt, headpiece to Luke with the Birth of John the Baptist, headpiece to John with the Anastasis, and the standard evangelist portraits. The Flight to Egypt as an illustration for the Matthew headpiece is found, to this writer's knowledge, only in these two manuscripts [26] and thus is a telling detail. The books do not agree in the subject preceding the Gospel of Mark, Parma 5 having John baptizing the people and E. D. Clarke 10 having John the Baptist teaching. Yet neither conforms to the usual practice of depicting the Annunciation or the Baptism of Jesus in this location,[27] and certainly the events chosen are related. Finally, Parma 5 has a few other miniatures not present in the Oxford codex, and hence the above conclusions concerning the representations of the *Maiestas Domini* can be extended to the entire program; that is, the illustrations of E. D. Clarke 10 may be seen as an abridgment of the unusual cycle found in Parma 5.[28]

GOSPEL BOOKS IN BRESCIA AND MT. SINAI

In addition to the Irenaean introduction to the Gospels as a whole, the "Epiphanios" preface also served as the basis for images of Christ in Majesty, although the latter text, unlike the former, does not explicitly prescribe such a composition. The clearest connection of miniature and prologue is to be found in a Gospel book in Brescia, Bibl. Civica Queriniana A.VI.26.[29] Its f. XIIIv (fig. 35) has an unusual format of a small circle with an inscribed portrait of St. Epiphanios (ὁ ἅγιος ᾽Επιφάνιος) and below a larger circle with a variant of the "Epiphanios" preface as printed in von Soden.[30] At the end of the prologue there are four Greek participles, which, as von Soden notes, are sometimes joined to the prologue and are taken from the liturgy.[31] The opposite page, f. XIVr, has a rectangle filled with five circles (fig. 36). The Virgin and Child occupy the central one and the four symbols the corners, creating a variant on the *Maiestas Domini* theme.

The two pages show definite signs of repainting, and it is difficult to untangle the confused decoration of the book and to choose between the proposed dates for the manuscript in the tenth, twelfth, and fourteenth centuries.[32] The three preserved evangelists (f. XIVv, fig. 37; f. 58v; f. 97v) are Palaeologan, possibly fourteenth century, because of the proportions of the figures, especially the inflated hips and thighs. These aspects may be compared, for example, with the figure of Matthew in a late-thirteenth-century Gospel book in Leningrad, Publ. Lib. gr. 101 (fig. 40). Although the Brescia evangelist probably belongs to the following century, both portraits of Matthew share the same general Palaeologan characteristics. The evangelists in the Brescia codex are not, however, part of the original decoration of the manuscript, as a close examination of f. 58r indicates. At present, the latter page contains only a frame of an evangelist portrait that has completely flaked away, but the ink color of the title above, ἅ(γιος) Μάρκος, is the same as that of the script of the text, and hence this must be the original portrait. The Palaeologan evangelists probably are replacements for similarly damaged miniatures that were simply removed from the manuscript. One can argue that ff. XIIIv and XIVr, instead of being replaced, have been extensively repainted in the later period, because the head of St. Epiphanios is similar to that of Matthew from the fourteenth century, and the highlighting of the drapery of the Virgin and Child resembles the other evangelist portraits of the Palaeologan date. The symbols also are redone, and in this case one cannot even be certain that the animals were originally in these same positions.[33]

The script of the book may fit best into the twelfth century, as Mioni suggested,[34] and to this period should be attributed the original scheme of decoration. The headpiece of f. 1 with an arcuated lintel embellished by gold ornament on blue ground explains perhaps the suggestion of a tenth-century date. The ornament here is much like the "Laubsäge" style Weitzmann identified with that period.[35] However, it is also possible that this is only a copy of such decoration, and a parallel case would be a twelfth-century manuscript written in the Studios Monastery in Constantinople and now in the Vatican (gr. 2564).[36] The headpiece to the Gospel of Matthew in the latter follows closely another ornamental style of the tenth century, presumably because the illuminator or scribe had a model of that date at his disposal.

The inscriptions for each symbol have been rubbed out except for that of the man, but the survival of the one label is evidence that there were previously symbols here and that they were inscribed, most likely according to the system of the preface on the confronting page. The MP ΘU beside the Virgin also seems to be original, so that probably the central medallion contained a bust of the Virgin, and she probably held the Christ child in her arms as now. As for f. XIIIv, the identification of St. Epiphanios was written by the twelfth-century scribe of the prologue, confirming that the smaller circle always had such a portrait. In sum, the initial twelfth-century decoration of both pages consisted of an elaborate prologue illustration, comprising the portrait of St. Epiphanios on one page and facing it the Virgin and probably the infant Jesus, together with the four symbols. Most likely the symbols were inscribed with the evangelists' names according to the system of the adjacent preface.

A similar juxtaposition of the *Maiestas Domini* with prologues about the evangelist symbols is encountered in a Gospel book at Mt. Sinai, gr. 178. A badly deteriorated miniature depicts a bust of Christ framed by a square and accompanied by the four apocalyptic beasts (fig. 38). On the opposite recto four texts, one of which is the prologue of Epiphanios, mention the symbols.[37] The symbols appear not to have been labeled, so that no explicit reference is made to the latter text. Furthermore, it is likely that this miniature and the evangelist portraits were added later in the Palaeologan period on previously vacant pages of the book.[38] Probably the theme of the *Maiestas Domini* in this case was merely a convenient vehicle for representing the four symbols together or the subject of the adjacent texts.

THE INFLUENCE OF PREFACES

The miniatures in the preceding four manuscripts have a direct and tangible connection with prologues. Although this is the extent of the evidence so far noted, three other Gospel books do contain illustrations that may reflect earlier models in which miniature and preface were coordinated. The earliest are Paris, Bibl. Nat. gr. 81 (fig. 39), copied by the monk Nicephoros in 1092,[39] and Vienna, Nat. Lib. Suppl. gr. 164, written in 1109;[40] in both, the *Maiestas Domini* is placed on the verso of a folio opposite the portrait of Matthew on the next recto. The unusual selection of prefaces in these two books of mediocre quality is much alike. Besides a standard set of prologues to the Gospels (von Soden, no. 120), they include biographies of the evangelists taken from the *Menaion* reading for the saint's day and a text about the cherubim attributed in both cases to St. Basil the Great.[41] The latter prologue in fact is simply a version of Irenaeus' discussion of the fourfold nature of the Gospels, the faces of the cherubim, and the character of each Gospel, a somewhat more extensive borrowing from Irenaeus than is found in the usual Gospel preface (von Soden, no. 82). The text might be considered to be the basis for the miniatures of Christ in Majesty in the two books, yet in each the passage is written between the Gospels of Matthew and Mark. Perhaps in a more refined version of the program preface and image were more closely linked. That this is a definite possibility in the case of Paris gr. 81 is indicated by the other miniatures paired with Mark (figs. 52–53), Luke, and John, illustrations to be analyzed shortly.

Accompanying figures in Leningrad, Publ. Lib. gr. 101 of the late thirteenth century, also may be derived originally from a prototype in which prologues were illustrated.[42] The miniature relevant to the present discussion is the portrait of Matthew in which the *Maiestas Domini* is pictured directly above the evangelist (fig. 40). Although the Leningrad manuscript contains a series of prefaces derived from Cosmas Indicopleustes (von Soden, nos. 121–22), as well as other comments on the origins of the Gospels,[43] no account explicitly mentions such a heavenly vision in connection with Matthew. However, it should be remembered that the Irenaean prologue on Matthew (von Soden, no. 108) is frequently combined with the general introduction to the Gospels (von Soden, no. 82), as seen, for example, in the Oxford and Parma manuscripts. Thus, the theme of Christ in Majesty in the prototype for Leningrad gr. 101 could have been paired with Matthew in order to illustrate the two combined prefaces. More can be said about this probability shortly, when the other miniatures in the book are examined.

After the foregoing seven manuscripts, the evidence even of the indirect association of the *Maiestas Domini* with prefatory texts ends, for although the theme is found in other books there is no specific reason to relate these miniatures to prefaces. For instance, the two opening pages in the Nicomedia Gospels, a late-twelfth-century manuscript in Kiev, State Public Library of the Ukrainian Academy of Sciences, No. 25, illustrate a youthful Christ enthroned with the symbols (f. 1v) and opposite the Virgin and Child (f. 2r), yet the manuscript has no prefaces.[44] The same is true of the twelfth-century Gospel book in the collection of the University of Chicago, MS 131,[45] and another in Venice, Bibl. Marc. gr. Z540.[46] The badly damaged headpiece to Matthew in the former contains five medallions, depicting an enthroned Christ in the center and the four symbols at the corners (fig. 41). Though the composition has analogies with the headpieces of Parma, Bibl. Palat., MS gr. 5, and Oxford, E. D. Clarke 10, the Chicago manuscript has no prologues relating to the image.

In the Venice Gospel book the *Maiestas* (f. 11v, fig. 42) may be connected with an illustration of Christ blessing the four evangelists (f. 12v), although the corresponding rectos of each folio are blank, and it is not even certain if these pages are in their original positions.[47] In the Venice Gospels as in the Parma manuscript, Christ is seated on a rainbow and is surrounded by a multicolored mandorla. The four symbols fly out from behind the oval, and below Isaiah and Ezekiel hold scrolls prophesying the theophany. The text of Isaiah is, "I saw the Lord sitting on a high and exalted throne" (Isaiah 6:1); that of Ezekiel, "I saw the likeness of a throne and on the throne the likeness of a kind of man; this was the appearance of the likeness of the glory of the Lord" (Ezekiel 1:26 and 2:1). On the scroll of Christ is written part of his last instructions to the disciples from the Gospel of Matthew (28:18); "All authority in heaven and on earth has been given to me." [48] While the references to the throne on which the Lord sits have a vague similarity to the Irenaean preface to the Gospels, this is not enough to connect the image with any specific prologue, and indeed the manuscript contains no prefaces. Perhaps because of the lack of any explanatory text for the *Maiestas Domini,* it was thought desirable to depict the two prophets below.

Another example of the theme not associated with prologues is a miniature in a Psalter and New Testament in the Vatican Library, gr. 1210, of the eleventh or twelfth century.[49] Its illustrations, however, probably date to the fifteenth century and include a full-page representation of Christ in Majesty (fig. 43). It is now bound at the end of the book, but this is probably not its original position; and considering the other illustrations in the manuscript, the miniature may have once served as the frontispiece to the New Testament in analogy to the above examples. This iconography of the *Maiestas* appearing at the beginning of a Gospel book or lectionary subsequently spread beyond the political borders of Byzantium and was taken up in Russia in the fifteenth century, probably at the instigation of Byzantine itinerant artists. Thus, the scene is found on f. 1v of a fifteenth-century Slavic Gospels in Moscow, Hist. Mus. Eparch. 436 (fig. 45).[50] The drapery style of the enthroned Christ and the polygonal mandorla with its spiky rays show strong affinities with the Palaeologan miniature inserted into Vat. gr. 1210 and further attest to the ultimate Byzantine origin of the composition.[51]

THE IMPACT OF THE LITURGY

It is a moot point whether or not these miniatures in the above four Greek manuscripts are ultimately based on prologues, since there is another factor contributing to the appearance of theophanic illustrations at the beginning of Greek Gospel books, namely the influence of the liturgy. In his study of the images of the Ancient of Days, Christ Emmanuel, and Christ Pantocrator in the headpieces of the Gospel book in Paris, Bibl. Nat. gr. 74, Tsuji pointed to the interpretation of the section of the liturgy involving the reading of the Gospels, as presented in the *Historia Ecclesiastica,* a liturgical commentary most recently attributed to Germanos, patriarch of Constantinople from 715 to 730.[52] For Germanos the procession of the Lesser Entry that brought in the *Evangelion* symbolized the παρουσία, or the coming of Christ.[53] The Gospel itself is said to be "the coming of the Son of God by which he was shown to us." [54] The προκείμενον, or responsorial psalm, in this portion of the liturgy "tells again the revelation of the prophets, and the prophecy of the coming of Christ the King, like soldiers running forward and shouting: 'Thou who sit upon the cherubim, manifest thyself and come deliver us.' " [55] Germanos employs the Irenaean definition of the four Gospels, the one that is the basis of the Gospel preface (von Soden, no. 82) and thus speaks of the apocalyptic appearance of God sitting on the cherubim.[56] Tsuji links this theophanic interpretation of the Gospel that was read in the mass with the appearance of God in three forms in the headpieces of Paris, gr. 74. Furthermore, he suggests that scenes of the Maiestas Domini in a twelfth-century lectionary in Athens (Nat. Lib. cod. 2645) and one of the thirteenth century in S. Giorgio dei Greci, Venice, are occasioned by this conception of the Lesser Entry and the reading of the lections.[57]

More evidence can be added to his discussion of both illustration and liturgy. First, the interpretation of the Lesser Entry as the coming of Christ neither began nor ended with Germanos. Maximus, writing in the seventh century in his *Mystagogia*, the other important early liturgical commentary, relates the first entry of the priest to the first coming of Christ in the flesh into the world.[58] The twelfth-century commentary traditionally attributed to Sophronius defines the εὐαγγέλιον as the "revelation of the coming of Christ, the Son of God, who was shown to us not through riddles but openly." [59] The treatise is a compilation based on the eighth-century *Historia Ecclesiastica* and the eleventh-century *Protheoria* of Nicholas of Andida,[60] and this particular section is a good illustration of the mixture of sources. The statement just quoted is based on Germanos,[61] the very next sentence is taken from the *Protheoria*.[62] The latter commentary, itself, departs from the pattern and says instead that the Lesser Entry symbolizes the appearance of Christ at the Jordan, the same thought that appears in a liturgical commentary written in verse by Michael Psellos and based on the *Protheoria*.[63] Finally, in the fourteenth century the *Sacrae liturgiae interpretatio* (c. 1350) by Nicholas Cabasilas speaks about the ceremony involving the Gospel lection in terms similar to those that Germanos used centuries before.

When these [the antiphones] are over, the priest, standing in front of the altar, raises the Gospel book and shows it to the people, thus symbolizing the manifestation of the Lord when he began to appear to the multitudes. . . . After the Trisagion the reading from the Apostolic book takes place; this is followed by the Gospel. Before each the Church sings praises to God. . . . What do the readings from the Holy Scripture at this point in the liturgy signify? I have already told you their practical purpose; they prepare and cleanse in readiness for the great sanctification of the holy mysteries. Their significance, however, is this: they represent the manifestation of the Savior, by which he became known soon after his showing. The first showing of the Gospel with the book closed represents the first appearance of the Savior. . . . But that which is represented here is his more perfect manifestation.[64]

Such interpretations of the reading of the Gospel passages may have influenced the subjects chosen to decorate the initial pages of lectionaries or Gospel books, and furthermore some of the above miniatures may be a product of this influence. Unfortunately, all has to remain conjecture except for the *Maiestas Domini* in Vat. gr. 1210 (fig. 43). This miniature is specifically related to the liturgy by means of the epithets given to the four beasts surrounding Jesus. In addition to the abbreviated names of the evangelists, the symbols are inscribed with the following participles: ἄδοντα (lion), βοῶντα (calf, mostly effaced now), κεκραγότα (eagle), καὶ λέγοντα (man). These words are pronounced out loud by the celebrant of either the liturgy of St. John Chrysostomos or St. Basil and refer to the myriad of angels, archangels, cherubim, and seraphim who surround the Lord, "singing, crying out, shouting, and saying the triumphal hymn." [65] The terms were applied to the symbols in the context of the Majesty of the Lord as early as Cappadocian apse frescoes of the tenth and eleventh centuries, and they appear later on fifteenth-century liturgical veils again in association with the symbols. [66] The concept survives the demise of the Byzantine Empire and is encountered in an unpublished Post-Byzantine liturgical manuscript at the Iviron Monastery on Mt. Athos, cod. 1438 (fig. 45). Here the four symbols framed by gold roundels are placed in the margin beside the passage in question from the liturgy of St. John Chrysostomos. Furthermore, it will be recalled that the entire phrase from the liturgy was occasionally added to the conclusion of the prologue of Epiphanios, and the pertinent example in this regard is the Brescia Gospels discussed previously (fig. 35). Thus these varied examples, both textual and artistic, demonstrate the strong and continuing impact of the divine service.

Finally, the liturgy may be the key for understanding another series of *Maiestas* images—those coupled with the scene of Moses receiving the law. The iconography appears in two Gospel books, Paris, Bibl. Nat. suppl. gr. 1335 from the second half of the twelfth century, [67] and Florence, Bibl. Laur. Plut. VI. 32, slightly later in date (fig. 47). [68] In both a full-page miniature of Christ and the four symbols on the recto of a folio is placed opposite the scene of Moses receiving the law (fig. 46). The latter is inscribed with the first portion of John 1:17, "For the law was given through Moses," and the *Maiestas* with the continuation, "grace and truth came through Jesus Christ." It has been convincingly argued that a third manuscript, the Rockefeller McCormick Gospels, once had the same iconography, for this particular passage from John accompanies the image of Moses receiving the law (f. 8v), and most likely on the facing recto in the analogous position to the other two manuscripts there once appeared the *Maiestas* with the remainder of the inscription. [69] In all three cases the miniatures follow the canon tables and immediately precede the portrait of Matthew (also not extant in the Rockefeller McCormick Gospels) and the opening of the Gospel of Matthew. One other Gospel book, Mt. Athos, Dionysiou 4, has a preliminary miniature of Moses, but the entire text of John 1:17 is written on this page, and there is no *Maiestas*.[70] The same also occurs in Berlin, Staatsbibl. quarto 66, and in this case the scene is found before the Gospel of John.[71]

Brockhaus noted long ago that John 1:17 was the last verse of the pericope of John read on Easter Sunday, the first reading in a lectionary.[72] The uncial lectionary in the Vatican (gr. 1522) contains at the beginning a miniature of Moses receiving the law and opposite a poem about Christ and Moses. Both the miniature and these folios of the manuscript seem to be from the tenth century, so this is an early example of the theme in a lectionary.[73] Another piece of evidence in this regard is provided once more by the *Historia Ecclesiastica*. Germanos interprets the Gospel lection read in the mass in these terms:

The Gospel-lection is the coming of the Son of God in which he was shown to us, no longer speaking to us through clouds and riddles as once to Moses through voices and lightning and sounds and in darkness and fire on the mountain, or to the prophets of old through dreams, but he appeared openly as a true man and was seen by us as a gentle and quiet king, who came down as rain silently on a fleece. We saw his glory, glory as the only-begotten by the Father, and he was full of grace and truth. Through him the God and Father spoke to us, mouth to mouth and not through riddles. The Father bears witness about this and says this is my beloved Son, Wisdom and Reason and Power. He was proclaimed to us in prophets; in the Gospels he was made manifest.[74]

Germanos is thus presenting an elaborate contrast of the Old and New Dispensations peppered with colorful biblical quotations, such as God now, since Christ, speaking to us "mouth to mouth." The same thought is paraphrased later in the previously mentioned twelfth-century liturgical commentary attributed to Sophronius. While there is no specific proof of a definite causal relation between this type of liturgical exegesis and the frontispiece illustrations to the Gospel books or the poem in Vat. gr. 1522, it has been suggested by others in addition to Tsuji that ideas contained in the *Historia Ecclesiastica* did have an impact on art, chiefly in regard to its interpretation of ecclesiastical architecture and the Middle Byzantine system of church decoration.[75] Together with certain generalized theophanic images in Gospel books, then, the iconography of the *Maiestas* paired with Moses receiving the law probably also should be considered to be a theme related to the liturgy. These miniatures thus do not belong in the category of *Maiestas* representations linked to prologues. However, such liturgical interpretations are not irrelevant, for they will aid in understanding more about the origins of the prologues themselves, a matter to be discussed at the conclusion of this study.

NOTES

1. B. Brenk, *Spätantike und frühes Christentum* (Berlin, 1977), 186, is the latest reference to the mosaic. In fig. 159 the detail of the symbol of the man is illustrated. This symbol, which is not inscribed in the mosaic, is here said to be that of Matthew. In view of the evidence presented in the preceding chapter, it might be more proper to avoid making any identification at all.

2. C. Ihm, *Die Programme der Christlichen Apsismalerei vom vierten Jahrhundert bis zur Mitte des achten Jahrhunderts* (Wiesbaden, 1960), 42–51.

3. K. Weitzmann, *The Monastery of Saint Catherine at Mount Sinai, the Icons, Volume One: From the Sixth to the Tenth Century* (Princeton, 1976), 41–42.

4. A. Grabar, *L'Iconoclasme byzantin dossier archéologique* (Paris, 1957), 241–57 (hereafter, *L'Iconoclasme*). Also see J. Lafontaine-Dosogne, "Théophanies-Visions auxquelles participent les prophètes dans l'art byzantine après la restauration des images," *Synthronon* (Paris, 1968), 135–43 (hereafter, "Théophanies-Visions"), and below, Chapter V, pages 100ff.

5. On the appearance of the Deesis in the apses of Middle Byzantine churches see Th. von Bogyay, "Deesis," *RBK*, cols. 1183–85; J. Lafontaine-Dosogne, "L'Evolution du programme decoratif des églises," *XVᵉ congrès international d'études byzantines, Rapports, III. Art et archéologie* (Athens, 1976), 143; N. Thierry, "À propos des peintures d'Ayvali köy (Cappadoce). Les programmes absidaux à trois registres avec Deisis, en Cappadoce et en Georgie," *Zograph*, 5 (1974), 16–22.

6. C. Nordenfalk, *Codex Caesareus Upsaliensis* (Stockholm, 1971), 103–12.

7. H. L. Kessler, *The Illustrated Bibles from Tours* (Princeton, 1977), 36–42, esp. 36, n. 5, with bibliography (hereafter, *Tours*). The principal general study of the theme is F. van der Meer, *Maiestas Domini: théophanies de l'Apocalypse dans l'art chrétien* (Rome, 1938). Much useful material is to be found in Neuss, *Ezechiel*.

8. Kessler, *Tours*, 40–41. Christ in Majesty also was sometimes connected with the Priscillian prologue to Matthew. The latter is illustrated in the Carolingian Lorsch Gospels with an image of Christ enthroned in glory and surrounded by the generations of his ancestors. See Walker, *ArtB*, 30 (1948), 9–10. P. Bloch in turn suggests that an Ottonian portrait of Matthew placed below the mandorla of a seated Christ may be related to the earlier Lorsch miniature. See "Die beiden Reichenauer Evangeliare im Kölner Domschatz," *Kölner Domblatt*, 16–17 (1959), 12–15.

9. There are only a few scattered references. See Kessler, *Tours*, 39; G. Galavaris, *The Illustrations of the Liturgical Homilies of Gregory Nazianzenus* (Princeton, 1969), 121–23; Nordenfalk in *ZKunstg*, 8 (1939), 75; Tsuji, "Paris, Gr. 74," 175–87; G. Millet, *La dalmatique du Vatican* (Paris, 1945), 69–70.

10. Lazarev, *Storia*, 191, 249; E. Martini, *Catalogo di manoscritti greci esistenti nelle Biblioteche Italiane*, I, pt. 1 (Milan, 1893–96), 149–53; M. Bonicatti, "Per una introduzione alla cultura mediobizantina di Constantinopoli," *RIASA*, N.S., 9 (1960), 211–49, 252–53; Belting, "Stilzwang," 228; Athens, *Byzantine Art, An European Art*, 315–16.

11. The emperor is misidentified as Constantine the Great in Athens, *Byzantine Art, An European Art*, 315.

12. Belting, "Stilzwang," 227–28; Tsuji, "Paris, Gr. 74," 173.

13. Von Soden, I, 1, 311.

14. Ibid.

15. Martini, *Catalogo di manoscritti greci esistenti nelle Biblioteche Italiane*, I, 1, 149–53. The cur-

rent folio numbers in the manuscript are slightly different from the ones he gives.

16. Cf. a Beatus manuscript in Turin (E. Kitzinger, "World Map and Fortune's Wheel: A Medieval Mosaic Floor in Turin," *PAPS*, 117 [1973], fig. 12); a Romanesque floor mosaic also in Turin (ibid., figs. 2–5); and the Byzantine miniature in the Barberini Psalter in the Vatican, Barb. gr. 372, f. 219v (D. V. Ainalov, *The Hellenistic Origins of Byzantine Art* [New Brunswick, 1961], fig. 126). In the above the winds are placed at the corners of the rectangular area. In the following they occupy the sides: the Octateuch in Istanbul, Topkapi Sarai, MS 8, f. 32v (Th. Ouspensky, *L'Octateuque de la Bibliothèque du Sérail à Constantinople* [Sofia, 1907], pl. X, 18); the Vatican illustrated manuscript of Cosmas Indicopleustes, Vat. gr. 699 (C. Stornajolo, *Le miniature delle Topografia Christiana di Cosma Indicopleuste Codice Vaticano Greco 699* [Milan, 1908], pl. 7.

17. See above, Chapter I, pages 8–9.

18. Isaiah is also an appropriate prophetic figure because of his well-known description of a divine vision (Isaiah 6:1–3) and his later account of Hezekiah praying to the Lord God (37:16), "who sittest upon the cherubim" (ὁ καθημένος ἐπὶ τῶν χερουβίμ)—the same words David uses in Psalm 79:1, quoted in the preface.

19. On the Gospel headpieces see Meredith, "Codex Ebnerianus," 421.

20. See below, Chapter III, page 59.

21. For example, there is no title cited in the following editions of the letter: von Soden, I, 1, 388–89; Gregory, *Textkritik*, II, 863–64; Migne, *PG*, 22, cols. 1276–77; E. Nestle, *Novum Testamentum graece* (Stuttgart, 1968), 32–33. The text is translated by H. H. Oliver, "The Epistle of Eusebius to Carpianus, Textual Tradition and Translation," *Novum Testamentum*, 11 (1958), 138–45. He too fails to mention the title in question. Some examples of the title prior to the Parma Gospels: Rossano Gospels, sixth century (Haseloff, *Codex purpureus Rossanensis*, 6, pl. XIII); Venice, Bibl. Marc. cod. gr. I, 8, tenth century (Weitzmann, *Byzantinische Buchmalerei*, fig. 92); Leningrad, Publ. Lib. gr. 72, A.D. 1061 (Treu, *Griechische Handschriften*, 56); Leningrad, Publ. Lib. gr. 291, A.D. 1067 (ibid., 123); Moscow, Hist. Mus. gr. 9, ninth century (ibid., 237). In Vat. gr. 354 of A.D. 949

the title is applied to an introduction to the chapter lists, another example of its transference to a different context (R. Devreesse, *Codices Vaticani Graeci II, Codices 330–603* [Vatican, 1937], 38).

22. Belting also emphasized that the image showed the harmony of the Gospels. See "Stilzwang," 228.

23. Madan, *Summary Catalogue*, IV, 300–301; Lazarev, *Storia*, 190, 249, with bibliography; A. van Buren in *Illuminated Greek MSS*, 193; Oxford, *Greek Manuscripts* (1966), 41; Hutter, *Corpus*, I, 56–57, fig. 208.

24. The condensation of this and other miniatures in the Oxford manuscript may be the result of the size of the book, as it measures 112 × 143 mm, versus 228 × 298 mm for Parma 5.

25. *Greek Manuscripts* (1966), 41.

26. Meredith, "Codex Ebnerianus," 421.

27. Ibid.

28. The opposite conclusion, namely that Parma 5 is an elaboration upon the simpler cycle of Clarke 10, is less plausible. Consider the two scenes of the Nativity and the Journey to Egypt in the former. They form a logical narrative unit before the Gospel of Matthew. Clearly the Nativity, a major feast scene, is the principal subject and conforms to the usual iconography (cf. Meredith, "Codex Ebnerianus," 421). The representation of only the Flight to Egypt in Clarke 10 makes little sense by itself and suggests that this manuscript is derived from one with a larger series of images.

29. Martini, *Catalogo di manoscritti greci esistenti nelle Biblioteche Italiane*, I, 2, 259–60; A. Muñoz, "Miniature bizantine nella Biblioteca Queriniana di Brescia," *Miscellanea Ceriani* (Milan, 1910), 173–78, figs. 1–2; Lazarev, *Storia*, 252; E. Mioni in *Venezia e Bisanzio*, no. 48.

30. Παρασημείωσις τοῦ ἁγίου ἐπιφανίου περὶ τῶν τεσσάρων εὐαγγελίων. Ὅτι τό μὲν κατὰ ματθαῖον ἐγράφη ἐν ὁμοιώματι ἀν[θρώπ]ου τῶν χερουβίμ. Τὸ κατὰ [μάρχον] ἐν ὁμοιώματι μόσχου. Τὸ κατὰ λουκᾶν ἐν ὁμοιώματι λέοντος. Τὸ κατὰ ἰωάννην εἰς ὁμοίωμα ἀετοῦ, ἀδόντα, βοῶντα, κραυγάζοντα, καὶ λέγοντα.

Note of St. Epiphanios on the four Gospels. The Gospel according to Matthew was written under the symbol of the man of the cherubim; the Gospel according to Mark under the symbol of the calf; the Gospel according to Luke under the symbol of the lion; the Gospel according to John under the symbol of the eagle. Singing, crying, shouting, and saying.

31. Von Soden, I, 1, 304; F. E. Brightman, *Liturgies Eastern and Western* (Oxford, 1896), I, *Eastern Liturgies,* 323 (hereafter, *Liturgies*). On the connection between these words and the symbols see G. de Jerphanion, "Les noms des quatre animaux et le commentaire liturgique du Pseudo-Germain," *La Voix des monuments* (Paris, 1930), 250–54 (hereafter, "Les noms").

32. Mioni (*Venezia e Bisanzio,* no. 48) cites the literature. Lazarev (*Storia,* 252) puts it in the twelfth century.

33. This repainting of earlier manuscripts was not uncommon. According to V. Lazarev, the Chludov Psalter was restored not before the end of the twelfth century ("Einige Kritische Bemerkungen zum Chludov-Psalter," *BZ,* 29 [1929–30], 279; I thank R. Achilles for this reference). I. Hutter has described the overpainting of the eleventh-century Octateuch, Vat. gr. 747 ("Paläologisches Übermalungen im Oktateuch Vaticanus Graecus 747," *JÖB,* 21 [1972], 139–47). A. W. Carr noted the Palaeologan retouching of Brit. Lib. Harley 1810, a Gospels in the style of the so-called Nicaea school ("The Rockefeller McCormick New Testament," 52). This is evident in the style of the published miniature of the Crucifixion (O. M. Dalton, *Byzantine Art and Archaeology* [Oxford, 1911], fig. 261). The "spirited drôleries" in the margins of the miniatures are not contemporary, as O. Demus believed (*The Mosaics of Norman Sicily* [London, 1949], 435), but also are Palaeologan and compare with those in Mt. Athos, Stavronikita cod. 50 (J. R. Martin, *The Illustration of the Heavenly Ladder of John Climacus* [Princeton, 1954], figs. 133–71), and in Mt. Athos, Iviron cod. 548 of 1433 (S. M. Pelekanides et al., *The Treasures of Mount Athos,* II [Athens, 1975], figs. 133–36). The Harley miniatures were redone because of deterioration. The response of the Palaeologan restorer of another "Nicaea" manuscript in the H. P. Kraus collection was to remove the old flaked illustrations and add new ones in the contemporary style, an analogous case to the Brescia Gospels (H. Buchthal, "An Unknown Byzantine Manuscript of the Thirteenth Century," *The Connoisseur,* 155 [1964],

217–24; R. P. Bergman in *Illuminated Greek MSS,* 181–82). Not all such restoration is Byzantine. Scores of miniatures in the Menologium of Basil II were retouched, most likely after the book was already in Italy. On the later owners of the manuscript see *Il Menologio di Basilio II* (Turin, 1907), v–ix.

34. Mioni, *Venezia e Bisanzio,* no. 48.

35. Weitzmann, *Byzantinische Buchmalerei,* 18–22.

36. For Vat. gr. 2564 see C. Giannelli, "Un nuovo codice di provenienza studita," *Bullettino dell'Archivio Paleografico Italiano,* N.S., 2–3 (1956–57), pt. 1, 347–59, pl. III, 1. This headpiece can be compared with Baltimore, Walters Art Gallery cod. W.524, f. 149r (Vikan, *Illuminated Greek MSS,* fig. 7); Florence, Bibl. Laur. Plut. LXXXI, 11, f. 1r (Weitzmann, *Byzantinische Buchmalerei,* fig. 36); and London, Brit. Lib. Harley 5787, f. 41r (ibid., fig. 289).

37. V. Gardthausen, *Catalogus codicum graecorum sinaiticorum* (Oxford, 1886), 35; Hatch, *Facsimiles,* pl. LII; K. W. Clark, *Checklist of Manuscripts in St. Catherine's Monastery, Mount Sinai* (Washington, D.C., 1952), 23; M. Kamil, *Catalogue of All Manuscripts in the Monastery of St. Catherine on Mount Sinai* (Wiesbaden, 1970), 69. The other miniatures are unpublished, but there are photographs at the Library of Congress and Dumbarton Oaks. The texts are nos. 84, 87–89 in von Soden, I, 1, 303–4.

38. Ff. 2r–4r contain the complete canon tables. At the top of each, two partial circles are drawn, and these continue on ff. 4v–6v, apparently through lack of coordination in the design of the tables. The *Maiestas* miniature is painted on one of these pages. Without examining the actual manuscript, which I know only from the Library of Congress microfilm, it seems that the other portraits may have also been painted on empty pages. Matthew (f. 9v), Luke (f. 90v), and John (f. 146v) resemble the corresponding evangelists in Mt. Athos, Stavronikita cod. 43 (Weitzmann, *Byzantinische Buchmalerei,* figs. 169, 171–72). For the impact of the Stavronikita Gospels in the Palaeologan period see K. Weitzmann, "The Character and Intellectual Origins of the Macedonian Renaissance," *Studies in Classical and Byzantine Manuscript Illumination* (Chicago, 1971), 216–17; Belting, *Das illuminierte Buch,* 9; H. Belting and H. Buchthal, *Patronage in Thirteenth-Century Constantinople, An Atelier of Late*

Byzantine Book Illumination and Calligraphy (Washington, D.C., 1978), 17–20 (hereafter, *Patronage*). As for the script, the catalogue entries cited in the previous note assign the manuscript to the thirteenth century, but a twelfth-century date also seems possible.

39. H. Omont, *Inventaire sommaire des manuscrits grecs*, I (Paris, 1886), 11; Gregory, *Textkritik*, I, 175; F. Halkin, *Manuscrits grecs de Paris, Inventaire hagiographique* (Bruxelles, 1968), 3; Lake, *Minuscule Manuscripts*, V, 10, pls. 306–7. The manuscript was written in the Monastery of Meletius. Its miniatures are unpublished.

40. Buberl and Gerstinger, *Die byzantinischen Handschriften*, 46–49, pl. XIX, 1.

41. For the contents of the Vienna manuscript see Hunger, *Katalog . . . Supplementum Graecum*, 101–2, and E. Gollob, *Verzeichnis der griechischen Handschriften in Österreich auszerhalb Wiens* (Vienna, 1903), 60–68. There is no detailed description of Paris gr. 81 published. I have examined the latter but not the former. The title, incipit, and explicit of this preface in Paris gr. 81 is the same as quoted by Gollob for the Vienna manuscript.

42. Lazarev, *Storia*, 281–82, 333, fig. 397 (f. 10v); E. E. Granstrem, "Katalog grecheskikh rukopisei leningradskikh khranilishch, vyp. 4," *VizVrem*, 23 (1963), 185–86; V. N. Lazarev, "Novyĭ pamíatnik konstantinopol'skoĭ miniatíury XIIIv.," *VizVrem*, 5 (1952), 178–90; I. P. Mokretsova, "Novye dannye o miniatíurakh Evangeliía grech. 101 Gos. publichnoĭ biblioteki im M. E. Saltykova-Shchedrina v Leningrade," *VizVrem*, 33 (1972), 203–5; Treu, *Griechische Handschriften*, 63–67; A. Bank, "Les monuments de la peinture byzantine du XIIIᵉ s. dans les collections de l'URSS," *L'Art byzantin du XIIIᵉ siècle* (Belgrade, 1967), 95–96; Belting, *Das illuminierte Buch*, 8, 38, 62; R. Naumann and H. Belting, *Die Euphemia-Kirche am Hippodrom zu Istanbul und ihre Fresken* (Berlin, 1966), 162, 167; *Iskusstvo Vizantii*, III, 24; V. D. Likhachova, *Byzantine Miniature* (Moscow, 1977), 19–20, pl. 41 in color; Buchthal and Belting, *Patronage*, 66, 71. A miniature in a Gospel book on Mt. Athos, Dochiariou 21, may belong to this category of illustrations indirectly connected with prologues. On f. 4v there is an image of a large tetramorph facing the beginning of Matthew on f. 5r. The miniature is clearly a

later addition to the manuscript, possibly of Post-Byzantine date, but the Irenaean preface (von Soden, no. 82) does appear in conjunction with the notice on Matthew (von Soden, no. 108) at the end of his Gospel.

43. Treu, *Griechische Handschriften*, 64–67.

44. N. I. Petrov, "Miniatíury i zastavski grecheskogo evangeliía XIII veka," *Iskusstvo*, 1 (Kiev, 1911), 117–30; 2, 170–92; Lazarev, *Storia*, 335; Bank, "Les monuments," 94–95; Treu, *Griechische Handschriften*, 339–41; Carr, "Rockefeller McCormick," 14, 42; *Iskusstvo Vizantii*, III, 22.

45. K. W. Clark, *A Descriptive Catalogue of New Testament Manuscripts in America* (Chicago, 1937), 235–38, with further bibliography (hereafter, *New Testament MSS*); E. C. Colwell, *The Four Gospels of Karahissar*, I (Chicago, 1936), 35–37. The quincunx format also appears in the Matthew headpiece of Vat. Barb. gr. 449, f. 8r, in which Christ is accompanied by four prophets: H. R. Willoughby, *The Four Gospels of Karahissar*, II (Chicago, 1936), pl. X. The Barberini Codex is a member of the "Nicaea" school or more specifically the "Family 2400," for which see Cutler and Carr, *REB* 34, 306. Chicago 131 may also be connected in a more general way with these manuscripts, as R. W. Allison noted in an unpublished description of the book written in 1971 and available at the University of Chicago Library.

46. G. Galavaris, *The Illustrations of the Liturgical Homilies of Gregory Nazianzenus* (Princeton, 1969), 122; Lazarev, *Storia*, 193; Athens, *Byzantine Art, An European Art*, 319; T. G. Leporace, *Biblia Patres Liturgia, Catalogo di mostra presso la Biblioteca Nazionale Marciana* (Venice, 1961), 8–9; G. Millet, *Dalmatique*, 69–70; H. Buchthal, "An Illuminated Byzantine Gospel Book of about 1100 A.D.," *Special Bulletin of the National Gallery of Victoria* (Melbourne, 1961), 2–12; A. Grabar, "Une pyxide en ivoire à Dumbarton Oaks. Quelques notes sur l'art profane pendant les derniers siècles de l'Empire byzantin," *DOP*, 14 (1960), 142; Belting, "Stilzwang," 225, 228; Kessler, *Tours*, 39, 48, 50.

47. Ff. 11 and 12 constitute a single sheet of parchment that now interrupts the chapter lists to Matthew on ff. 10r–v and 13r–v. Ff. 10 and 13 were most likely meant to be in the center of a quire. Presently the quire is arranged as follows:

Perhaps the positions of the bifolios ff. 11–12 and 10–13 have been interchanged.

48. Millet, *Dalmatique*, 69–70.

49. See above, Chapter II, p. 34.

50. Lazarev, *Theophanes*, 94; O. Popova, *Les miniatures russes du XIe au XVe siècle* (Leningrad, 1975), 152, fig. 72.

51. Another miniature that might be included at this point is the *Maiestas Domini* in Montreal, McGill Univ. 1, cited by Lazarev, *Storia*, 423, and Clark, *New Testament MSS*, 131. However, according to G. Vikan (*Illuminated Greek MSS*, 220–21), the illustration is a modern forgery.

52. Tsuji, *DOP* 29, 179–82. For the matter of the attribution to Germanos see Bornert, *Commentaires*, 142–60.

53. Brightman, "Historia Mystagogica," 265. On the actual form of the procession in the early liturgy see T. F. Mathews, *The Early Churches of Constantinople: Architecture and Liturgy* (University Park, 1971), 138–47.

54. Brightman, "Historia Mystagogica," 388.

55. Ibid., 387. Translated by Tsuji (*DOP* 29, 179–80), who unfortunately uses the Greek text printed in *PG*, 98, col. 412, which, as explained previously, has numerous later interpolations. See above, Chapter II, pages 39–41.

56. Brightman, "Historia Mystagogica," 388–89.

57. Tsuji, *DOP* 29, 181–82.

58. *PG*, 91, col. 688.

59. *PG*, 87³, col. 3997.

60. Bornert, *Commentaires*, 211.

61. Brightman, "Historia Mystagogica," 389.

62. *PG*, 140, col. 436C.

63. See Bornert, *Commentaires*, 208.

64. Τούτων δὲ ἀσθέντων, ὁ ἱερεὺς ἐν μέσῳ πρὸ τοῦ θυσιαστηρίου ἱστάμενος ὑψοῦ τὸ εὐαγγέλιον αἴρει, καὶ ἀναδείκνυσι· τὴν ἀνάδειξιν τοῦ κυρίου σημαίνων, ὅτε ἤρξατο φαίνεσθαι. . . . Μετὰ δὲ τὸν τρισάγιον ὕμνον, ἀποστολικὸν ἀναγιγνώσκεται βιβλίον· εἶτα τὸ εὐαγγέλιον αὐτὸ, πρότερον ὕμνου τῷ θεῷ παρὰ τῆς ἐκκλησίας ἀσθέντος. . . . Ἀλλὰ τί βούλεται ἐνταῦθα ἡ ἀνάγνωσις τῶν ἱερῶν γραφῶν; Εἰ μὲν τὴν χρείαν βούλει μαθεῖν, εἴρηται· παρασκευάζουσι γὰρ ἡμᾶς, καὶ προκαθαίρουσι πρὸ τοῦ μεγάλου τῶν μυστηρίων ἁγιασμοῦ. Εἰ δὲ τὴν σημασίαν ζητεῖς, τὴν φανέρωσιν τοῦ κυρίου δηλοῦσιν, ἣν ἐφανεροῦτο κατὰ μικρὸν μετὰ τὴν ἀνάδειξιν.

Πρῶτον μὲν γὰρ τὸ εὐαγγέλιον ἀναδείκνυται συνεπτυγμένον, τὴν ἐπιφάνειαν τοῦ κυρίου σημαῖνον· . . . . Ταῦτα δὲ τῆς φανερώσεώς ἐστι σημαντικὰ τῆς τελειωτέρας . . .

PG, 150, col. 412, 416. Translated by J. M. Hussey and P. A. McNulty, *Nicholas Cabasilas, A Commentary on the Divine Liturgy* (London, 1960), 59, 61–62.

65. Brightman, *Liturgies*, I, 323.

66. G. de Jerphanion, "Les noms," 252–54; S. Kostof, *Caves of God, The Monastic Environment of Byzantine Cappadocia* (Cambridge, Mass., 1972), 82–83; Bornert, *Commentaires*, 124–28; I. D. Stefănescu, *L'Illustration des liturgies dans l'art de Byzance et de l'Orient* (Bruxelles, 1936), 83; J. Lafontaine-Dosogne, "Théophanies-Visions," 139; N. Thierry, "À propos des peintures d'Ayvali köy (Cappadoce)," 6; P. Johnstone, *The Byzantine Tradition in Church Embroidery* (Chicago, 1967), 37.

67. Willoughby, *The Rockefeller McCormick New Testament*, III, pls. II, XCIX.

68. See above, Chapter II, page 34.

69. Willoughby, *The Rockefeller McCormick New Testament*, III, 9–12.

70. Pelekanides, *Treasures*, I, 393–94, fig. 14; S. Der Nersessian, "A Psalter and New Testament Manuscript at Dumbarton Oaks," *DOP*, 19 (1965), 175.

71. Hamann-MacLean, "Der Berliner Codex," 228, fig. 8. The scene of Moses receiving the law appears by itself at the beginnings of two other manuscripts: Mt. Sinai, gr. 149, f. 4v (unpublished, photograph at the Library of Congress) and Manchester, John Rylands Library, MS. Gr. 17, f. 2v (unpublished). Both may date to the late twelfth or early thirteenth century. Also see A. Xyngopoulos, "Εὐαγγελιστὴς Ἰωάννης-Μωϋσῆς," **Δελτ. Χριστ. Ἀρχ. Ἑτ.,** 8 (1975/76), 101–8, for an illustration of John being given his Gospel by the hand of God in the same pose used for Moses receiving the law. Xyngopoulos correctly sees the miniature as a version of the iconography under discussion.

72. H. Brockhaus *Die Kunst in den Athos-Klöstern* (Leipzig, 1924), 188.

73. Der Nersessian, *DOP* 19, 175; Weitzmann, *Byzantinische Buchmalerei*, 6, figs. 25–26; Bonicatti, *Bibliofilia*, 145; Willoughby, *The Rockefeller McCormick New Testament*, 11–12.

He gives a partial translation of the poem. The full text is printed in B. de Montfaucon, *Palaeographia graeca* (Paris, 1708), 228. On the date of the manuscript see above Chapter II, pp. 28.

74. Τὸ εὐαγγέλιόν ἐστιν ἡ παρουσία τοῦ υἱοῦ τοῦ θεοῦ καθ' ἣν ὡράθη ἡμῖν, οὐκέτι διὰ νεφελῶν καὶ αἰνιγμάτων λαλῶν ἡμῖν ὡς ποτὲ τῷ Μωϋσῇ διὰ φωνῶν καὶ ἀστραπῶν ἤχων καὶ γνόφῳ καὶ πυρὶ ἐπὶ τοῦ ὄρους, ἢ τοῖς πάλαι προφήταις δι' ἐνυπνίων, ἐμφανῶς δὲ ὡς ἄνθρωπος ἀληθὴς ἐφάνη καὶ ὡράθη ἡμῖν ὁ πραῢς καὶ ἡσύχος βασιλεὺς ὁ καταβὰς ὡς ὑετὸς ἀψοφητὶ ἐν πόκῳ, καὶ ἐθεασάμεθα τὴν δόξαν αὐτοῦ, δόξαν ὡς μονογενοῦς παρὰ πατρὸς πλήρης χάριτος καὶ ἀληθείας δι' οὗ ἐλάλησεν ἡμῖν ὁ θεὸς καὶ πατὴρ στόμα πρὸς στόμα καὶ οὐ δι' αἰνιγμάτων· περὶ οὗ ὁ πατὴρ μαρτυρεῖ καὶ λέγει οὗτός ἐστιν ὁ υἱός μου ὁ ἀγαπητός, σοφία <καὶ> λόγος καὶ δύναμις, ὁ ἐν προφήταις μὲν προκηρυχθεὶς ἡμῖν, ἐν εὐαγγελίοις δὲ φανερωθείς. . . .

Brightman, "*Historia Mystagogica*," 388. The text is partially translated by Tsuji, *DOP* 29, 180.

75. The concrete symbolism of the church and liturgy in the commentary has often been cited in discussions of the theological basis of the Middle Byzantine system of church decoration. See Stefănescu, *L'Illustration des liturgies*, 41–42; Bornert, *Commentaires*, 179; S. Der Nersessian, "Le décor des églises du IXe siècle," *Actes du VIe Congrès international d'études byzantines*, 2 (Paris, 1951), 318–19; H. J. Schulz, *Die byzantinische Liturgie* (Freiburg im Breisgau, 1964), 123–24; O. Demus, *Byzantine Mosaic Decoration* (London, 1947), 15. It should be pointed out that some of this symbolism existed much earlier. See A. Grabar, *L'Iconoclasme byzantin dossier archéologique* (Paris, 1957), 234 (hereafter, *Iconoclasme*).

IV   The Inspired or Inspiring Evangelist

Greek Gospel prologues also deal with topics other than the apocalyptic visions described in the general prefaces of Irenaeus and Epiphanios. Many texts constitute small biographies of the particular author, and a genre of evangelist portraits may be related to this latter category. In particular, the present discussion will focus on the association of the evangelist with various figures who instruct or are instructed by him. Pictorially this often takes the form of the teacher lecturing or dictating to the pupil, who then copies down the revealed Word. Theologically several issues are involved. In one case it is the relationship of the evangelist to Jesus; that is, whether or not the writer was an original disciple of Christ or only a follower of one of the apostles. Second, the illustrations and texts address the question of how the account of the evangelist was disseminated to the church at large. By making a relevant statement on the origins of each narrative, both text and image are thus valid introductions to the Gospel to which they are appended.

The first to investigate the problem of such accompanying figures was A. Baumstark in an article of 1915 on a Byzantine manuscript in the library of the Greek Patriarchate in Jerusalem (Τάφου 56). In the latter, Mark is represented with Peter, Luke with Paul, John with Prochoros, and Matthew is alone (figs. 50–51). Concerning the first two miniatures, Baumstark called attention to the statement of Irenaeus that Peter and Paul inspired the accounts of Mark and Luke, respectively, and noted other examples of the iconography in Byzantine and Coptic manuscripts.[1] The next scholar to take up the matter was J. Weitzmann-Fiedler, who in an often cited article added other illustrations of accompanying figures (the translation of her term—*Begleitfiguren*) and sought to separate the scene of John dictating to Prochoros from the disussion. She pointed to several examples of secondary characters with portraits of Matthew and noted that the preserved manuscripts with accompanying figures are provincial. Like Baumstark, she thought that the origins of the iconography were not metropolitan but were to be found in the "east of the Byzantine Empire." [2] The most recent reporting on these matters is the short treatment of H. Hunger in the *Reallexikon zur byzantinischen Kunst,* where he lists a few new monuments and, more important, suggests a reading for the inscription on a Lavra miniature.[3]

In addition to these three studies specifically pertaining to the theme, the earlier articles of Baumstark and Weitzmann-Fiedler have been used in discussions of the persistently puzzling portrait of Matthew in the Lindisfarne Gospels, an early-eighth-century English manuscript. A third person, besides the evangelist Matthew and his symbol, the man, is shown peering out from behind a curtain. Nordenfalk, referring to the earlier studies on the Greek accompanying figures, thought that the model of the miniature was a Greek manuscript, presumably of pre-Iconoclastic date.[4] In the commentary volume to the facsimile of the manuscript, Bruce-Mitford suggested that the model was a "sixth-century Italo-Greek MS. and apparently from Vivarium." According to him, the third figure is not a scribe but Christ himself, in spite of the fact that he lacks a cross nimbus.[5] The problems raised by the Lindisfarne Gospels and by another early medieval manuscript in Ghent published by Koehler are intriguing, and so too are those of the occasional Western illustrations of the inspiring apostles, as, for example, in a late-ninth-century Gospel book in Prague.[6] However, all such issues must remain outside the purview of the present inquiry, whose concern, as before, is the Greek Gospel book and its own textual and iconographic traditions.

MARK AND LUKE

A Gospel Book in Baltimore

The clearest instances of the relation of miniature and prologue are to be found in the subject of Mark and Luke taking dictation from Peter and Paul, respectively. Although Baumstark noted that according to the early Christian tradition of Irenaeus, Mark's Gospel was based upon the account of Peter and Luke's upon that of Paul,[7] at that time he was not aware of the continuous dissemination of this legend in the Middle Byzantine period through the Gospel prefaces paraphrasing Irenaeus (von Soden, no. 108). The portraits of Peter and Paul below the headpiece of the *Maiestas Domini* in the Parma Gospels (frontispiece), it will be remembered, refer to that series of texts. Yet this late-eleventh-century miniature is not the first illustration of the concept, for an early-tenth-century Gospel book in the Walters Art Gallery in Baltimore (W.524), recently published by Weitzmann, depicts Mark and Luke in the company of Peter and Paul (figs. 48–49).[8] In each miniature the evangelist at the left writes in a book, while the apostle sits nearby and extends his right hand toward the evangelist in the traditional gesture of speech. Thus, Mark and Luke are meant to be recording the words of the two apostles.

As Weitzmann noted, the Walters Gospel book has suffered some mutilation.[9] A number of miniatures have been removed, and some are now in a private collection in Switzerland. Others still in the book have been displaced, so that at present Luke and Paul are found before the Gospel of Matthew, James precedes the Gospel of Luke, and Matthew is entirely missing. There also is a lacuna in the canon tables, and folios from the Gospels of Luke and John are commingled. Nevertheless, the pictorial and textual contents of the Gospels section of the manuscript can be fairly easily restored. Weitzmann has accomplished the former with the discovery of the missing feast scenes,[10] and Clark has sorted out the confused latter half of the manuscript and has noted some of its subsidiary texts.[11] Besides the standard letter of Eusebius to Carpianus, the canon tables, and the chapter lists, there are prefaces to Luke and John by Cosmas Indicopleustes (von Soden, no. 122).[12] Apparently no prologues were intended for Matthew or Mark, a lack of consistency that is not uncommon in Byzantine Gospel books.

The prologue to Luke by Cosmas makes no mention of the apostle Paul, but other texts in the manuscript do pertain to the evangelist portraits under discussion. Short poems, heretofore unnoticed, are written before the Gospels of Mark and Luke. They may be rendered in prose as follows:

Πέτρου μνηθεὶς τοῖς ἀπορρήτοις λόγοις,

Τὴν τοῦ Θεοῦ κένωσιν εἰς βροτῶν φύσιν,

Ἐν ᾗ τὸ διπλοῦν, ὢν Θεάνθρωπος, φέρει,

Ταύτην καθεξῆς συντίθησι πανσόφως

Ὁ δευτερεύων Μάρκος ἐν θεογράφοις.[13]

Initiated by the ineffable words of Peter, Mark, who is second among the divinely inspired authors, writes very wisely of God's reducing Himself to the nature of mortals, in which being at once God and man, He bears a double nature.

Τρίτος δὲ Λουκᾶς ῥητορεύει μειζόνως
Τοῦ μέχρις ἡμῶν μετριωθέντος Λόγου
Τὴν παιδικὴν αὔξησιν· εἶτα καὶ
    μέσην,

Καὶ τὴν τελείαν τῆς θεώσεως χάριν·
Παῦλον γὰρ ἔσχε τεχνικὸν παι-
    δοτρίβην.[14]

Luke, the third, recounts grandly the growth of the Word as a child, then as an adult man and [finally] the ultimate grace of deification; for he had Paul as his skillful instructor.

Both poems describe the student-teacher relationship of Mark to Peter and Luke to Paul, and thus it is significant that the texts are placed near the evangelist portraits. The epigram on Mark appears on f. 88v, and the portrait follows on f. 89v (fig. 48). Since the miniature of Luke and Paul (fig. 49) is presently displaced, its precise physical relation to the verses about Luke on f. 145r is not known, but certainly the image was placed shortly before the opening of the Gospel of Luke on f. 149r and most likely occupied the facing verso.

In Byzantine Gospel books such poems are not infrequently written beside evangelist portraits, creating a close association of the text and the image, and so, for example, a series of poems included in the famed collection of Greek poetry, the *Palatine Anthology*,[15] accompanies the tenth-century evangelist portraits of Paris, Bibl. Nat. Coislin gr. 195,[16] and the somewhat later and clearly related, unpublished miniatures of Mt. Athos, Lavra A12.[17] In the eleventh century the evangelists in Paris, Bibl. Nat.Coislin gr. 21,[18] and Rome, Vat. gr. 358,[19] have the identical verses, and those inscribed around the portraits of the Codex Ebnerianus in Oxford, Bodl. Lib. Auct. T. inf. 1.10,[20] of the twelfth century recur beside the evangelists added in the fourteenth century to Venice, Bibl. Marc. gr. I.8.[21] Also, one finds in the later century the same set of poems with the evangelist portraits of Mt. Athos, Lavra A46 of 1333, and Patmos, cod. 81 of 1335, two Gospel books that also agree textually in other respects, according to Belting.[22]

All the above demonstrate the close connection at times between portraits of the evangelists and epigrams, and furthermore the existence of such pairs of related manuscripts indicate that both picture and text were occasionally copied together. Yet what separates any of these books from the Walters Gospels is that only in the latter do the illustrations make reference to the content of the poems. Many epigrams mention the affiliation of Mark and Peter and Luke and Paul, but few evangelist portraits actually illustrate it. As a result, the poems, in most cases, serve as textual ornament to the pictures.

Other Miniatures Related to Prologues

The coordination of the visual and verbal, then, is more the exception; hence the importance of the Walters Gospel book. Another interesting case is the Jerusalem manuscript, Τάφου 56, for here the evangelist portraits (figs. 50–51) are inscribed with single explanatory sentences that function like cartoon captions:

Τέκνον Μάρκε, ἅ ἐγώ σοι ἐντέλλομε [sic] ταῦτα γράφε.

[My] son Mark, write this which I order you.

Τέκνον Λουκᾶ, ἅ οἶδας καὶ ἤκουσας ταῦτα γράφε.

[My] son Luke, write this which you know and have heard.[23]

In each instance the standing apostle at the right gestures to the evangelist who writes in a book. Except for the fact that the apostles stand, the composition corresponds to that of Walters, W.524. The portrait of John dictating to Prochoros in the Jerusalem manuscript is inscribed with a similar text,[24] and thus there is a pictorial and literary unity to these three portraits. However, as Weitzmann-Fiedler observed, the portrait of John with Prochoros has a different origin than those of Mark and Luke; therefore by the time of this crude, provincial Gospels in Jerusalem the iconography of apostles as accompanying figures is becoming mixed with other themes.[25]

Besides poems on the evangelists or the unique inscriptions of Τάφου 56, the relationship of these evangelists and apostles is treated in several prefaces to the Gospels, and the latter are also illustrated occasionally. Mention has been made of the Irenaean prologues to each Gospel (von Soden, no. 108) depicted in the Parma headpiece. In the Paris manuscript also discussed earlier, Bibl. Nat. gr. 81, the portraits of Mark (fig. 53, f. 96r) and Luke (f. 151r) are paired with separate full-page miniatures of Peter (fig. 52, f. 95v) and Paul (f. 150v) on the facing verso. Each set occupies a separate bifolium of the manuscript. Preceding both pairs are two prose discussions about the evangelist—one a Gospel preface (von Soden, no. 120) and the other a selection or adaptation from the readings in the *Menaia* on Mark and Luke (April 25 and October 18, respectively).[26] Whereas the former, the prologues, are not particularly specific concerning affiliations with the apostles and describe Mark and Luke in the same terms as the "pupil of Peter and the fellow traveler of Paul" (ὁ μαθητὴς Πέτρου καὶ συνέκδημος Παύλου),[27] the passages for the saints' own days are more properly explicit. The latter are written on pages immediately preceding the miniatures (ff. 94r–95r and f. 149v) and fully explain them.

The Gospel book in Leningrad, Publ. Lib. gr. 101 (figs. 54–55),[28] and another in Athens, Nat. Lib. cod. 151 (fig. 56),[29] similarly illustrate either prefaces or epigrams on the two evangelists. The portraits of Mark in both books represent Peter standing behind his pupil, whereas in the miniature of Paul and Luke in Leningrad gr. 101 (fig. 55) the apostle is placed before the evangelist in a composition more akin to the same portrait in Walters W.524 (fig. 49). Athens 151 contains the Irenaean prologues to the individual Gospels (von Soden, no. 108), as well as poems describing what is illustrated. The prefaces of the Leningrad Gospels (von Soden, no. 122) mention Peter but not Paul, yet both are singled out in the verses for Mark and Luke, written shortly before the images.[30] In view of the possible association of the aforementioned miniature of Matthew and the *Maiestas Domini* in Leningrad gr. 101 (fig. 40) with the Irenaean prologue to Matthew (von Soden, no. 108) and the Gospels as a whole (von Soden, no. 82), one might also imagine a model for the manuscript in which the prefaces to Mark and Luke were present and occasioned the iconography of those portraits. The result would have been a program that was as logically consistent as that of the Parma Gospels.

Miniatures without Accompanying Texts

In these five manuscripts dating from the tenth to the fourteenth century the illustrations of the apostles and evangelists directly correspond to prefaces or epigrams in the books. Although this is the extent of the evidence so far uncovered, there are in addition representations of the theme in other manuscripts in which this direct dependence of illustration on text does not exist. Once more the assumption made here is that such examples are in some manner derivative from cases where that association with prologues or epigrams was made. For instance, neither of the two Lavra manuscripts that Weitzmann-Fiedler illustrated has prefaces or epigrams pertaining to their portraits of Luke and Paul.[31] One book, Mt. Athos, Lavra cod. A7, perhaps of the twelfth century, now contains only the miniatures of Matthew and a youth (fig. 67, f. 13v), the Baptism of Christ (f. 102r) before the Gospel of Mark, and Luke and Paul (fig. 57, f. 161v).[32] The presence of the Baptism probably means that in addition to portraits of Mark and John the manuscript is also lacking the initial feast scenes for the other Gospels. The book has prefaces to Matthew (von Soden, nos. 121 and 122), Mark (no. 122), and Luke (no. 122), but the latter makes no reference to Paul. The other Lavra Gospel book, cod. A104, has drawings of Luke and Paul (fig. 58, f. 89v) and John and Peter (fig. 59, f. 133v) but no prologues at all.[33] Perhaps as a result the theme of the inspiring apostles has become curiously distorted. Although Mark and Luke were not considered to have been among the first followers of Jesus and thus had to depend upon the accounts of Peter and Paul, John was always counted among the original disciples, so that there is no reason that he should be paired with Peter.

The iconographic misunderstanding might also be due to the artist involved, for certainly he lacked training in the style of metropolitan Byzantine art. In fact, the entire manuscript resembles products of southern Italy.[34] The neat, upright letters of the text are thinner as a rule than the Middle Byzantine *Perlschrift* and seem to follow Italian conventions.[35] To that area also may be attributed the large expansive β at the beginning of Matthew. The stem with its interlaced ends and the loops filled with vines and human and animal heads are certainly Italian.[36] In the miniatures, details such as the segmented, interlaced arch above the heads of Paul and Luke (fig. 58) and the technique of simple line drawings recall the much finer products of Montecassino or other Italian centers.[37] Textually also the manuscript should be connected with Italy. One unmistakable piece of evidence is the inscription on the book John holds, for the language here is Latin, not Greek.[38] Furthermore, there is the matter of a particular subscription that appears at the end of each of the four Gospels. The one for Matthew reads as follows: "The Gospel according to Matthew was written and collated in 2500 verses from old Jerusalem copies kept on the Holy Mountain." [39] The texts have been investigated by A. Schmidtke, who has found them to be associated in many cases with manuscripts written in southern Italy, and for this and other reasons he assigns the manuscript to that region.[40]

All that remains to be explained is why a manuscript of clear Italian inspiration is now on Mt. Athos. Although some Greek books from that region are presently in Eastern Mediterranean collections, such as the Monastery of St. John the Theologian on Patmos or the National Library in Athens,[41] this is a comparatively rare phenomenon and in the case of the Patmos collection may be due to special circumstances.[42] However, it is not surprising for the Lavra

Monastery, if it is remembered that during the Middle Ages there was a monastery of the Amalfitans located nearby. By 1287 the once prosperous but now deserted monastery was given to the Lavra, which inherited its property and, more important its archives.[43]

In the two Lavra codices as well as all the previous examples of apostles as accompanying figures, Peter or Paul stand or sit beside the evangelist in a pose that ultimately may be based, as Baumstark thought, on the inspiring muse of ancient art.[44] In addition, though, another configuration is encountered in two manuscripts: the Alaverdy Gospels, a Georgian manuscript now in Tbilisi, the MSS Institute of the Academy of Sciences of the Georgian SSR. MS No. A484, and written in 1054 A.D. in a Georgian monastery near Antioch,[45] and a Greek lectionary at the Koutloumousiou Monastery on Mt. Athos, cod. 61.[46] In the former the half figure of Peter, framed by a segment of sky in the upper right corner of the miniature, gestures down to the seated Mark below (fig. 60). Such a composition is most likely based upon a Greek model, as the evangelists in the manuscript are decidedly Byzantine in appearance and the accompanying inscriptions are in Greek. Furthermore, the basic composition recurs in the Koutloumousiou lectionary (fig. 61). The pose of Mark with his right hand placed on a book in his lap is the same as the corresponding evangelist in the Alaverdy Gospels, and Peter is again placed in the upper right corner. The apostle gestures with his right hand and carries a scroll in his left, as in the Georgian miniature. There is no mention of prologues in the Alaverdy Gospels by Khakhanov, who described it in 1898,[47] but given the reliability of much more recent cataloguers in this respect, his account should not necessarily be trusted. Whether or not Georgian Gospel manuscripts contain texts corresponding to the Greek prefaces under discussion is an unexplored question. The Koutloumousiou manuscript definitely does not have any supplementary texts, and thus by the stage of Lavra A104 and the last two books the iconography of the inspiring apostles has moved rather far from its original context.[48]

MATTHEW AND JOHN

In the majority of preceding manuscripts Mark and Luke were the only evangelists to be shown with apostles. None were needed for Matthew and John, because they were inspired directly by Christ. At times, however, attempts were made to supplement the illustrations of the latter two authors. One method was to differentiate between the relative status of Matthew and John versus that of Mark and Luke. An unambiguous example is the set of evangelist portraits in a twelfth-century Gospels in Leningrad, Publ. Lib. gr. 98.[49] Each author is placed in an arch; Matthew and John (fig. 62) stand, and Mark and Luke (fig. 63) sit on a bench. Inside the lunettes above there are roundels; the ones for the two senior evangelists contain the bust of Christ; those for Mark and Luke, representations of Peter and Paul. Thus, the comparative prestige of the evangelists is clearly shown.

Such an idea could be based upon any number of texts, but Gospel prologues should be seen as one of the more important sources. Although the Leningrad Gospels has no prefaces,[50] pertinent ones are present in an illustrated Gospels in Florence, Bibl. Laur. Plut. VI.18, of the eleventh or early twelfth century (figs. 64–65).[51] In the manuscript there is a set of prefaces (von Soden, no. 120) that states as usual that Mark and Luke are the pupils of Peter and Paul.[52] In addition, the prologue to Matthew says that he is a disciple of the Lord, and the one for John says that he is the brother of James, the son of Zebedee. The latter is in reference to Matthew 4:21: "And going on from there he [Jesus] saw two other brothers, James the son of Zebedee and John his brother, in the boat . . . and he called them." Thus, the evangelist John is identified as the apostle John selected by Christ and the person who, in the words of the preface, "leaned on the breast of the Lord." [53] Finally, this concept is described in a more direct fashion in a note about Matthew written just before his portrait. It says that "there are four evangelists; two of these, Matthew and John, were among the choir of the twelve [apostles]." [54]

All this is accurately illustrated in the manuscript. In the upper right corners of the portraits of John (fig. 64) and Matthew there is a small figure of Christ, holding a scroll in his left hand and gesturing with his right arm to the evangelist below. The composition recalls the representations of Peter and Mark in the Alaverdy Gospels and Koutloumousiou 61 (figs. 60–61). In contrast, the portraits of Mark and Luke (fig. 65) in Plut. VI.18 have only a blessing hand projecting from the arc of heaven. Hence, in the Florence Gospels, John and Matthew are shown receiving their inspiration directly from Christ himself, whereas Mark and Luke are accorded the lower status of being directed by the more remote hand of God.

Matthew is associated with Jesus in a few other miniatures as well, and the examples of the *Maiestas Domini* paired with Matthew in Leningrad gr. 101 and Paris gr. 81 may belong to this category. More pertinent, however, is the portrait of Matthew in the Alaverdy Gospels (fig. 66), where the half figure of Christ, clearly designated by his cross nimbus, appears in the upper right corner of the miniature and extends one arm down toward the seated evangelist. The resulting composition is the same one employed in the Georgian manuscript for the other portraits in the book (fig. 60). Matthew is also shown with Jesus in a bilingual Coptic and Arabic Gospels in the Vatican, Copt. 9 of 1204/5, and as in the Alaverdy Gospels the inscriptions on the miniature are in Greek.[55] Moreover, the same figures have also been thought to appear together in Syrian illumination.[56] Yet again with the miniatures of these three East Christian cultures it is not known if the portraits are dependent upon prefaces in these languages or alternatively if artists are simply following Byzantine pictorial models.

Finally, mention must be made of the ostensibly relevant representations of a bust of Christ combined with a Gospel headpiece and placed opposite an evangelist portrait. A number of examples survive of headpieces to Matthew with such decoration, but the problem is that other Gospels are also so honored, especially, but not exclusively, that of John.[57] Thus, no consistent pattern emerges, and no specific relation with prologues can be established.

The second accompanying figure that is occasionally shown with Matthew is a youth, who in the two twelfth-century manuscripts on Mt. Athos, Lavra A7 (fig. 67),[58] and Koutloumousiou 61 (fig. 68), stands respectfully at the left of the old, gray-haired evangelist. An eleventh-century Gospel book in the Pierpont Morgan Library in New York, M748, contains a related portrait of Matthew writing in a book as a young man observes at the right (fig. 69).[59] The beardless youth in all three instances seemingly performs no function, since he is not writing down the words of the evangelist as a secretary would do. Nevertheless, Weitzmann-Fiedler considered him to be a scribe, for he could not be an apostle, because Matthew was not inspired by such a person and because the humble devotional gesture would be inappropriate in that context. Perhaps the youth was added, she thought, only in analogy to the accompanying figure of the other evangelists,[60] a reasonable hypothesis and a procedure certainly known in other cases.[61]

The young man is not identified in Koutloumousiou 61 or in Morgan 748, but there are traces of an inscription in Lavra A7. The latter is most difficult to decipher, and Weitzmann-Fiedler thought it was impossible,[62] but Hunger read "ὁ ἅ[γιος] Ἰάκων[ος]." According to him, then, this should be Ἰάκωβος Ἀδελφόθεος, or James the Brother of Jesus, who according to tradition translated Matthew's Gospel into Greek.[63]

The Lavra manuscript contains a preface to Matthew from Cosmas Indicopleustes (von Soden, nos. 121–22), but it says nothing about any translator of the Gospel of Matthew. However, this is a subject common to several texts found in Gospel manuscripts. By far the most common is the prologue to Matthew derived from Irenaeus (von Soden, no. 108), which has been often mentioned before. It says that the Gospel of Matthew was written in Hebrew and "translated by John."[64] In another preface (von Soden, no. 113) the translator is said to be either Bartholomew or John, and in a third preface taken from Dorotheus (von Soden, no. 106) he is identified as James the Brother of the Lord.[65] The matter is also sometimes discussed in subscriptions to the Gospel of Matthew, some saying that John was the translator and others James.[66]

In terms of frequency of occurrence, John, by virtue of being cited in preface no. 108, one of the most common prologues, is the more widely attested. None of the above texts is to be found in Lavra A7, but the manuscript is of decidedly modest quality and from the twelfth century, ample time for the disassociation of text and image. A version of preface no. 108 to Matthew is found, for example, as early as Coislin 195 of the tenth century, although its evangelist portraits have no accompanying figures.[67] If Hunger's reading of the inscription above the youth's head in Lavra A7 is correct, then he is to be identified as James. Although the evidence in the prologues and subscriptions is not unanimous as to the identity of the translator of the Gospel of Matthew, nevertheless the texts should be considered for the problem of an accompanying figure for Matthew. Because of their widespread use, they popularized the probably fictitious legend of the translation of the Gospel of Matthew from Hebrew to Greek.[68] The young man's subservient or respectful attitude in all these manuscripts may be best explained if he is considered the future translator.

The last evangelist to be studied is John, and two iconographic schemes are found in his portraits, one as rare as the other is common. The first, the association of the Virgin with John, occurs in Paris, Bibl. Nat. gr. 81, and as was the case with the other portraits in that book, there is a preface that explains the iconography of this miniature also. The prologue is based on the reading from the **Μηναῖον** for September 26, the feast day of the evangelist.[69] It recounts events from John's life, beginning with his family background. He was the son of Zebedee and Salome, who was one of seven children of Joseph. Though the familial relations are somewhat ambiguous, Jesus is said to be the uncle of John, because Jesus was the brother of Salome. Thus, John was in some sense related to Mary, the mother of Jesus. More important, however, the passage declares that after the Crucifixion, John "took the Mother of God to his own home and looked after her until her death." Only afterward did he begin his missionary activity. The portrait of the Virgin is on f. 242v of Paris, gr. 81, facing that of John on the opposite page (f. 243r). The above text on ff. 240v–241v immediately precedes the miniatures, as f. 242r is blank.

The Paris portraits are the only examples of this theme so far encountered among Greek manuscripts. Yet Mary and John do appear in the Coptic manuscript, Rome, Vat. copt. 9 of 1204/5 (fig. 70), previously cited. There the Virgin stands in an orant position next to the seated evangelist, who holds his Gospel in his hands. The book is inscribed in Greek with the first words of that text, and the Virgin is labeled MP ΘU, her standard epithet in Byzantine, but not earlier Coptic art. The style of the evangelist portraits in the Vatican manuscript is clearly dependent upon Byzantine models, as Weitzmann noted.[70] Such factors, then, open the possibility that the iconography of the book also follows Greek practices, and indeed beside the miniature of Matthew and Christ there are portraits of Mark and Luke taking dictation from angels.[71] Perhaps the latter, in analogy to Florence, Plut. VI.18, represent a variation on the concept of the younger evangelists receiving indirect divine inspiration, because they were not immediate followers of Jesus.

Far more common than the association of the Virgin with John is the scene of the evangelist dictating the Gospel to his disciple Prochoros on the island of Patmos. It becomes increasingly popular in the Middle Byzantine period, gradually replacing the portraits of John seated pensively in a high-backed wicker chair.[72] The iconography has been investigated by Baumstark, Weitzmann-Fiedler, and Weitzmann and has been shown to be based upon a legend presented initially in the fifth-century *Acts* of John and subsequently repeated in a somewhat condensed form in the life of John written in the tenth century by Simeon Metaphrastes and included in his Menologium.[73] Thus, the group of John and Prochoros seemingly could not be inspired by prefaces.

However, there is some evidence of Prochoros being cited in supplementary texts to the Gospels. The only example in von Soden's study is the following subscription to the Gospel of John: [74]

Τέλος τοῦ κατὰ Ἰωάννην εὐαγγέλιον· ἐγράφη διὰ Πρόχορου μαθητοῦ αὐτοῦ   ἐν Πάτμῳ τῇ νήσῳ μετὰ χρόνους λβ τῆς Χριστοῦ ἀναλήψεως.

The end of the Gospel according to John. It was written by Prochoros, his disciple, on the island of Patmos in   the 32nd year after the Ascension of Christ.

Similar information is given in another prologue, not noticed by von Soden. It appears in a Gospel book of the late eleventh or early twelfth century in Naples, Bibl. Naz. Suppl. gr. 6, which presently contains only portraits of Matthew and John (fig. 71), the other two having been removed.[75] Besides the Eusebian letter, canon tables, and chapter lists, there are brief two-line prefaces or subscriptions to Mark, Luke, and John. The latter is preceded by a short text almost identical to the subscription above: "The Gospel according to John was written by Prochoros, his disciple, on the island of Patmos in the 32nd year after the Ascension of Christ." This note on f. 315r is found shortly before the miniature of John and Prochoros on f. 316v (fig. 71); thus, one might suppose that, as noted many times before, the appearance of the text occasioned the illustration. Yet in this case there is abundant room for doubt. By the period of the Naples Gospel book, the pictorial tradition of John dictating to Prochoros was well established; in contrast, prologues or subscriptions merely mentioning Prochoros are rare. Therefore, one can legitimately ask if image might not have influenced text in this instance.

Such is the range of evidence concerning the theme of the evangelist and an accompanying figure. Many but not all of the foregoing examples owe their origins to prologues. However, other factors also influenced the iconography, and one of these certainly was the predilection for visual uniformity. If Mark and Luke were to be accompanied by two apostles, then it was felt desirable to pair Matthew and John with someone also. Leningrad gr. 101 is a case in point. With Matthew there is the *Maiestas Domini* (fig. 40), perhaps ultimately related to the combination of the prologue of Irenaeus on the four Gospels with his introduction to the Gospel of Matthew. The portraits of Mark and Luke (figs. 54–55) likewise follow prefaces or epigrams, but the illustration of John and Prochoros does not.[76] In Athens 151 this desire for formal unity is even more apparent. Someone in each portrait is shown seated and writing in a book. That position is naturally accorded to the evangelist in the pictures of Matthew, Mark (fig. 56), and Luke; but to Prochoros in the fourth portrait (fig. 72). John is placed behind his pupil, and the resulting composition departs from both the established iconography and the original legend in order to conform to the pattern of the other miniatures in which Peter and Paul stand in back of Mark and Luke, and an angel is behind Matthew.[77] Thus, a pictorial correspondence has been created at the expense of iconographic logic.

The Athens manuscript demonstrates the effect an individual artist can have on the disposition of the miniatures. He might rearrange figures to suit his taste or follow sources different from those of the book's scribe, thereby severing the connection of text and illustration. Such a process may explain the disparate evidence presented in the foregoing three sections on the evangelist symbols, the *Maiestas Domini*, and evangelists with accompanying figures. Therefore, the instances in which there is no relation between supplementary text and miniature do not necessarily disprove the basic contention of this study that these three themes in Byzantine manuscripts are ultimately dependent upon prefaces or epigrams. In this respect, then, it is significant that the earliest examples of each subject, Athens 57, Parma 5, or Walters W.524, were intimately linked to these texts. This is not to imply, however, that these were the first illustrations of prologues or poems. It is entirely possible that earlier ones once existed, and the crucial question here is when this phenomenon began. With miniatures the investigation perforce leads quickly to conjecture, because there is little additional evidence. This is not true, however, of the texts. The number of illustrated Greek Gospel books is only a small percentage of those containing prologues or epigrams. For this reason if the above question is posed differently to look instead at the larger body of material, the prospects are more favorable, and thus what follows is an attempt to supplement the foregoing iconographic analyses through an examination of the textual history of prologues.

NOTES

1. A. Baumstark, "Eine antike Bildkomposition in Christlich-orientalischen Umdeutungen," *Monatshefte für Kunstwissenschaft*, 8 (1915), 113–21, pl. 30 (hereafter, Baumstark 1915). On Τάφου 56 see below, pages 79ff.

2. J. Weitzmann-Fiedler, "Ein Evangelientyp mit Aposteln als Begleitfiguren," *Adolph Goldschmidt zu seinem siebenzigsten Geburtstag* (Berlin, 1935), 30–34 (hereafter, Weitzmann-Fiedler).

3. H. Hunger, "Evangelisten," *Reallexikon zur byzantinischen Kunst*, II (Stuttgart, 1971), cols. 467–69.

4. C. Nordenfalk, "Eastern Style-Elements in the Book of Lindisfarne," *ActaArch*, 13 (1942), 165.

5. Bruce-Mitford, *Codex Lindisfarnensis*, 164–68.

6. W. Koehler, "Die Denkmäler der Karolingischen Kunst in Belgien," *Belgische Kunstdenkmäler*, 1 (1923), 11–26, pls. 2–3. On the Prague manuscript see H. Swarzenski, "The Role of Copies in the Formation of the Styles of the Eleventh Century," *Romanesque and Gothic Art, Studies in Western Art*, I (Princeton, 1963), 15; P. Bloch and H. Schnitzler, *Die ottonische Kölner Malerschule*, II (Düsseldorf, 1970), 113–15, figs. 411, 425. Peter with Mark is found in Hildesheim, cod. 18 (Bloch and Schnitzler, II, fig. 412).

7. Baumstark 1915, 115.

8. K. Weitzmann, "An Illustrated Greek New Testament," 20–23, figs. 10, 12.

9. Ibid., 19.

10. Ibid., 26–29.

11. Clark, *New Testament MSS*, 351–352.

12. Von Soden, I, 1, 319–20. To be specific, the preface to Luke (ff. 147r–v) is the Cosmas preface with the first παραγραφή, but not the second that von Soden gives (ibid., 319). The preface to John (f. 247r) omits the παραγραφή, a common feature according to von Soden (ibid., 321).

13. Ibid., 379.

14. Ibid.

15. W. R. Paton, *The Greek Anthology*, I (New York, 1927), 36–37.

16. H. Omont, *Miniatures des plus anciens manuscrits*, 45, pl. LXXXI. The portrait of John has an additional four-line poem, and each miniature also has a brief note about the publication of the evangelist's Gospel. The latter are basically the same as the common subscriptions to the Gospels. Cf. von Soden, I, 1, 297. It should be noted that Omont has slightly revised the poems in his transcription.

17. Kominis, "Συναγωγή ἐπιγραμμάτων," 263, 266, 270, 273, 276; Spyridon and S. Eustratiades, *Catalogue of the Greek Manuscripts in the Library of the Laura on Mount Athos* (Cambridge, Mass., 1925), 2 (hereafter, *Catalogue*). The texts in the latter, repeated in the former, are rather inaccurate. The Lavra manuscript also contains the second poem on John and the same notes on the Gospels as found in

Coislin 195. As in the latter codex, the additional passages are written below the miniatures. Since the manuscript was examined on a microfilm at the Library of Congress, the date of the miniatures is difficult to determine, but the script and ornament of the book may belong in the eleventh century.

18. Omont, *Miniatures des plus anciens manuscrits,* 46, pl. LXXXIII; R. Devreesse, *Le fonds Coislin* (Paris, 1945), 17–18; B. de Montfaucon, *Bibliotheca Coisliniana* (Paris, 1715), 65–66. The manuscript was brought from the Orient to Paris in the mid-seventeenth century by Athanasius (H. Omont, *Missions archéologiques françaises en Orient aux XVII*ᵉ *et XVIII*ᵉ *siècles,* II (Paris, 1902), 853–54.

19. Bonicatti, "Per un introduzione," 213, 228, 230, 256, fig. 11. He argues that the manuscript was made in Constantinople on the basis of its high quality and its connection with Vat. gr. 463 written there in 1062. Most likely the manuscript remained there until an agent for the Vatican purchased it in that city in 1438. On the acquisition see R. Devreesse, *Le fonds grec de la Bibliothèque Vaticane des origines à Paul V, ST,* 244 (Vatican, 1965), 8; Devreesse, *Codices Vaticani graeci,* II, 43–45. Beyond the agreement of these epigrams, the two Gospels have other features in common. Both have commentaries by the Pseudo-Peter Laodicenus, Synaxaria and Menologia, canon tables, the letter of Eusebius to Carpianus with the optional ending of κανόνες . . . . εὐαγγελισταῖς (von Soden, I, 1, 389), chapter lists, and prefaces (ibid., no. 120), and at the end there is written the pericope on the woman taken in adultery.

20. H. O. Coxe, *Catalogi codicum manuscriptorum Bibliothecae Bodleianae pars prima recensionem codicum Graecorum continens* (Oxford, 1853), cols. 703–4; Hutter, *Corpus,* I, figs. 236–39.

21. E. Mioni, *Bibliothecae Divi Marci Venetiarum, Codices graeci manuscripti,* I (Rome, 1967), 13–14. He omits the poems. On another occasion I hope to analyze in greater detail the relationship of the two manuscripts.

22. Belting, *Das illuminierte Buch,* 67. The same set of epigrams are written with the evangelist symbols of Mt. Athos, Iviron cod. 66, though neither the pictures nor the texts are mentioned by Lambros, *Catalogue,* II, 6. E. W. Saunders (*A Descriptive Checklist of Selected Manuscripts in the Monasteries of Mount Athos* [Washington, D.C., 1957], 6) notes that the symbols are added later (hereafter, *Checklist*). The same probably applies to the verses. This series of poems is very common, and E. Follieri lists over twenty manuscripts with them. See "Epigrammi sugli Evangelisti dei codici Barb. gr. 352 e 520," *BGrottaf,* N.S., 10 (1956), 79–80.

23. Baumstark 1915, 114. See also W. H. P. Hatch, *Greek and Syrian Miniatures in Jerusalem* (Cambridge, 1931), 86–87.

24. Baumstark 1915, 115.

25. Weitzmann-Fiedler, 30–31, 34.

26. Μηναῖον τοῦ Ἀπριλίου (Athens, 1904), 146; Μηναῖον τοῦ Ὀκτωβρίου (Athens, 1904). 140.

27. Von Soden, I, 1, 314–15.

28. See above, page 62.

29. Lazarev, *Storia,* 422; Buberl, *Die Miniaturenhandschriften,* 24–25, figs. 88–89; A. Delatte, *Les manuscrits à miniatures et à ornements des bibliothèques d'Athènes* (Paris, 1926), 20–24; I. Sakkelion, Κατάλογος τῶν Χειρογράφων τῆς Ἐθνικῆς Βιβλιοθήκης τῆς Ἑλλάδος (Athens, 1892), 29; V. J. Djurić, "Über den 'Cin' von Chilandar," *BZ,* 53 (1960), 349, where the miniatures are assigned to c. 1360.

30. Treu, *Griechische Handschriften,* 64.

31. Weitzmann-Fiedler, 31–32, figs. 1–2, 5–6.

32. Ibid., figs. 1–2; Spyridon, *Catalogue,* 1; Saunders, *Checklist,* 7.

33. Weitzmann-Fiedler, 31–32, figs. 5–6; Spyridon, *Catalogue,* 11; Saunders, *Checklist,* 9; Bruce-Mitford, *Codex Lindisfarnensis,* 164.

34. Hunger thought the manuscript was from some Western province. See *RBK,* II, col. 469.

35. Hunger's term in *Geschichte der Textüberlieferung,* I, 96. Cf. H. Follieri, *Codices graeci Bibliothecae Vaticanae,* pl. 36, from Vat. gr. 2000 of 1102 written in Calabria.

36. The size of the letter, the dragon heads, and the interlace may be compared with the initial β also for the Gospel of Matthew in Milan, Bibl. Ambros. B. 56, written in Calabria in 1022. See Grabar, *Les manuscrits grecs,* 72–73, fig. 320. The β of Matthew in Paris, Bibl. Nat. gr. 83, dated 1168, is similarly filled with thick vine stems. Cf. Lake, *Minuscule Manuscripts,* V, pl. 322. The Lavra initial is unpublished but may be seen in the microfilm of the manuscript at the Library of Congress.

37. Cf. Montecassino MS 99 in C. R. Dodwell,

Painting in Europe 800–1200 (Baltimore, 1971), 136, fig. 151.

38. "In principio erat verbum et verbum erat. . . ." Transcribed by von Soden, I, 1, 166.

39. Von Soden lists these as nos. 59–60; see I, 1, 299.

40. *Neue Fragmente und Untersuchungen zu den Judenchristlichen Evangelien* (Leipzig, 1911), 3, 12–15. It should be pointed out that the subscription is not used exclusively in Italy, for it is found in Vat. Urb. gr. 2, an illustrated manuscript of the twelfth century produced in Constantinople. On the subscription of the latter see H. C. Hoskier, "Evan. 157 (Rome, Vat. Urb. 2)," *JTS*, 14 (1913), 78–79, 86, and Metzger, *Text of the New Testament*, 63–64.

41. E.g., Patmos gr. 29, gr. 33, gr. 39, gr. 43, gr. 70, gr. 72, gr. 171; Athens, Nat. Lib. cod. 74, 149, 210, 211. Grabar, *Les manuscrits grecs*, passim.

42. Ibid., 50.

43. P. Lemerle, "Les archives du monastère des Amalfitains au Mont Athos," Ἐπ. Ἑτ. Βυζ. Σπ., 23 (1953), 555. For the location of the monastery near Lavra see the map of Mount Athos in P. Lemerle et al., *Actes de Lavra* (Paris, 1970), 62–63, map II. I wish to thank Professors P. Magdalino and N. Oikonomides for this reference. A recent general discussion of Amalfi and its role as an intermediary between East and West is M. Balard, "Amalfi et Byzance (Xᵉ–XIIᵉ siècles)," *Travaux et Mémoires*, 6 (1976), 85–95.

44. Baumstark 1915, 117–18. Certainly pertinent in this regard is the portrait of Mark in the sixth-century Rossano Gospels (Haseloff, *Codex*, pl. XIV).

45. S. Amiranashvili, *Gruzinskaiā Miniatiūra* (Moscow, 1966), 20, pls. 21–25; idem, *Istoriiā Gruzinskogo Iskusstva* (Moscow, 1963), 231; Lazarev, *Storia*, 169; H. Machavariani, *Georgian Manuscripts* (Tbilisi, 1970), pls. 13–15; A. S. Khakhanova, "Ekspeditsii na kavkaz, 1892, 1893 i 1895 g.," *Materialy po arkheologii Kavkaza*, 7 (1898), 11. The manuscript's colophon is published and translated by W. Z. Djobadze, *Materials for the Study of Georgian Monasteries in the Western Environs of Antioch on the Orontes* (Louvain, 1976), 12–20.

46. Weitzmann-Fiedler, 31, fig. 4; Pelekanides, *Treasures*, I, 452–53, fig. 303; Lambros, *Catalogue*, I, 280; P. Huber, *Athos, Leben,*

Glaube, Kunst (Zürich, 1969), 212–14, 233, figs. 129, 136; T. Jirat-Wasuitynski in *Illuminated Greek MSS*, 157. According to G. Mercati, "Origine antiochena di due codici greci del secolo XI," *AnalBoll*, 68 (1950), 215–17, the manuscript was made in Antioch. As noted by A. W. Carr, the precise codicological relation of the miniatures to the manuscript is not known.

47. See note 45 above.

48. The same may be true for the occasional appearance of the iconography in Coptic illumination. Cf. M. Cramer, *Koptische Buchmalerei* (Recklinghausen 1964), 83, figs. 92–93. A Coptic-Arabic Gospels in Paris, Institut Catholique, Copte-Arabe 1, of 1249/50 contains a representation of Peter with Mark. An inscription below in Arabic says that "Peter is giving him the Gospel." Translated by J. Leroy, *Les manuscrits coptes et coptes-arabes illustrés* (Paris, 1974), 166, pl. E (hereafter, *Manuscrits coptes*). The manuscript apparently contains no prologues. On its contents see ibid., 157.

49. Treu, *Griechische Handschriften*, 12; E. E. Granstrem, "Katalog grecheskikh rukopiseĭ Leningradskikh khranilishch," *VizVrem*, 23 (1963), 186; Lazarev, *Storia*, 253; Bank, *L'art byzantin du XIIIᵉ siècle*, 100–101; *Iskusstvo vizantiĭ*, II, 65.

50. Treu, *Griechische Handschriften*, 61.

51. Lazarev, *Storia*, 175; Bandini, *Catalogus . . . graecorum*, I, 130–36.

52. Bandini, *Catalogus . . . graecorum*, I, 133–34, for the beginnings of these prefaces.

53. The phrase is borrowed from Irenaeus, *Adversus Haereses*, III, 1, 1 (*PG*, 7, col. 845), and refers to John 13:23.

54. Bandini, *Catalogus . . . graecorum*, I, 133.

55. Cramer, *Koptische Buchmalerei*, 79–80, fig. 87; Leroy, *Manuscrits coptes*, 148–50; H. Buchthal and O. Kurz, *A Hand List of Illuminated Oriental Christian Manuscripts* (London, 1942), 58–59.

56. Baumstark 1915, pl. 33 (Paris, Bibl. Nat. Syr. 41); J. Leroy, *Les manuscrits syriaques à peintures conservés dans les bibliothèques d'Europe et d'Orient* (Paris, 1964), 254, is uncertain of the identification of the evangelist. In Paris, Syr. 41, the miniature of the evangelist facing toward Christ and holding his Gospel also is related to the iconography of the evangelists presenting their work to Jesus, seen in Vat. gr.

756 and elsewhere, as Leroy, *Manuscrits syriaques*, 255, noted.

57. For examples, see Carr, "Rockefeller McCormick New Testament," figs. 40, 137, 147, 150, 164, 175, 193, 195; Hamann-MacLean, "Der Berliner Codex," figs. 33–34; Colwell, *Four Gospels of Karahissar*, II, pls. XI, XLV, LXVII, CXV; Buberl, *Die Miniaturenhandschriften*, figs. 58, 62; Belting, *Das illuminierte Buch*, fig. 5.

58. Weitzmann-Fiedler, fig. 1.

59. Ibid., 32, fig. 7; J. C. Anderson, in *Illuminated Greek MSS*, 92–95; C. Nordenfalk, "The Apostolic Canon Tables," *GBA*, 62 (1963), 22–25, 32; Clark, *New Testament MSS*, 168–69, with further bibliography.

60. Weitzmann-Fiedler, 32.

61. See below, page 87.

62. Weitzmann-Fiedler, 31.

63. Hunger, *RBK*, II, col. 469. Also on the translators of Matthew see D. T. Schermann, *Propheten- und Apostel-legenden, TU*, 31, 3 (1907), 276. On the microfilm of Lavra A7 at the Library of Congress one can see ὁ . . . . φ_c. The last two letters could be from Ἀδελφός, so Hunger's general interpretation is plausible, but the inscription may have read ὁ ἅ[γιος] Ἰάκων[ος] Ἀδελφός, the more common title for St. James. A detailed examination of the actual miniature and a resolution of this matter would certainly be desirable.

64. Von Soden, I, 1, 311.

65. Ibid., 307, 312.

66. Ibid., 298.

67. The preface is not exactly the same as no. 108, but it states that the Gospel "was translated by John the Apostle into the Greek language." The text is not mentioned in the catalogue of Devreesse (*Le fonds Coislin*, 173–74).

68. Modern scholarship rejects the idea that the Gospel of Matthew was originally written in either Hebrew or Aramaic. See Lawson, *Biblical Theology*, 43; F. L. Cross and E. A. Livingstone, *The Oxford Dictionary of the Christian Church* (London, 1974), 891.

69. Μηναῖον τοῦ Σεπτεμβρίου (Athens, 1904), 231.

70. K. Weitzmann, "The Ivories of the So-Called Grado Chair," *DOP*, 26 (1972), 78–79, where the matter of the inscription is also discussed (hereafter, "Grado Chair").

71. Cramer, *Koptische Buchmalerei*, pl. XII, fig. 98.

72. H. Buchthal, "A Byzantine Miniature of the Fourth Evangelist and Its Relatives," *DOP*, 15 (1961), 132.

73. Baumstark 1915, 111; Weitzmann-Fiedler, 30–31; K. Weitzmann, "The Constantinopolitan Lectionary, Morgan 639," *Studies in Art and Literature for Belle da Costa Greene*, ed. D. Miner (Princeton, 1954), 373.

74. Von Soden, I, 1, 299. The manuscript he cites for this subscription is ε 1230 or Athens, Nat. Lib. cod. 128. Sakkelion (Κατάλογος, 22) mentions no illustrations in the book.

75. E. Martini, "Sui codici Napoletani restituiti dall'Austria," *Atti della Reale Accademia di archeologia, lettere e belle arti*, N.S., 9 (1926), 165; G. Perleoni, *Catalogus codicum graecorum Bibliothecae Nationalis Neopolitanae*, I (Rome, 1962), 11–12.

76. Lazarev, *Storia*, fig. 399.

77. This is a common pose for an inspiring figure. Cf. Milan, Bibl. Ambros. cod. 54 (H. Buchthal, *The Miniatures of the Paris Psalter* [London, 1938], fig. 23); Mt. Athos, Chilandari cod. 13 (Pelekanides, *Treasures*, II, figs. 420–22); Washington, D.C., Dumbarton Oaks, cod. 3 (S. Der Nersessian, *DOP* 19, 178, fig. 42); Leningrad, Publ. Lib. MS No. F. 1, 591 of 1429 (S. Radojčić, "La pittura bizantina dal 1400 al 1453," *RSBN*, N.S., 5 [1968], fig. 4).

V   The Origins of Greek Gospel Prefaces and Their Illustration

The study of the varieties of supplementary texts found in the thousands of extant copies of the Greek Gospel books has scarcely begun. Von Soden's haphazard collection of prefaces, epigrams, and subscriptions, mostly published without manuscript citations, remains the sole source for these texts, and limited as it is, without his book the present investigation would have been far more difficult. Although von Soden noted that some prologues were derived from the writings of early authors, such as Irenaeus or Cosmas Indicopleustes,[1] neither he nor anyone else has considered the key question of when these and other texts were first excerpted, abridged, or paraphrased and used as prologues. This is a complex problem, because the introduction of some pieces, such as the prefaces to each Gospel based on Theophylact of Bulgaria (d. 1108),[2] must be rather late; and the origin of others, such as the Irenaean prefaces, could be quite early. Thus, one is presented with a possible field of inquiry that stretches in these particular cases from the second to the twelfth century.

In order to make definitive statements about the history and origin of Gospel prologues, it would be necessary first to examine the hundreds of manuscripts that are reported in the works of New Testament scholars such as Gregory,[3] von Soden,[4] or Aland;[5] to make careful notes on all the prefaces; to collate the results; and finally to prepare critical editions of every piece. Such work would prove useful for many purposes, and most likely relationships among various Gospel books would become apparent from the supplementary texts they contain. The latter methodology has been used for Latin Gospels,[6] and similar relations have been postulated above. In spite of the potential value, the effort involved would be enormous and well beyond the limits of the present study.

Instead, a more modest and necessarily more tentative investigation of the origins of prefaces has been made with the aid of the unparalleled collection of microfilms of New Testament manuscripts at the Institut für Neutestamentliche Textforschung in Münster. The purpose was to determine patterns of appearance of prefaces in early Greek Gospel books, for it is assumed that this is the factor most relevant to the history of book illumination. Illustrated manuscripts for the most part are deluxe productions often valued as much or more for their decoration as for their subject matter, and hence the types of texts found in such books tend to be conservative if not antiquated. Thus, for the present purposes it is sufficient to define general trends in the usage of the prologues that have been connected with pictorial themes.

Accordingly, all the surviving uncial copies of the Gospels and a selection of the earliest minuscules were examined at Münster for any kind of subsidiary text. This procedure insures a survey of all early manuscripts, because of the history of Greek writing. The uncial script is found on ancient scrolls and continued to be used as late as the eleventh century A.D. for certain liturgical codices.[7] It was gradually supplanted by the minuscule script beginning in the late eighth century or the early ninth century.[8] For two or three hundred years both scripts were employed for religious manuscripts, until the minuscule ultimately prevailed and became the standard mode of writing. About 250 uncial manuscripts are listed in the *Kurzgefasste Liste der Griechischen Handschriften des Neuen Testaments* prepared by K. Aland.[9] Most of these are small fragments of a few pages and thus furnish no information about prologues, unless they happen to contain the end of one Gospel and the beginning of another. Nevertheless, an adequate number of manuscripts are sufficiently preserved to afford some understanding of the composition of uncial Gospels.

The early minuscules were isolated by means of the dates assigned to manuscripts in the *Kurzgefasste Liste*. These attributions in turn are based on the judgments of New Testament scholars or the cataloguers of various collections.

Some of these opinions, often made decades ago, would not be accepted today, but they must be used, because a redating of thousands of manuscripts for the present purpose is impossible. All minuscule Gospels assigned to the ninth century, amounting to only 14 books, were examined, as were the three manuscripts placed in the category, "ninth–tenth century." Many more were listed for the tenth century, or in total, 122 copies of some portion of the New Testament. From that period, all dated and about 50 undated Gospel books were studied in order to gain an impression of the texts found at this time. The following comments on prologues are based upon this work in Münster.

If the uncial Gospels, the earliest manuscripts, are taken as a group, certain patterns emerge. Many books have no supplementary texts, but at most a typical early Byzantine Gospel manuscript may contain chapter lists, canon tables, and the letter of Eusebius about his tabulation, but no prefaces, epigrams, or subscriptions whatsoever.[10] Thus, it has only the essential subsidiary material—tables of contents and the system of concordance of Eusebius and a note by him explaining its use. There are a few uncial Gospels with texts other than these, but none has been dated before the ninth century by palaeographers.

The most common texts found in the latter group are subscriptions concerning the time when each Gospel was written or issued. These occur in four manuscripts: Hamburg, Univ. Bibl. cod. 91; Paris, Bibl. Nat. gr. 63; Rome, Vat. gr. 354, dated 949; and Mt. Athos, Dionysiou 10.[11] All but Vat. gr. 354 have been assigned to the ninth century. In addition, an introductory or concluding text of St. Hippolytus (von Soden, no. 150) appears in two manuscripts: Paris, Bibl. Nat. gr. 48, and Moscow, Hist. Mus. gr. 9 (399), both of the ninth century;[12] a Gospels in Princeton (Univ. Lib., Garrett 1) from the same period has verses about the evangelists.[13] Two manuscripts have original prefaces—Cambridge, Univ. Lib., Add. 6594, and Moscow, Hist. Mus., gr. 9 (399).[14] Another, Brit. Lib., Harley 5684, has a preface to Matthew (von Soden, no. 120), but this passage is written in minuscule script by another and possibly later hand.[15] Of the books with prologues, the Gospels in Cambridge, Add. 6594, contains prefaces to Mark, Luke, and John based on Irenaeus (von Soden, no. 108), and the Moscow manuscript has a brief introduction to the Gospels excerpted from a homily of John Chrysostomos (von Soden, no. 80).[16] Finally, Vat. gr. 354 of 949 has a note about the chapter lists in the book.[17] Only the Cambridge Gospels has texts that pertain to the iconographic problems discussed previously, for preface no. 108 to Mark and Luke mention Peter and Paul, respectively. There are no texts discussing the evangelist symbols or Christ enthroned on the cherubim.

As for the Gospels in minuscule script, here too there are certain observable characteristics. The standard minuscule Gospel book as described by Devreesse, for example, contains the letter of Eusebius, canon tables, a definition of the Gospels, chapter lists, prefaces to the Gospels, and subscriptions specifying the number of verses in each book or the date and place of publication.[18] Hundreds of manuscripts conform to this pattern, which in turn probably influenced the supplementary texts in the Middle Byzantine uncial Gospels just described.

The use of these texts in minuscule Gospels begins early and gradually becomes universal. The very first dated example, the Uspenski Gospel book (Leningrad, Publ. Lib. gr. 219), is an important specimen in this regard. It was completed on May 7, 835, by the scribe Nicholas, who later became abbot of the Studios Monastery in Constantinople.[19] In addition to scribal chapter lists and several hymns, verses, and other texts added to it in the thirteenth to fifteenth centuries, there are the following texts in the hand of the scribe: a genealogical table of the ancestors of Jesus (f. 1r) in uncials, a chronology of the life of Christ (ff. 340r–341r, von Soden, no. 151), another similar chronology attributed to Maximus (ff. 341r–342r; von Soden, no. 152), notices of the deaths of three monks (f. 344r), and the colophon (f. 344v).[20] From a study of a microfilm of the manuscript in Münster, there is no question that the preface and the two postscripts are in fact original.[21] Such chronologies continue to be used in later Gospels, and so, for example, the passage of Maximus appears in Vat. gr. 1254 of the tenth century and in London, Brit. Lib. Add. 17470 of 1034.[2] The other text is to be found in Vat. Urb. gr. 2 of the twelfth century.[23] Though von Soden lists both as postfaces, they are not always written at the end of Gospels, and the first three such texts that he notes (nos. 150–52) frequently serve as prefaces.[24]

Minuscule Gospels from later in the ninth century do not always have supplementary texts, and apparently the custom established itself only gradually. Thus, the second-oldest-dated minuscule manuscript of the New Testament, Leningrad, Academy Lib. gr. 74 of 891, has no prologues or verses and only the briefest of subscriptions.[25] The same is true of the other seven Gospel books attributed to the ninth century in the *Kurzgefasste Liste*. Other manuscripts without prefaces or verses are the following: Paris, Bibl. Nat. suppl. gr. 1257; Mt. Athos, Lavra A78; Leningrad, Publ. Lib. gr. 210; and Megaspelaion cod. 1.[26] Leningrad, Publ. Lib. gr. 54, has a scribal note comparing the genealogies of Matthew and Luke,[27] and London, Brit. Lib. Add. 33277, includes poems about Matthew and Mark.[28] The only book with the standard prologues is Mt. Athos, Lavra A15, which contains both the Irenaean introduction to the four Gospels and the brief notices on each evangelist (von

Soden, nos. 82 and 108). It might be more conservative to date the script of the book to the ninth or the tenth century,[29] but the Lavra Gospels is certainly one of the earliest examples of the two sets of Irenaean prologues that have been discussed often in the preceding pages.

Two of the three New Testament manuscripts listed by Aland in the category "ninth-tenth centuries" are Gospels. One, Leningrad, Publ. Lib. gr. 220, has no prologues or verses; the other, a Gospel book in a theological seminary in Chicago, contains the same poems as London, Add. 33277.[30] Manuscripts survive in much greater numbers from the tenth century proper. Among the 122 New Testament manuscripts of this period enumerated by Aland, not all of which have been examined, there are examples of most of the prefaces and verses that have been linked to Gospel iconography. The prologues of Irenaeus on each evangelist (von Soden, no. 108) and to the Gospels as a whole (von Soden, no. 82) as well as those of Cosmas Indicopleustes (von Soden, no. 122) are found in Paris, Bibl. Nat. gr. 89.[31] Another common preface (von Soden, no. 120) appears in Paris, Bibl. Nat. gr. 177; Paris, Bibl. Nat. Coislin gr. 20; and Budapest, Univ. Lib. cod. gr. 1.[32] During the tenth century, prologues and epigrams became common, and the tradition is thereby established for the remainder of the Middle Ages and beyond.

The evidence, then, from a survey of uncial and minuscule Gospels, points to the hypothesis that Gospel prologues are not a feature of the earliest Greek manuscripts but appear only in the early ninth century. No preserved uncial Gospels before that time had supplementary texts (excluding the Eusebian letter), whereas two are found in the Uspenski Gospels of 835. Discoveries of new manuscripts, such as the still unpublished cache of early books found recently at Mt. Sinai,[33] could of course alter these findings, and future students of the textual history of Gospel prologues may detect clues that would suggest an earlier history for certain prefaces. However, it is not likely that hundreds of unknown books will be revealed that would measurably alter the basic direction of the foregoing evidence. Thus, it is significant that prologues begin to become common only in the ninth and tenth centuries and that there is no apparent reason to suppose that their usage dates earlier than the eighth or early ninth century.[34]

The Uspenski Gospels is, therefore, the earliest-dated example of two features that are characteristic of Middle Byzantine Gospel books—the minuscule script and supplemental texts—and there is reason to believe that the appearance of both elements may not be coincidental. At the period of the proposed introduction of these ancillary tracts, the transliteration of texts from uncial to minuscule was the major literary enterprise; Lemerle, for instance, considers this to be a decisive moment in the history of medieval Greek manuscripts, comparable in its own time with the later invention of printing.[35] Because of the use of connecting ligatures and the rounded, more cursive shapes of the letters, books written in minuscule could be copied faster and on fewer pages of valuable parchment. Word division now becomes common, since groups of letters were connected. Not only was there usually no separation of words in uncial texts, but marks of accent and punctuation were seldom written either.[36] Thus, the transliteration of a text from uncial to minuscule letters involved more than simply recopying, and often editorial work was done. As Dain says, the act of transliteration is at the same time "un travail critique." Those who study the textual history of classical authors often identify the stage of transcription from the types of errors resulting from the process. At this time a new collation of a text was frequently made, and marginal variants were given.[37]

Is there any evidence of such development in the text of the four Gospels? Zuntz thought that with the victory of Orthodoxy in 843 there was a new Byzantine "ecclesiastical text" of the Gospels,[38] and Lake suggested that the Byzantine text may have been connected with the introduction of the minuscule.[39] Recently Birdsall was more cautious, as he showed that Photius, at least, used an older type of text. According to him, Zuntz did not give precise enough evidence for the theory that the Byzantine text is a consequence of the restoration of Orthodoxy; but he nevertheless believes that "a number of codicological facts point in that direction," exactly what, he does not say.[40] Unfortunately, there the matter rests, without enough information on which to form an opinion.

Whether or not there was a significant change in the canonical text of the Gospels at the time of the shift to minuscules, it is tempting to see the appearance of supplementary texts in the early ninth century, given the manuscript evidence presented above, as a part of the general editorial and literary activity of an age, which witnessed new critical editions of classical authors. Certainly the inclusion of prologues reflects a changed attitude toward the Gospels. These anecdotal and didactic passages are akin to the marginalia of classical treatises and are indicative of a more scholarly interest in the Gospels. The addition of such passages to the canonical scriptures represents a breakdown of the rigid formality of an uncial manuscript, containing solely the four Gospels and possibly chapter lists and canon tables. As such, this informal approach matches the change from the hieratic uncial to the more prosaic minuscule, a script whose origins most likely are to be found in humble notary hands.[41] The distinction in prestige between the minuscule and uncial continues to be observed in later periods, so that the latter will be employed for titles or for particularly ornate liturgical books.

The little that has been learned so far from the text of the prologues themselves does not contradict this hypothesis. The sources of many of the prologues are early authors, such as Irenaeus (second century), Cosmas Indicopleustes (sixth century), or St. Maximus (seventh century). Usually no evidence is available about when passages from such writers were chosen for prefaces, but there are suggestions that the origins of two other prologues are relatively late. The best-documented case, a preface to Luke, unfortunately encountered only rarely, is attributed in manuscripts to St. Methodius, presumably the first patriarch after Iconoclasm (843–47). Chapman discovered that the text is a Greek translation of a prologue for Luke commonly seen in Latin Gospels,[42] a circumstance that is historically quite plausible. Methodius, who was born in Syracuse and later became a monk in a monastery in Constantinople, went to Rome after the second outbreak of Iconoclasm about 815 and returned to Constantinople in 821.[43] While in Rome it is known that he devoted himself to literary work at St. Peter's.[44] Thus, this Greek prologue, if by the same Methodius, presumably has a *terminus post quem* of the early ninth century.

The second example is the prologue of Hippolytus of Thebes (von Soden, no. 150), who wrote sometime between 650 and 750, and more likely in the latter half of this period according to Diekamp.[45] The prologue found, for example, in the Patriarchate Gospels, cod. 3, is taken from the concluding chapter of his chronicle. The earliest example of the preface known to this writer is found in a tenth-century Gospels in Paris, Bibl. Nat. gr. 177.[46] If Diekamp's theory is correct, the *terminus post quem* of the text would be the latter half of the seventh, or preferably the first half of the eighth century, perhaps not much earlier than the introduction of such chronicles of the life and genealogy of Jesus into Gospel books. The Uspenski Gospels contains a similar text.[47]

There are a number of implications of the foregoing hypothesis that supplementary texts were introduced into Gospel books only in the eighth or early ninth century, and a few of them may be examined in the following pages. One factor certainly to be considered is the Iconoclastic controversy (726–843) itself. The widespread adoption of a preface such as the general introduction to the Gospels of Irenaeus (von Soden, no. 82) may be even later than the early ninth century, for the sentiments expressed there seem incompatible with Iconoclastic theology and more appropriate for Iconophile circles. The language is graphic and explicit. The four faces of the tetramorph are the "pictures" (εἰκόνες) of the "dispensation of the Son of God." Further, each of the animals "depicts" and "represents" an attribute of Christ.[48] Such concrete visual metaphors do not seem to be the type that an Iconoclastic theologian would have chosen to place at the beginning of his Gospel book, especially when the addition of such a supplementary text would have broken a centuries-old tradition.

Rather, the Irenaean preface fits better the theological position of the Iconophiles. In his book on Iconoclasm, Grabar has written a stimulating section on the importance of visions of God to the Iconophiles both during and after the controversy, and some of his comments are appropriate for the present problem.[49] In the first period up to the Ecumenical Council of 787, which temporarily restored icons, the issues revolved around accusations of idolatry. The role of the Incarnation, though important before, becomes decisive in the later stages of the dispute. The Incarnation gave to man the gift of contemplating God, who before was seen only by the angelic beings and by a few chosen prophets of the Old Testament. This is the argument, for instance, of a homily attributed to Theodore Studites, a principal leader of the Iconodules.[50] He goes on to say that after the Incarnation man resembles the "Zodia" and that like the cherubim, he is furnished with many eyes opened to God.[51] Icons offer to everyone the opportunity to relive the experiences of the prophets of old. Later, the office of the Sunday of Orthodoxy, the feast established to celebrate the return of icons, twice quotes Gospel texts about heavenly visions of God and angels.[52]

That this conception of the Incarnation and divine visions was more than an abstract theory during these years of controversy over icons is attested by the story of the miraculous discovery of the early Christian mosaic of Christ and the four beasts at Hosios David in Thessaloniki (fig. 54). According to the account of the monk Ignatius, the apse mosaic was long covered up. One day during the reign of Emperor Leo V (813–20), the Egyptian monk Senouphios had a vision in which Christ told him to go to the Latomos Monastery in Thessaloniki, and there he would find the image of the Second Coming he so earnestly desired to contemplate. Senouphios did as directed but found no such image, until one day during an earthquake the mosaic was revealed. Senouphios was so awestruck that he died on the spot.[53]

Although the earliest manuscript of the story is from the eleventh or twelfth century,[54] there is no apparent reason to doubt the main outlines of the account within the parameters of medieval hagiographic legends. The image could have been covered up during Iconoclasm and then forgotten;[55] moreover, the theophany of Christ and the four beasts was the type of divine vision by an ordinary man that Iconophile writers defended. Even if the account is entirely spurious, it still illustrates the reverence the monks, the principal supporters of images, had for the *Maiestas Domini*. Such visions of God had a corresponding significance in post-Iconoclastic art as well, and Grabar discussed several examples.[56] More recently Mango's researches on the ninth- or tenth-century mosaic programs of Hagia Sophia have disclosed new evidence of a monumental Pantocrator and angels in the nave of the church and the Pentecost, Baptism, and Pantocrator with seraphim and cherubim in the galleries.[57] The common denominator here is the fact that all are theophanies.

The Irenaean preface about David's vision of the Lord sitting on the cherubim fits well, then, into this intellectual position of the Iconophiles during the second period of Iconoclasm and after 843. Conversely, there is evidence that such a subject was not favored by the Iconoclasts, if one can trust the statements made by Patriarch Nicephorus in his *Refutatio et Eversio*. Written between 820 and 828, according to Alexander,[58] the treatise contains a rebuttal of the findings of the Iconoclastic Council of 815. In particular, Nicephorus accuses the Iconoclasts of attacking the Bible, because they consider the cherubim of the Old Testament to be idols, that is, "the golden cherubim above the mercy seat, the images in Solomon's temple, the vision of Ezekiel." [59] Nicephorus' argument recalls a similar one made repeatedly by John of Damascus in his orations on images. He cites the example of the golden cherubim that God ordered Moses to make for the Ark (Exodus 25:18–20) as a potential contradiction of the prohibition against images in Deuteronomy 5:8: "You shall not make a carved image for yourself nor the likeness of anything in the heavens above, or on the earth below, or in the waters under the earth." [60] John's purpose in emphasizing the possible conflict is perhaps best explained by Leontios of Naples, whom John quotes. According to Leontios, God directed Moses to make the cherubim, and therefore an objection lodged against such images would be a condemnation of God.[61]

Thus, both the cherubim and the Old Testament theophanies figure explicitly in the doctrines of several of the Iconodule writers, and furthermore it seems that these themes were not popular among the Iconoclasts. Yet why should this discussion of the four Gospels and the four faces of the cherubim have been selected as a prologue in the first place? The problem of certain heretics who refused to accept the canonical four Gospels, the issue that aroused Irenaeus, had long since been resolved, and surely among the writings of earlier theologians there must have been innumerable other choices for an introduction to the Gospels.

One answer may lie in the subsequent history of the passage of Irenaeus. As discussed earlier, the text was repeated by a number of later authors, one of whom was Patriarch Germanos (715–29), writing in his liturgical commentary, the *Historia Ecclesiastica,* and it may be proposed that this association contributed to a wider knowledge of these few paragraphs out of the whole of Irenaeus' long treatise on heresies. Because of his opposition to the imperial Iconoclastic policy, Germanos was deposed by Emperor Leo III at the beginning of the controversy, thereby guaranteeing the veneration of later Iconophiles. Germanos' standing was further enhanced when he was condemned by the Iconoclastic Council of 754. Subsequently two of his letters were quoted in the Council of 787, which temporarily restored icons.[62] Germanos and three other patriarchs were especially singled out for veneration at the Feast of Orthodoxy, and the group was given a prominent place next to the apostles in the mosaic decoration from the second half of the ninth century in the room over the southwest vestibule of Hagia Sophia.[63] Thus, Germanos was an honored and respected man to the supporters of icons, both during and after Iconoclasm.

Furthermore, there is the context in which the passage of Irenaeus appears in the *Historia Ecclesiastica*. Tsuji, who mentioned Germanos' text in connection with the prologue, termed the former "a variation of the Preface." [64] The relation, on the contrary, may be the opposite. Although both have textual variants with each other, and both are probably based on Irenaeus independently,[65] it is the *Historia Ecclesiastica* that may have contributed to the adoption of this text of Irenaeus. It will be recalled that Germanos uses it in his discussion of the Lesser Entry and that the whole ceremony is seen by him as "the advent [παρουσία] and the entry of the son of God into the Cosmos," that is, a theophany.[66] The "Holy Gospel" is the παρουσία of the Son of God that was revealed to us, not obscurely as it was to Moses and the other prophets, but openly; and this symbolism, whose appeal to Iconophiles is now clear, may have influenced Gospel iconography.[67] The Gospel is further discussed in those Irenaean terms: "Four are the Gospels, because there are four universal winds," and so on.[68] Although the same passage was quoted by earlier authors in various learned theological treatises probably of limited dissemination, it is Germanos who takes it out of this more restricted milieu and makes it the definition of the Gospels in a work of a quite different nature. The influence of the *Historia Ecclesiastica*, according to Bornert,[69] was widespread, to judge from the number of surviving manuscripts, and its proposed impact on art has already been noted. Given the evidence that both the Iconoclastic controversy and the liturgical commentary antedate prefaces, the possibility must be considered that the *Historia Ecclesiastica* served to popularize the text of Irenaeus and influenced its adoption as a prologue to the four Gospels.[70]

The second implication of the textual evidence about prefaces involves the three iconographical themes discussed earlier: evangelist symbols, the *Maiestas Domini*, and evangelists with accompanying figures. If it is accepted that each is inspired originally by Gospel prologues, then all presumably postdate the introduction of such texts in the eighth or early ninth century, and because of Iconoclasm, their widespread use, if not origin, would not have occurred until after the restoration of images in 843. This is not to say that any of the three subjects did not exist before this time, because obviously there are earlier representations of Christ in Majesty and possibly of Peter dictating to Mark.[71] However, their appearance in Greek Gospel books is another matter. The earliest versions of all three themes were intimately connected with Gospel prologues, and for this reason the ultimate models for the symbols in Athens 57, the *Maiestas Domini* in Parma 5, or the accompanying figures of Walters W.524 are most likely post-Iconoclastic.

This proposed date for the origin of evangelist symbols in Byzantine manuscripts is contrary to the opinions of some that there once were pre-Iconoclastic manuscripts with evangelist symbols and supports the doubts of others about the existence of such models. Further, the observed close connection of the symbols to prologues based on Greek Patristic authors renders more difficult the position of those who suggest that Byzantine evangelist symbols in general were originally influenced by Western medieval art. Although the situation in the Palaeologan era may be different, the pairing of symbols in many Middle Byzantine manuscripts depends upon indigenous Greek texts, and thus a case based upon a purely visual transmission of motifs from the West to the East is not easily defensible on those grounds.

In sum, the history of the prologues and poems found in Byzantine Gospel books involves a number of different issues. The present study has concentrated more on the art-historical aspects, but further research might pursue other directions. For instance, in the foregoing, several lines of evidence converged on what Mango has called the Iconophile intelligentsia of the late eighth and early ninth centuries.[72] Prefaces were associated, not with early uncial manuscripts, but with the new minuscule script, and the first dated minuscule book, the Uspenski Gospels, happens also to be the earliest documented example of supplementary texts. It and an early copy of the Epistles with a preface (Moscow, Hist. Mus. gr. 93) were most likely written in the Studios Monastery, the same one in which Theodore, an important theorist of images, served as abbot. One preface was a translation by Methodius, later the first patriarch after Iconoclasm; another, the Irenaean introduction to the four Gospels, may have been inspired by the liturgical commentary of the last Iconodule patriarch before Iconoclasm.

Another track to pursue would be the examination of the history of the prologues to the other books of the New Testament, and there one of the principal problems would be the so-called Euthalian material, a collection of tables of contents and introductions to Acts and the Pauline and Catholic Epistles. Portions of these texts, especially the chapter lists, may go back to the fourth century; other passages seem to be later, and it is thought that the material exists in chronologically different strata.[73] In probing these matters a detailed investigation of early New Testament manuscripts would be a major desideratum, and afterward it would be interesting to survey the categories of Acts and Epistles illustration, particularly author portraits, to see if such texts might contribute to the explication of the images.

Finally, for the manuscripts of the four Gospels under discussion in the foregoing pages, more information on the patterns of appearance of prefaces would be desirable. At times it has been possible to demonstrate the affiliation of two books, like the Gospels in Parma and Oxford (E. D. Clarke 10) by comparing the nature of their supplementary texts. This effort could be profitably extended to a larger body of manuscripts. Probably by collating data on their contents, groupings by region, monastery, or scribe could be formed.[74] The information thus obtained would be of interest to the wider audience of students of medieval Greek manuscripts, and when combined with an analysis of illumination, palaeography, codicology, and textual criticism of the New Testament, it should provide a more comprehensive history of the Byzantine Gospel book.

NOTES

1. For example, von Soden, I, 1, 302–3, 311, 316. On the latter see also F. Halkin, *Bibliotheca hagiographica graeca*, 3d ed. (Bruxelles, 1957), 28, 57–58, 78, 104.

2. Von Soden, I, 1, 321–26.

3. Gregory, *Textkritik*, I.

4. Von Soden, *Schriften des Neuen Testaments*, I, 1.

5. Aland, *Kurzgefasste Liste*.

6. For example, see the study of D. Wright, "The Codex Millenarius and Its Model," *MünchJb*, 15 (1964), 37–54, esp. 37–38, with further references.

7. V. Gardthausen, *Griechische Palaeographie*, II (Leipzig, 1913), 88–158; G. Cavallo, *Ricerche sulla maiuscola biblica* (Florence, 1967); idem, "Funzione e strutture," *Paléographie grecque*. For a review of the earlier literature see J. Iri-

goin, "Les manuscrits grecs 1931–1960," *Lustrum*, 7 (1962), 39–44 (hereafter, *Lustrum*).

8. C. Mango, "La culture grecque et l'occident au VIIIᵉ siècle," *I problemi dell' occidente nel secolo VIII*, 2, *Settimane di studio del Centro Italiano di studi sull'alto medioevo*, 20 (1973), 717–20; P. Lemerle, *Le premier humanisme byzantin* (Paris, 1971), 112–18; Irigoin, *Lustrum*, 44–48; see the articles by E. Follieri, A. Blanchard, C. Mango, and F.-J. Leroy in *Paléographie grecque*, 139–90.

9. More are known. At the latest recording the number was 266. See K. Aland, *Studien zur Überlieferung des Neuen Testaments und Seines Texts* (Berlin, 1967), 207.

10. In the present study the letter of Eusebius to Carpanius is not considered as a prologue to the Gospels. It is of a different character and

merely explains the use of the canon tables. The inclusion of the latter to a certain extent requires the former. The system naturally begins with Eusebius in the fourth century. See C. Nordenfalk, *Die spätantiken Kanontafeln* (Göteborg, 1938), 45–51.

11. These manuscripts have the following numbers of Gregory in the *Kurzgefasste Liste:* 013, 017, 028, 045; cf. pp. 37–39, 41. The subscriptions are of the type listed in von Soden, I, 1, 297 (nos. 40–51).

12. Aland, 38, 40 (nos. 021, 031).

13. Aland, 41 (no. 047). The epigram to Luke is visible in the illustration in Vikan, *Illuminated Greek MSS,* 56–57, fig. 2, with bibliography. The verses are unpublished, not even being mentioned in the description of the manuscript by Clark, *Greek New Testament MSS,* 61–63.

14. Aland, 40 (nos. 034, 031).

15. Ibid., 37 (no. 011).

16. Treu, *Griechische Handschriften,* 237.

17. Von Soden, I, 1, 402, and see above, Chapter III, note 21.

18. Devreesse, *Introduction,* 168–69. These are the items he lists under the heading, "la présentation 'byzantine' des livres du N.T."

19. Treu, *Griechische Handschriften,* 85–86; A. Diller, "A Companion to the Uspenski Gospels," *BZ,* 49 (1956), 332–33; T. W. Allen, "The Origin of the Greek Minuscule Hand," *JHS,* 40 (1920), 2–3; Lemerle, *Humanisme,* 113. The latest study on Nicholas as a scribe is F.-J. Leroy, "Un nouveau manuscrit de Nicolas Stoudite: *Le Parisinus Graecus 494,*" *Paléographie grecque,* 181–87.

20. Treu, *Griechische Handschriften,* 86.

21. The flourish at the end of the first postface (f. 341r) is in the same style as others in the book. Folios 340–42 are part of quire 44 (MΔ) numbered in the same manner as the rest of the gatherings. Quire 44 contains four folios, and the next, number 45 (ME, ff. 343–44), only two folios including the colophon. The script of the two postfaces and the colophon is the work of the scribe of the main text.

22. There is no published catalogue description of Vat. gr. 1254. Von Soden, I, 1, 362, cites the British Museum manuscript.

23. Ibid.

24. Ibid., 361–62. For example, text no. 150 is a prologue appearing in the Patriarchate Gospels, Istanbul, Ecumenical Patriarchate, cod.

3, and in Vat. Urb. gr. 2. No. 151 is also found in the latter.

25. Treu, *Griechische Handschriften,* 207–9. As stated before, chapter lists, canon tables, or the letter of Eusebius are not being considered in this discussion.

26. Aland, 129, 139, 173, 177; MSS ε1295, 1500, 2142, 2224, respectively.

27. Ibid., 91, MS ε566; Treu, *Griechische Handschriften,* 49.

28. Aland, 109, MS ε892. The verses are published by von Soden, I, 1, 378 (nos. 5–6).

29. Aland, 118, ε1080, ninth century; Eustratiades, *Catalogue,* 3, fourteenth century; Gregory, *Textkritik,* I, 240, ninth or tenth century; von Soden, I, 1, 256. A few uncial letters appear, so this is no longer a pure minuscule, suggesting a more recent date. Later evangelist portraits have been inserted on separate bifolios, and arches have been painted on the other three pages of each bifolio.

30. Aland, 82, ε399; and ibid., 136, ε1424, Chicago, Lutheran School of Theology, Gruber MS 152.

31. Ibid., 62, ε29. Venice, Bibl. Marc. Gr. I, 18 (ibid., 83, ε411), of the tenth century has prefaces nos. 121 and 122.

32. Ibid., 77, 63, 66; MSS 299, 36, 100, respectively.

33. The discovery was publicized by an article in the Greek newspaper, Καθημερινή, May 21–22, 1978 (a reference I owe to Dr. Temily Mark-Weiner), and was discussed by Professors I. Ševčenko and B. Narkiss at the fall 1978 meeting of the Byzantine Studies Association of America.

34. No study has been made of prefaces to other parts of the New Testament, either of their possible relation to illustrations or of their textual history. However, concerning the latter, it is interesting to note that prologues are found in a manuscript of the Epistles in Moscow (State Hist. Mus. gr. 93) of the ninth century. Diller thought that its minuscule script was by the same scribe as the Uspenski Gospels (*BZ* [1956], 332–33). Treu (*Griechische Handschriften,* 281–82) does not accept this attribution, because he thinks the manuscript may instead have merely been written in the same center as the Uspenski Gospels, that is, the Studios Monastery. The book does have the types of quire signatures that usually, but

not always, indicate a Studite origin. Also see F.-J. Leroy, "Un nouveau manuscrit," *Paléographie grecque,* 187.

35. Lemerle, *Humanisme,* 121.

36. Ibid., 119.

37. Ibid., 118–20; A. Dain, "La transmission des textes littéraires classiques de Photius à Constantin Porphyrogénète," *DOP,* 8 (1954), 36; idem, *Les manuscrits* (Paris, 1964), 128–33.

38. G. Zuntz, *The Text of the Epistles* (London, 1953), 151.

39. K. and S. Lake, "The Byzantine Text of the Gospels," *Mémorial Lagrange* (Paris, 1940), 255.

40. J. N. Birdsall, "The New Testament Text," *The Cambridge History of the Bible,* I (Cambridge, 1970), 320–21.

41. See the literature cited in note 8 to this chapter.

42. Chapman, *History of the Vulgate Gospels,* 237. The Latin text, he thinks, was composed c. 435–40 (ibid., 286). Also see von Soden, I, 1, 327, 365–66; J. Regul, *Die Antimarcionitischen Evangelienprologe* (Freiburg, 1969), 14; R. G. Heard, "The Old Gospel Prologues," *JTS,* N.S., 6 (1955), 7–11, 16.

43. Beck, *Kirche,* 496; Mango, "La culture grecque," 716.

44. See the passage quoted by Mango, ibid., 720. Proof also of his relations with the Latins is the papal discourse in support of icons that he presented to the Iconoclast emperor, Michael II, after Methodius returned from Rome. Michael's reaction was to throw him in prison (G. Ostrogorsky, *History of the Byzantine State* [New Brunswick, 1969], 204). On other translations from Latin to Greek at this period see Mango, "La culture grecque," 709–10. For example, a passion of St. Anastasia the Widow was translated in Rome in 824 (F. Halkin, *Légendes grecques de 'Martyres Romaines'* [Bruxelles, 1973], 7).

45. F. Diekamp, *Hippolytos von Theben* (Münster i.W., 1898), 157 (hereafter, *Hippolytos*).

46. Aland, 77, MS ε299.

47. Treu, *Griechische Handschriften,* 86; von Soden, I, 1, 362 (no. 151). The text is printed in Diekamp, *Hippolytos,* 53–54.

48. Text and translation above in Chapter I, page 6.

49. Grabar, *Iconoclasme,* 241–57; see also Lafontaine-Dosogne, "Théophanies-Visions," 135–43. J. Gouillard, "Le synodikon de l'Orthodoxie: édition et commentaire,"

Travaux et Mémoires, 2 (1967), 172–74, provides an important analysis of the problem. See also idem, "Art et littérature théologique à Byzance au lendemain de la querelle des images," *CahCM,* 12 (1969), 8–13.

50. Grabar, *Iconoclasme,* 242–43.

51. Ibid., 242.

52. Ibid., 243.

53. The account is summarized by V. Grumel, "La mosaique du 'Dieu Sauveur' au monastère du 'Latome' à Salonique," *EO,* 29 (1930), 163, and by R. Janin, *Les églises et les monastères des grands centres byzantins* (Paris, 1975), 393–94. I wish to thank Professor A. Bryer for this reference. Also see R. Cormack, "Painting after Iconoclasm," *Iconoclasm* (Birmingham, 1977), 157–60.

54. Janin (*Centres,* 393) says eleventh century and cites Grumel, but the latter ("La mosaique," 165) gives a twelfth-century date.

55. Janin, *Centres,* 394.

56. Grabar, *Iconoclasme,* 246–57.

57. C. Mango, *Materials for the Study of the Mosaics of St. Sophia at Istanbul* (Washington, D.C., 1962), 98. See also Lafontaine-Dosogne, "Théophanies-Visions," 135–43.

58. P. J. Alexander, *The Patriarch Nicephorus of Constantinople* (Oxford, 1958), 183.

59. Ibid., 246–47. The quotation is from Alexander's summary.

60. P. B. Kotter, *Die Schriften des Johannes von Damaskos,* 3, *Contra imaginum calumniatores orationes tres* (Berlin, 1975), 88, 92, 95–97 (I, 15, 16, 20; II, 9).

61. Ibid., 178. The authenticity of the quotation from Leontios has been questioned, and thus its suitability for John's argument and for Iconodulic thought may not be accidental. See E. J. Martin, *A History of the Iconoclastic Controversy* (London, 1930), 141–42.

62. P. A. Underwood, "A Preliminary Report on Some Unpublished Mosaics in Hagia Sophia: Season of 1950 of the Byzantine Institute," *AJA,* 55 (1951), 369; P. van den Ven, "La patristique et l'hagiographie au concile de Nicée de 787," *Byzantion,* 25–27 (1955–57), 351; L. Lamza, *Patriarch Germanos I von Konstantinopel (715–730)* (Würzburg, 1975), 180–81.

63. Underwood, *AJA,* 369–70. Also see Grabar, *Iconoclasme,* 193–94, 213–14; Mango, *Materials,* 44–45; R. Cormack, "Painting after Iconoclasm," *Iconoclasm,* ed. A. Bryer and J. Herrin (Birmingham, 1977), 149–50. Now

most recently there is R. Cormack and E. J. W. Hawkins, "The Mosaics of St. Sophia at Istanbul: The Rooms Above the Southwest Vestibule and Ramp," *DOP,* 31 (1977), 175–252.

64. Tsuji, *DOP* 29, 181.

65. For example, two phrases in the first sentence of the preface from Irenaeus are not given by Germanos: καὶ οὔτε πλείονα οὔτε ἐλάττονα and παντοχόθεν πνέοντα τὴν ἀφθαρσίαν καὶ ἀναζωπυροῦντα τοὺς ἀνθρώπους. Thus, the prologue cannot be derived from Germanos, but instead probably quotes from Irenaeus or a repetition of the passage by another author.

66. Brightman, "Historia Mystagogica," 265.

67. Ibid., 388. See above, pages 67–68.

68. Brightman, "Historia Mystagogica," 388.

69. Bornert, *Commentaires,* 125.

70. In this connection there is an interesting unpublished preface in Oxford, Christ Church gr. 12. The text placed before the Gospel of Mark (f. 60r) is a version of Irenaeus' comments on the four Gospels and thus not the same as prologue no. 82. Its title states that it is from the *Historia Ecclesiastica* of St. Basil the Great. This probably refers to the treatise under discussion, because Basil is sometimes cited as its author (Bornert, *Commentaires,* 142–44).

71. One of the ivories of the so-called Grado Chair group shows Peter dictating to Mark (Weitzmann, "Grado Chair," fig. 14). Professor Weitzmann dates the ivories to the eighth century (ibid., 81) and thinks that the Mark plaque was one of an original series of four, each depicting an evangelist with an accompanying figure in analogy to illuminated manuscripts (ibid., 72). The dating of the ivories is still controversial. Volbach (*Elfenbeinarbeiten der spätantike und des frühen Mittelalters,* 2d ed. [Mainz an Rhein, 1976], 139) puts them in the eleventh century and assigns them finally to Sicily, as Weitzmann discusses ("Grado Chair," 50). See the latter (pp. 46–51) for a survey of the bibliography. The scene did exist in the West, and H. Graeven ("Der heilige Markus in Rom und in der Pentapolis," *RQ,* 13 [1899], 112–13) cites a miniature in the Gospel book of St. Bernward of Hildesheim (pl. VIII, 2) and says that the basis of the iconography is the prologue to Mark in the manuscript. Also see above, Chapter IV, note 6. It is entirely possible for the theme of Peter dictating to Mark to be represented

early, as the subject matter is known from the time of Irenaeus, but there is no preserved evidence to support Weitzmann's opinion that a Greek manuscript decorated with a series of evangelist portraits with accompanying figures, such as he describes, existed as early as the eighth century.

72. See his important study "The Availability of Books in the Byzantine Empire, A.D. 750–850," *Byzantine Books and Bookmen* (Washington, D.C., 1975), 43–45; and most recently, idem, "L'Origine de la *minuscule,*"*Paléographie grecque,* 175–80. One tantalizing question that still remains is that raised by Mango in both studies, namely the matter of Western influence during this period. It is a difficult and still unsettled problem, but it should be noted in this respect that prologues, like the minuscule script or zoomorphic letters he mentions, appear at an earlier date in Latin Gospels and that the preface of Methodius is a translation from Latin. On prefaces in Latin manuscripts see P. McGurk, *Latin Gospel Books from A.D. 400 to A.D. 800* (Paris, 1961); S. Berger, "Les Préfaces jointes aux livres de la Bible dans les manuscrits de la Vulgate," *MémAcInscr,* 11, 2 (1904), 1–78; R. M. Walker, "Illustrations to the Priscillian Prologues in the Gospel Manuscripts of the Carolingian Ada School," *ArtB,* 30 (1948), 1–10.

73. The issues are complex, and one finds little consensus in the secondary literature. Most recently see Birdsall in *The Cambridge History of the Bible,* I, 362–63; W. H. P. Hatch, "Euthalius," *The Twentieth Century Encyclopedia of Religious Knowledge,* I (Grand Rapids, Mich., 1955), cols. 399–401; B. Kraft, "Euthalios," *Lexikon für Theologie und Kirche,* III (Freiburg, 1959), cols. 1206–7. Among the earlier studies there is J. A. Robinson, *Euthaliana, Texts and Studies,* III, 3 (Cambridge, 1895). The recent doctoral dissertation of L. C. Willard ("A Critical Study of the Euthalian Apparatus," Yale University, 1970), cited in M. Geerard, *Clavis patrum graecorum,* II (Brepols, 1974), 301, was not available to me.

74. To a certain extent von Soden has done this for the Byzantine scribe Theodore Hagiopetrities. See I, 2, 781–93. The present writer hopes to elaborate on this material in a future study on the manuscript *oeuvre* of this scribe.

Appendix I

The Association of Symbol and Evangelist in Byzantine Art

The following tables are designed to accompany Chapter II. References to the examples listed in the first two tables will be found there. Most of the manuscripts in Table C are also discussed in the text, but none of the Post-Byzantine works of art are treated individually, and therefore bibliographic information is provided for that category. As explained in Chapter II, the degree of completeness within each chronological section varies.

The Middle Byzantine group, it is hoped, is reasonably comprehensive. More Palaeologan material probably can be found, and for the Post-Byzantine era scores of examples doubtlessly could be added. In the two latter periods, though, the general trends are basically clear from the monuments sampled to date. An exception might be Russian painting after c. 1400 where more research is certainly needed, but because this issue is tangential to a study of Byzantine illumination, the topic has been pursued only in a cursory fashion.

TABLE A. EVANGELIST SYMBOLS BEFORE THE EARLY THIRTEENTH CENTURY

	Mt.	Mk.	Lk.	Jn.
1. Rome. Vat. gr. 2138, 991 A.D.	man	lion	calf	eagle
2. Moscow. Hist. Mus. gr. 13, late 11th C.	lion	calf		eagle
3. Athens. Nat. Lib. cod. 57, second half of 11th C.	man	calf	lion	eagle
4. Corfu. Church of St. Mercurius, fresco, 1074–75.			lion	calf
5. Athens. Nat. Lib. cod. 163, late 11th–early 12th C.	man		lion	eagle
6. Vienna. Nat. Lib. suppl. gr. 164, 1109 A.D.	man	calf	lion	eagle
7. Mt. Athos. Vatopedi, pendant, 12th C.	lion	calf	man	eagle
8. Megaspelaion Monastery, cod. 8, 12th C.	lion	lion (restored?)	man	eagle
9. Mt. Athos. Dochiariou 52, 12th C.			calf	
10. Oxford. Bodl. Lib. Auct T. inf. 1.3, 12th C.	man	eagle	calf	lion
11. Bratislava. Lycaeum Augustanum, 12th C.	lion	calf	man	eagle
12. Istanbul. Ecumenical Patriarchate, cod. 5, 12th C.	?	?	?	eagle
13. Holkham Hall. Coll. of Earl of Leicester, MS 4, 12th C.	man	calf	lion	eagle
14. Moscow. Hist. Mus. gr. 14, late 12th C.	lion	calf	man	
15. Geneva. Bibl. Publ. et Univ. MS gr. 19, 12th C.	lion	calf	man	eagle
16. Washington, D.C., Freer Gallery of Art, No. 09.1685, 12th C.		eagle		man(?)
17. Istanbul. Ecumenical Patriarchate, cod. 3, late 12th C.	lion	man	calf	eagle
18. Athens. Nat. Lib. cod. 2251, late 12th–early 13th C.	man	lion		eagle
19. New York. Collection of H. P. Kraus, Gospel book.		lion	eagle	
20. Cambridge, Mass. Harvard College Lib. cod. TYP 215H and Washington, D.C., Dumbarton Oaks, acc. no. 58.105, early 13th C (?).	man	eagle	calf	lion
21. Manchester. John Rylands Lib. gr. 13, late 12th–early 13th C (?).		eagle	calf	lion
22. Athens. Gennadeion Lib. MS 1.5, 1226 A.D.	man	calf	lion	eagle
Texts				
1. "Epiphanios" preface (von Soden, I, 1, 303–4).	man	calf	lion	eagle
2. Milan. Bibl. Ambros. H. 13 sup., 11th C; Rome. Vat. gr. 1548, 11th C; Rome. Vat. gr. 1254, 10th or 11th C.	man	calf	lion	eagle
3. Paris. Bibl. Nat. gr. 93, 12th C.	man	winged form	calf	lion
4. Venice. Bibl. Marc. gr. Z 539, 12th C.	man	lion	calf	eagle
5. Rome. Vat. gr. 1506, 1024 A.D.	man	lion	calf	eagle
6. Rome. Vat. gr. 1974, 10th or 11th C.	man	lion	calf	eagle
7. Rome. Vat. gr. 1522, late 9th C.	man	lion	calf	eagle
8. Moscow. State Lenin Lib. gr. 10, 11th C.	man	lion	calf	eagle
9. Paris. Bibl. Nat. suppl. gr. 612, 1164 A.D.	man	eagle	calf	lion

Table B. The Association of Symbol and Evangelist in Manuscripts Prior to the Early Thirteenth Century

	Mt.	Mk.	Lk.	Jn.
I. *The Preface of Epiphanios.* Athens, Nat. Lib. cod. 57; Athens, Nat. Lib. cod. 163; Vienna, Nat. Lib. Suppl. gr. 164; Holkham Hall, cod. 4; Athens, Gennadeion Lib. MS 1.5; Tbilisi, MSS Institute MS No. A908, Ghelati Gospels (a Georgian manuscript).	man	calf	lion	eagle
II. *The Irenaean Preface.* Moscow, Hist. Mus. gr. 13; Geneva, Bibl. Pub. et Univ. MS gr. 13; Moscow, Hist. Mus. gr. 14; Vatopedi pendant; Bratislava, Lycaeum Augustanum; Megaspelaion cod. 8(?).	lion	calf	man	eagle
III. *Irenaeus.* Manchester, John Rylands Lib. gr. 13; Cambridge, Mass., Harvard College Lib. cod. TYP 215H; Oxford, Bodl. Lib. Auct. T. inf. 1.3.	man	eagle	calf	lion
IV. *St. Jerome.* Athens, Nat. Lib. cod. 2251; Rome, Vat. 2138.	man	lion	calf	eagle
V. *Miscellaneous.*				
Istanbul, Ecumenical Patriarchate, cod. 3.	lion	man	calf	eagle
New York, Collection of H. P. Kraus, Gospel book.		lion	eagle	
Washington, D.C., Freer Gallery of Art, No. 09.1685.		eagle		man(?)

TABLE C. EVANGELIST SYMBOLS IN THE PALAEOLOGAN PERIOD

	Mt.	Mk.	Lk.	Jn.
1. Leningrad. Publ. Lib. gr. 101, late 13th C.	man	lion	calf	eagle
2. Moscow. Hist. Mus. gr. 25, 14th C.	man	lion	calf	eagle
3. London. Brit. Lib. Add. 11838, 1326 A.D.	man	lion	calf	eagle
4. Megaspelaion Monastery, cod. 1, 14th C.	man	lion	calf	eagle
5. Mt. Athos. Vatopedi cod. 937, 14th C.		eagle	calf	lion
6. New York. General Theological Seminary Lib. cod. DeRicci 3, 14th C.	man	lion	calf	eagle
7. Mt. Athos. Stavronikita 43, symbols—13th–14th C.	man	eagle	calf	lion
8. Mt. Athos. Iviron cod. 548, 1433 A.D.	man	lion	calf	eagle
9. Rome. Vat. gr. 1210, 1447 (?) A.D.	man	lion	calf	eagle
10. Oxford. Bodl. Lib. Selden supra 6, late 13th–early 14th C.	man	lion	calf	eagle
11. Cambridge. Univ. Lib. MS Dd. 9. 69, 14th C.	man	lion	calf	eagle
12. London. Lambeth Palace, cod. 1176, 14th–15th C.	man	eagle	calf	lion
13. London. Brit. Lib. Egerton 2783, 14th C.	man	lion	calf	eagle
14. Munich. Bayerische Staatsbibl. cod. Slav. IV, 14th C.	man	not labeled	not labeled	eagle
15. Sofia. Nat. Mus. Poganovo Icon, late 14th C.	man	lion	calf	eagle
16. Trebizond. Frescoes in Hagia Sophia, c. 1260.	man	eagle	calf	lion
17. Athens. Byzantine Mus. Salonica epitaphios, 14th C.	man	lion	calf	eagle
18. Bucharest. Mus. of Art, Neamt epitaphios, 1437 A.D.	man(?)	lion(?)	calf	eagle
19. Epitaphios of St. Clement, c. 1295, location unknown.	man	lion	calf	eagle

Texts

	Mt.	Mk.	Lk.	Jn.
1. Poems of Manuel Philes.	man	lion		eagle
2. Mt. Sinai, gr. 176, 1286 A.D.	man	calf		lion
3. Venice. Bibl. Marc. gr. I, 14, later addition of Palaeologan, or Post-Byzantine date.	man	lion	calf	eagle
4. Venice. Bibl. Marc. gr. I, 15, 14th C.	man	eagle	calf	lion
5. Paris. Bibl. Nat. gr. 106, 14th C.	man	lion	calf	eagle
6. Rome. Vat. gr. 1254, late addition.	man	lion	calf	eagle
7. Patmos. cod. 81, 1335 A.D.	man	lion	calf	eagle
8. Paris. Bibl. Nat. Coislin 20, later note, 13th C.	man	lion	calf	eagle

TABLE D. EVANGELIST SYMBOLS IN POST-BYZANTINE ART, EXCEPTING RUSSIA

	Mt.	Mk.	Lk.	Jn.
1. Paris. Bibl. Nat. suppl. gr. 242, 1650 A.D. (Bordier, *Descriptions des peintures,* 293–96).	man	lion	calf	eagle
2. Jerusalem. Anastaseos, cod. 3, 1633 A.D. (Library of Congress photographs).	man	lion	calf	eagle
3. Jerusalem. Anastaseos, cod. 1, 1647 (?) A.D. (Library of Congress photographs).	man	lion		eagle
4. Mt. Sinai. gr. 2252, cover (Library of Congress photograph).	man	lion	calf	eagle
5. Mt. Sinai. gr. 2254, cover (Library of Congress photograph).	man	lion	calf	eagle
6. Mt. Athos. Lavra cod. ω142, 1653 A.D. (slides at Institute for Patristic Studies, Thessaloniki).	man	lion	calf	eagle
7. Mt. Athos. Karakallou, cod. 272, 1680 A.D. (slides at Institute for Patristic Studies, Thessaloniki).	man	lion	calf	eagle
8. Mt. Athos. Vatopedi cod. 247 (slides at Institute for Patristic Studies, Thessaloniki).	man	lion	calf	eagle
9. Mt. Athos. Xeropotamou, cod. 107, 16th C (Pelekanides, *Treasures,* I, figs. 418–20).		lion	calf	eagle
10. Mt. Sinai, gr. 208, cover (M. Beza, *Byzantine Art in Roumania* [New York, 1940], pl. 35).	man	lion	calf	eagle
11. Mt. Athos. Koutloumousiou, cod. 286, 18th C (Pelekanides, *Treasures,* I, figs. 349, 351, 352, 357).	man	lion	calf	eagle
12. Mt. Athos. Dionysiou, cod. 587, cover (Beza, *Byzantine Art,* pl. 30).	man	lion	calf	eagle
13. Jerusalem. Holy Sepulchre, Gospel of Prince Raresh (ibid., pl. 34).	man	lion	calf	eagle
14. Icon of Emmanuel Tzanes, Byzantine Museum, Athens, 1664 A.D. (M. Chatzidakis, *Byzantine Museum, Athens, Icons* [Athens, n.d.], fig. 29).	man	lion	calf	eagle
15. Vitza. Church of St. Nicholaos, frescoes of 1618 (Vokotopoulos in Ἀρχαιολογικὸν Δελτίον, 21 [1966], 300–301).	man	lion	calf	eagle
16. C. 20 liturgical veils on display at the Byzantine Museum, Athens.	man	lion	calf	eagle
17. Bilinzi. Bulgaria, Church of Archangel Michael, 17th C (E. Floreva, *Die Klosterkirche Archangel Michael in Bilinzi* [Sofia, 1973], pl. 6).	man	lion	calf	eagle
18. Icon of Christ Pantocrator, Byzantine Museum, Athens, 16th C (G. Sotiriou, *Guide du Musée Byzantin d'Athènes* [Athens, 1932], fig. 49).	man	lion	calf	eagle
19. Crucifix, Monastery of St. Panteleimon, Aghia, Thessaly, 16th C (J.T.A. Koumoulides and C. Walter, *Byzantine and Post-Byzantine Monuments at Aghia in Thessaly, Greece* [London, 1975], fig. 32).	man	lion	calf	eagle
20. Mt. Athos. Monastery of Dochiariou, dome fresco, 16th C (P. Huber, *Athos, Leben, Glaube, Kunst* [Zürich, 1969], fig. 180).	man	lion	calf	eagle
21. Dublin. Chester Beatty Library, cod. W135 (figs. 30–33).	man	lion	calf	eagle

Texts

	Mt.	Mk.	Lk.	Jn.
1. Painter's Manual of Dionysius of Fourna (P. Hetherington, *The 'Painter's Manual' of Dionysius of Fourna* [London, 1974], 53).	man	lion	calf	eagle

TABLE E. EVANGELIST SYMBOLS IN RUSSIA AFTER C. 1400

	Mt.	Mk.	Lk.	Jn.
1. Icon of Christ in Majesty, Recklinghausen, c. 1600 (Recklinghausen, *Ikonen-Museum* [Recklinghausen, 1965], pl. 51).	man	eagle	calf	lion
2. Icon of Trinity, 16th C (I. Grabar, *Istoriĭa russkago iskusstva*, VI, 1 [Moscow, n.d.], 301).	man	lion	calf	eagle
3. Icon of Trinity, c. 1610 (ibid., 373).	man	eagle	calf	lion
4. Icon of Trinity, 16th C (M. Farbman, *Masterpieces of Russian Painting* [London, 1930], pl. 39).	man	eagle	calf	lion
5. Icon of Christ in Majesty, 15th C. Metropolitan Museum, New York (L. Ouspensky and W. Lasky, *Der Sinn der Ikonen* [Bern, 1952], 72).	man	lion	calf	eagle
6. Icon of Christ in Majesty, Leningrad, 15th C (P. Schweinfurth, *Geschichte der Russischen Malerei im Mittelalter* [Haag, 1930], fig. 102).	man	eagle	calf	lion
7. Moscow, Khitrovo Gospels. Lenin Lib. M. 8657 (V. Lazarev, *Theophanes der Grieche und seine Schule* [Vienna, 1968], pls. 118–21).	man	lion	calf	eagle
8. Wings of altar doors (N. P. Likhachev, *Materiali istoriĭ russkago ikonopisaniĭa*, I [Leningrad, 1906], pl. 145).	man	eagle	calf	lion
9. Icon of God the Father at the Creation (ibid., pl. 243, no. 446).	calf	eagle	man	lion
10. Icon of Virgin and Child in Majesty, 16th C, Moscow, Tretĭakov Gallery (V. I. Antonov and N. E. Mnev, *Katalog drevnerusskoi zhivopisi*, II [Moscow, 1963], pl. 75).	man	calf	lion	eagle
11. Icon of Christ in Majesty, c. 1411, Moscow, Tretiakov Gallery (ibid., I, fig. 184).	man	eagle	calf	lion
12. Icon of the Paternity by Nicephorus Savin, 17th C, Moscow, Tretĭakov Gallery (T. T. Rice, *Icons* [London, 1960], pl. 62).	man	eagle	calf	lion

Appendix II
The Evangelist Symbols of Mt. Athos, Stavronikita 43

The Stavronikita Gospels is a well-known Byzantine manuscript with portraits of the evangelists, medallions of various saints, canon tables, and evangelist symbols. Weitzmann quite reasonably dated it to around the middle of the tenth century and considered its evangelist symbols to be the earliest examples in Byzantine illumination,[1] and his remains the standard opinion on the symbols.[2] However, further study of them from a microfilm of the manuscript at the Library of Congress has disclosed several incongruities, and the position taken here is that these symbols are not part of the original program of decoration but instead are later insertions into the manuscript.

Their placement in the book is unique in the history of Byzantine art. Each animal, framed by a medallion, is placed either in the exterior margin of a page or between the two text columns. There are four symbols in the Gospels of Matthew, Luke, and John, and three in Mark, or fifteen in all. Each symbol is associated with several dots placed in the text. A Greek number is written above each symbol, and the medallions for a single Gospel are numbered consecutively from one to three, or four. The medallion, dots, and number are all visible

115

in the second symbol of Matthew, placed between the columns of text (fig. 73). The four dots are in the left column, and the angel, like the other symbols, faces the passage so marked. In this instance it is clear that the symbol has been added after the text was written, because the roundel overlaps two letters here. The dots also do not fit well into the text, as they occupy about 1½ lines of space. Both factors suggest that the tenth-century scribe did not originally intend for the book to have these symbols. Furthermore, the styles of these roundels in no way equal the high quality of the various portraits in the book. The rendition of the cow (fig. 74), for example, is loose and sketchy and is not the work of a superior artist.

Although it is likely, then, that the symbols are later additions, it is not easy to assign a date to them, and the style of the various animals is of no help. But fortunately there are clues in the form of the letters used to number the symbols. The best letter for this purpose is the β on f. 187v (fig.74). The two loops of the β are tilted up, while the stem remains vertical, and the resulting cursive letter is quite different from the fine tenth-century hand of the text. The β is uncial, though a minuscule is normally used in the tenth century, unless it is found in a title or text, written in uncials.[3] Its round shape with the enlarged upper lobe, the crossbar at a diagonal, and the long stem resemble the β's in Vienna, Nat. Lib. Hist. gr. 125, f. 156r, assigned by Hunger to c. 1300, or those in Vienna, Nat. Lib. Suppl. gr. 91 (fig. 76).[4] Also comparable are the long, sharply bent tails to the letters α (fig. 75) and δ [5] in the Gospel book, and examples of such forms are also found in the Vienna manuscript. Both Viennese manuscripts are written in what Hunger terms the *Fettaugenstil*,[6] a mode of writing that appears in the second half of the thirteenth century and the first decade of the fourteenth century. This should be the date, then, of the letters and the symbols in the Stavronikita Gospels.

Yet one problem remains: Why were the medallions added at all? A partial solution is suggested by the position of the symbols in the manuscript. As stated before, each roundel is associated with groups of dots in the text (fig. 73), and thus the symbols function as some sort of marginal indicator of certain passages. Because of the dots, the precise texts so marked can be determined. Of the fifteen symbols in the book, twelve appear at the beginning of a Eusebian section of a Gospel. The three exceptions are from the Gospel of John. The symbols, then, come mostly at major divisions of the text, but the problem is that no pattern emerges from the places cited, because the passages marked have no common denominator. They do not pertain to a central theme, nor are they the readings for major feast days of the church.

Thus, although the added symbols do seem to serve as a type of marginal

notation, the rationale of their placement in the manuscript has yet to be discovered. The symbols have not been accurately described in any catalogue, and thus it seems useful in conclusion to note their locations in the Gospel text, their numbers, and their position on the page. Perhaps with this information someone may be able to discover the reason for their appearance in the manuscript.
Gospel of Matthew. Symbol of man.

f. 33r. In exterior margin; labeled α; section ξα; Matt. 7:24; symbol overlaps the text.

f. 48r. Between two columns; fig. 74, labeled β; faces inner column and Matt. 13:1; section ρλα; symbol covers up parts of some letters.

f. 67v. In exterior margin; labeled Γ; Matt. 19:16; sectionρζγ; chapter μα.

f. 82v. Between two columns; Matt. 24:36; section σξ; chapter νη; symbol covers up Eusebian section number and text initial.

Gospel of Mark. Symbol of eagle.

f. 111v. In exterior margin; labeled α; Mark 5:21; section μθ; fig. 76.

f. 122v. In exterior margin; labeled β; Mark 8:34; section πε in the inner column. There is no room for the symbol between columns because of an initial and section number. The symbol refers to the inner column, where the four dots are.

f. 137r. In exterior margin; labeled Γ; Mark 13:1; section ρλζ.

Gospel of Luke. Symbol of Calf.

f. 171v. In exterior margin; labeled α; Luke 6:17; section με. These passages are in the inner column, where the four dots are.

f. 187v. In exterior margin; labeled β; Luke 10:1; section ρζ; chapter λδ; fig. 75.

f. 205r. In exterior margin; labeled Γ; Luke 15:1; section ρπϛ.

f. 219r. In exterior margin; labeled δ; Luke 20:9; section σμα. These passages are in the inner column, where the four dots are.

Gospel of John. Symbol of lion.

f. 247v. In exterior margin; labeled α; John 4:43; section λδ.

f. 257r. In exterior margin; labeled β. The passage in the inner column begins after four dots and is John 7:14. Not a sectional division.

f. 267r. In exterior margin; labeled Γ. The passage after the four dots is John 10:17. Not a sectional division.

f. 277v. In exterior margin; labeled δ. The passage after the four dots in the inner column is John 13:31. Not a sectional division.

NOTES

1. Weitzmann, *Byzantinische Buchmalerei,* 23–24, figs. 169–78. Professor Weitzmann very graciously provided me with illustrations from the manuscript.

2. Vikan, *Illuminated Greek MSS,* 144; C. Nordenfalk, "An Illustrated Diatessaron," *ArtB,* 50 (1968), 133; Nilgen, "Evangelistensymbole," col. 527.

3. Ernest Colwell ("A Chronology for the Letters E, H, Λ, Π in the Byzantine Minuscule Book Hand," *Studies in Methodology in Textual Criticism of the New Testament* [Grand Rapids, Mich., 1969], 125–41) tried to study the progressive use of uncial forms in minuscule manuscripts as a dating criterion. The general idea is that minuscule manuscripts of the ninth or tenth century have few or no uncial letters, but the number of uncials increases in later centuries. Unfortunately, he does not consider any letter used with the symbols. Hunger (*Geschichte,* 95) mentions the penetration of uncial letters in the tenth century. It must be noted that uncial B is one of these letters that begins to be found in minuscule texts of the tenth century, so that its appearance in the Stavronikita Gospels does not absolutely rule out a tenth-century date.

4. Hunger, *Geschichte,* 100–101; H. Hunger, "Die sogennante Fettaugen-Mode in Griechischen Handschriften des 13. und 14. Jahrhunderts," *ByzF,* 50 (1972), 110, fig. 2.

5. Nordenfalk, *ArtB,* (1968), fig. 16b.

6. For the term: Hunger, *Geschichte,* 101–2. For a more precise dating of the style; Hunger, "Fettaugen-Mode," 109–13.

Appendix III

The Contents of Oxford, Bodl. Lib. E. D. Clarke 10, and Parma, Bibl. Palat. 5.

E. D. Clarke 10	Palat. 5
f. 1r headpiece of Eusebius and Carpianus	f. 3r headpiece of Eusebius and Carpianus
ff. 1r–2r letter of Eusebius to Carpianus	ff. 3r–4v letter of Eusebius to Carpianus
f. 2v *Maiestas domini*	f. 5r *Maiestas domini*
ff. 2v–3r prefaces: von Soden, no. 108 (Matthew); no. 82, no. 108 (Mark, Luke, and John)	ff. 5r–6r prefaces: von Soden, no. 108 (Matthew); no. 82, no. 108 (Luke and John—Mark has been cut out)
ff. 3v–4v chapter lists for Matthew	ff. 6v–7v chapter lists for Matthew

119

E. D. Clarke 10

Palat. 5

ff. 4v–5r definitions of words in Matthew by later hand

ff. 5v–10r canon tables

ff. 8r–12r canon tables
f. 12v miniature of Eusebius, Carpianus, and Ammonius
f. 13r miniature of Nativity and Constantine and Helena

f. 10v portrait of Matthew

f. 13v portrait of Matthew

f. 11r headpiece with Flight to Egypt

f. 14r headpiece with Flight to Egypt

ff. 11r–49v Gospel of Matthew

ff. 14r–89v Gospel of Matthew

ff. 50r–v chapter lists for Mark

ff. 90r–91r chapter lists for Mark

ff. 50v preface to Mark (von Soden, no. 108), definitions of words in Mark by a later hand

ff. 91v–92v three pages of Gospel scenes.

f. 51r blank

f. 93v blank

f. 51v portrait of Mark

f. 93v portrait of Mark

f. 52r headpiece of John the Baptist preaching and pointing to a tree with an ax in it

f. 94r John the Baptist baptizing the people

ff. 52r–75r Gospel of Mark

ff. 94r–135v Gospel of Mark

ff. 75v–76v chapter lists for Luke

ff. 136r–137v chapter lists for Luke, preface to Luke (von Soden, no. 108)

ff. 76v–77r definitions of words in Luke by later hand

f. 138r blank

f. 77v portrait of Luke

f. 138v portrait of Luke

f. 78r headpiece of Birth of John the Baptist

f. 139r headpiece of Birth of John the Baptist

ff. 78r–122v Gospel of Luke

ff. 139r–213v Gospel of Luke

f. 122v definitions of words in John by later hand

E. D. Clarke 10

f. 123r chapter lists for John, preface to John (von Soden, no. 108)

f. 123v portrait of John

f. 124r headpiece of Anastasis

ff. 124r–158r Gospel of John

f. 158v blank

ff. 159r–167r Synaxarium and Menologium

Palat. 5

ff. 214r–v chapter lists for John, preface to John (von Soden, no. 108)

f. 215r blank

f. 215v portrait of John

f. 216r head piece of Anastasis

ff. 216r–270r Gospel of John

ff. 270v–285v Synaxarium and Menologium

Illustrations

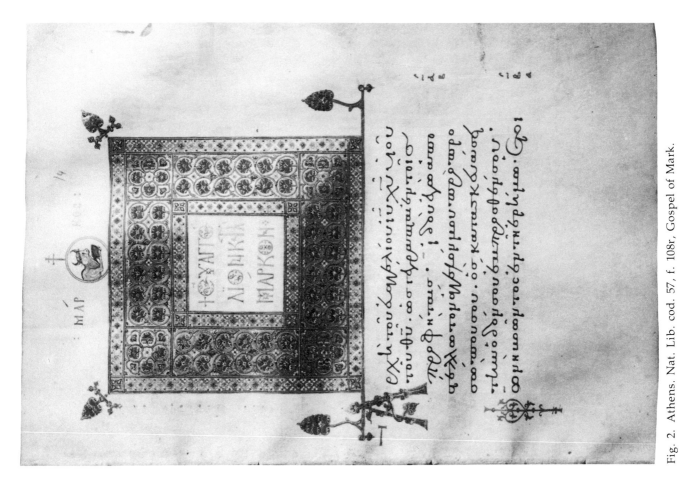

Fig. 2. Athens. Nat. Lib. cod. 57, f. 108r, Gospel of Mark.

Fig. 1. Athens. Nat. Lib. cod. 57, f. 107v, Mark.

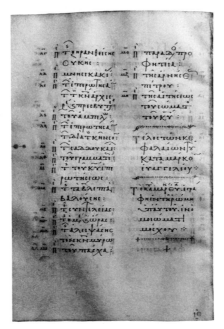

Fig. 3. Athens. Nat. Lib. cod. 57, f. 106v.

Fig. 4. Holkham Hall. Coll. Earl of Leicester, cod. 4, f. 280v, John and Prochoros.

Fig. 5. Tbilisi. MSS Institute of the Academy of Sciences, MS No. A908. Ghelati Gospels, Luke.

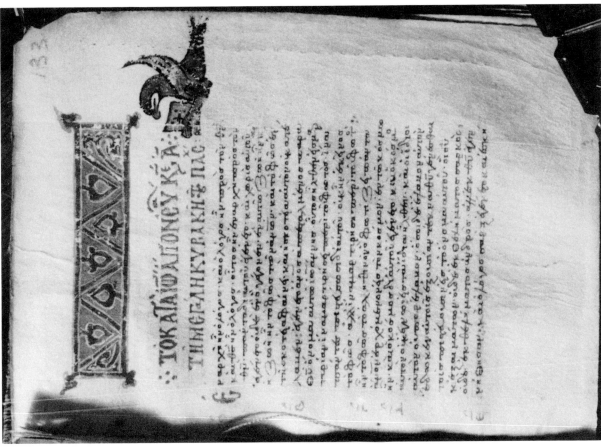

Fig. 7. Athens. Gennadeion Lib. MS 1.5, f. 133r, Gospel of John.

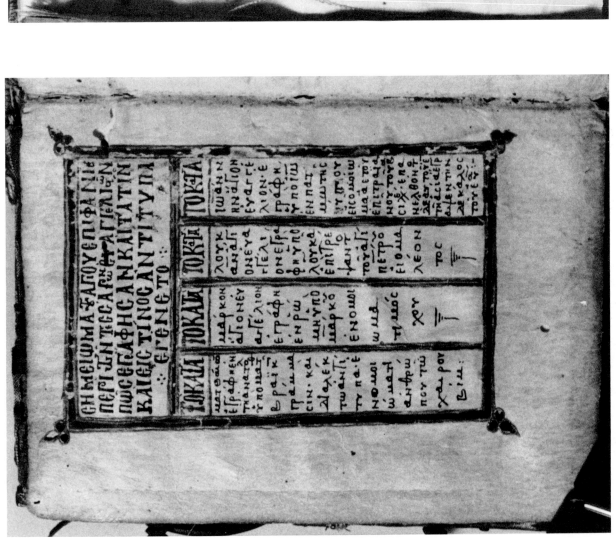

Fig. 6. Athens. Gennadeion Lib. MS 1.5, f. 1v.

Fig. 9. Geneva. Bibl. publ. et univ. cod. gr. 19, f. 382v, John and Prochoros.

Fig. 8. Moscow. Hist. Mus. gr. 14 (519), f. llv, Matthew.

Fig. 11. Bratislava. Lycaeum Augustanum, Gospel book, p. 192, Mark.

Fig. 10. Bratislava. Lycaeum Augustanum, Gospel book, p. 52, Matthew.

Fig. 13. Bratislava. Lycaeum Augustanum, Gospel book, p. 443, John.

Fig. 12. Bratislava. Lycaeum Augustanum, Gospel book, p. 282, Luke.

Fig. 14. Bratislava. Lycaeum Augustanum, Gospel book, p. 560.

Fig. 15. Basel. Universitätsbibl. MS A.N. IV.2, f. 265v, John and Prochoros.

Fig. 16. Oxford. Bodl. Lib. Auct. T. inf. 1.3, f. 153r, Gospel of John.

Fig. 17. Rome. Bibl. Vat. gr. 1522, f. 197r.

Fig. 19. Istanbul. Ecumenical Patriarchate cod. 3, f. 196v, Symbol of John.

Fig. 18. Istanbul. Ecumenical Patriarchate cod. 3, f. 83r, Symbol of Mark.

Fig. 20. Rome. Bibl. Vat. gr. 2138, f. 35r,
Symbol of Mark.

Fig. 21. Athens. Nat. Lib. cod. 2251, f. 149r, Symbol of
John.

Fig. 22. Mt. Athos. Dochiariou cod. 52, f. 108r, Symbol
of Luke.

Fig. 23. Washington, Freer Gallery of Art, No.
09.1685, f. Ir, Mark.

Fig. 24. Sofia. National Museum, Poganovo icon,
Maiestas Domini.

Fig. 25. Thessaloniki. Hosios David. *Maiestas Domini*.

Fig. 26. Megaspelaion, cod. 1, f. 18v,
Matthew.

Fig. 27. Megaspelaion, cod. 1, f. 147v,
Mark.

Fig. 28. Megaspelaion, cod. 1, f. 228v,
Luke.

Fig. 29. Megaspelaion, cod. 1, f. 357v,
John.

Fig. 30. Dublin. Chester Beatty Lib. W135, Matthew.

Fig. 31. Dublin. Chester Beatty Lib. W135, Mark.

Fig. 32. Dublin. Chester Beatty Lib. W135, Luke.

Fig. 33. Dublin. Chester Beatty Lib. W135, John.

Fig. 34. Oxford. Bodl. Lib. E. D. Clarke 10, f. 2v, Prefaces of Irenaeus.

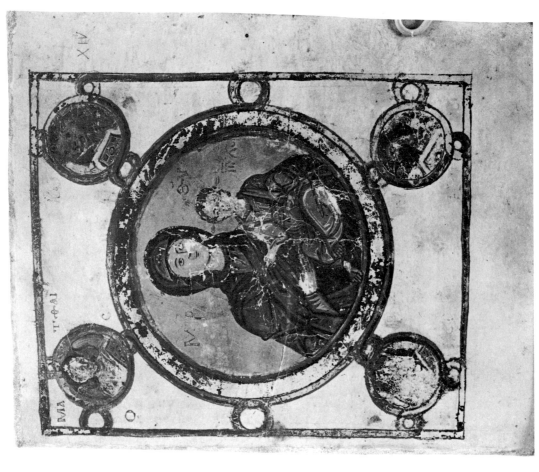

Fig. 36. Brescia. Bibl. Civica Queriniana A.VI.26, f. XIVr, Virgin and Child with evangelist symbols.

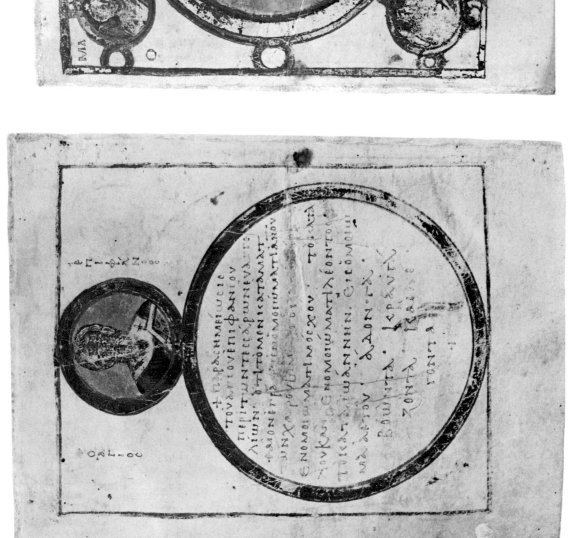

Fig. 35. Brescia. Bibl. Civica Queriniana A.VI.26, f. XIIIv, St. Epiphanios.

Fig. 37. Brescia. Bibl. Civica Queriniana A.VI.26, f.
XIVv, Matthew.

Fig. 38. Mt. Sinai. cod. 178, f. 6v, *Maiestas Domini.*

Fig. 39. Paris. Bibl. Nat. gr. 81, f. 7v,
Maiestas Domini.

Fig. 41. Chicago. University of Chicago Library, MS 131, f. 12r, *Maiestas Domini.*

Fig. 40. Leningrad. Publ. Lib. gr. 101, f. 10v, Matthew with *Maiestas Domini.*

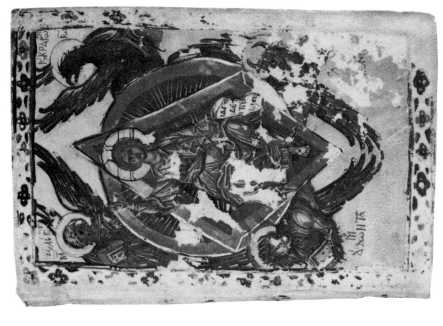

Fig. 43. Rome. Bibl. Vat. gr. 1210, f. 324r, *Maiestas Domini*.

Fig. 42. Venice. Bibl. Marc. gr. Z 540, f. 11v, *Maiestas Domini*.

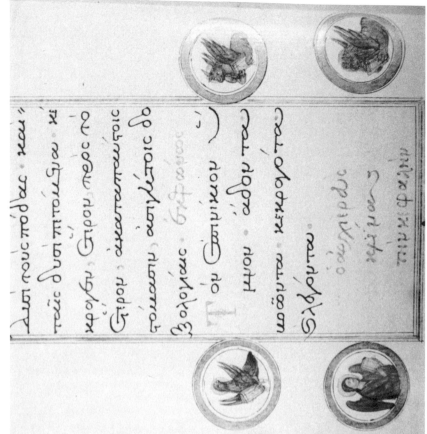

Fig. 45. Mt. Athos. Iviron cod. 1438, Four evangelist symbols.

Fig. 44. Moscow. Hist. Mus. Eparch. 436, f. 1v, *Maiestas Domini*.

Fig. 47. Florence. Bibl. Laur. Plut. VI.32, f. 8r, *Maiestas Domini*. (Upper inscription fully preserved in the original miniature.)

Fig. 46. Florence. Bibl. Laur. Plut. VI.32, f. 7v, Moses receiving the law.

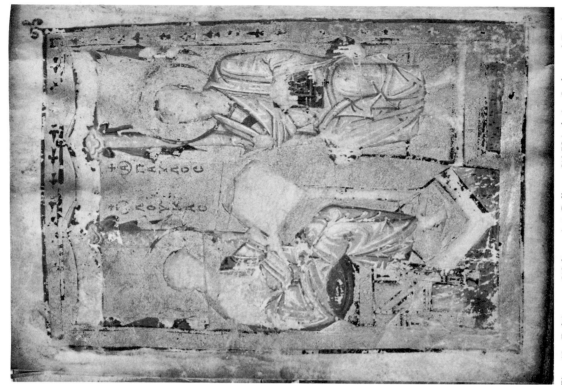

Fig. 49. Baltimore. Walters Art Gallery, W.524, f. 6v, Luke and Paul.

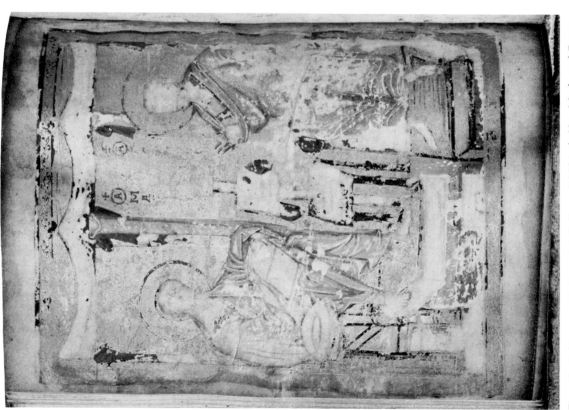

Fig. 48. Baltimore. Walters Art Gallery, W.524, f. 89v, Mark and Peter.

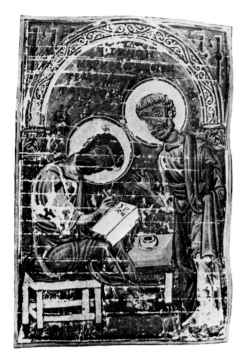

Fig. 50. Jerusalem. Greek Patriarchal Library, Τάφου 56, f. 68v, Mark and Peter.

Fig. 51. Jerusalem. Greek Patriarchal Library, Τάφου 56, f. 105v, Luke and Paul.

Fig. 52. Paris. Bibl. Nat. gr. 81, f. 95v, Peter.

Fig. 53. Paris. Bibl. Nat. gr. 81, f. 96r, Mark.

Fig. 54. Leningrad. Publ. Lib. gr. 101, f. 50v, Mark and Peter.

Fig. 55. Leningrad. Publ. Lib. gr. 101, f. 76v, Luke and Paul.

Fig. 56. Athens. Nat. Lib. cod. 151, f. 88v, Mark and Peter.

Fig. 57. Mt. Athos. Lavra cod. A7, f. 161v, Luke
and Paul.

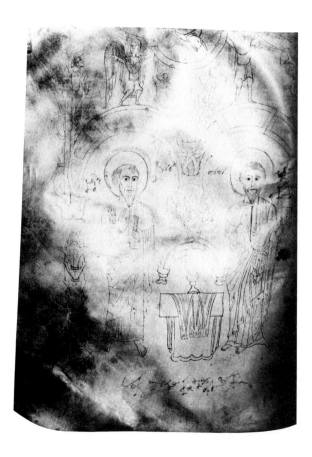

Fig. 58. Mt. Athos. Lavra cod. A104, f. 89v, Luke and
Paul.

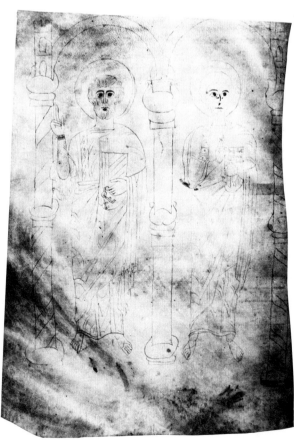

Fig. 59. Mt. Athos. Lavra cod. A104, f. 133v, John and
Peter.

Fig. 61. Mt. Athos. Koutloumousiou cod. 61, f. 112v, Mark and Peter.

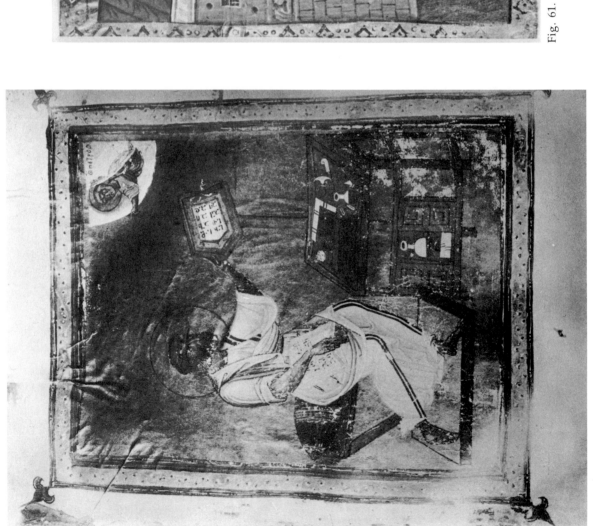

Fig. 60. Tbilisi. MSS Institute of the Academy of Sciences. MS No. A 484, f. 101v, Mark and Peter.

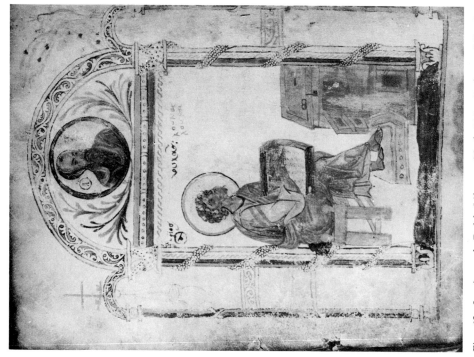

Fig. 63. Leningrad. Publ. Lib. gr. 98, f. 111v, Luke and Paul.

Fig. 62. Leningrad. Publ. Lib. gr. 98, f. 179v, John and Christ.

Fig. 65. Florence. Bibl. Laur. Plut. VI. 18, f. 139v, Luke.

Fig. 64. Florence. Bibl. Laur. Plut. VI. 18, f. 212v, John and Christ.

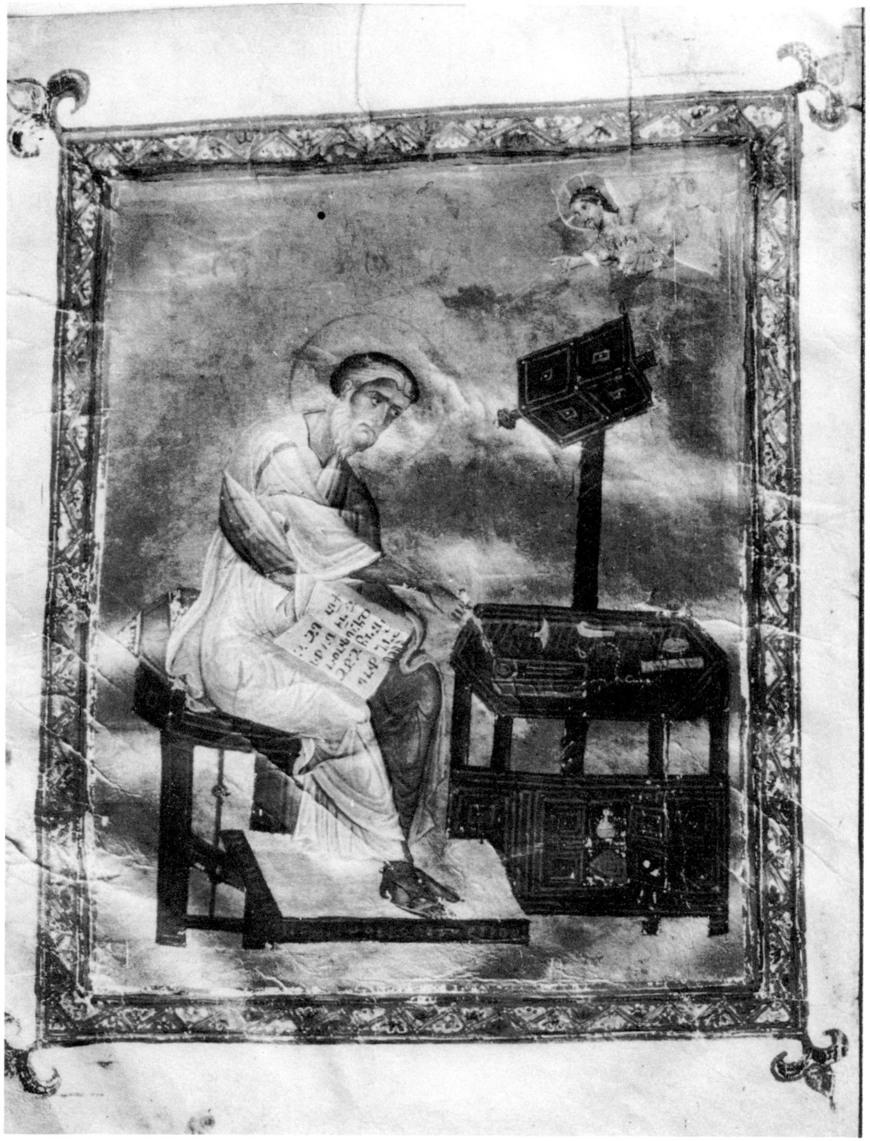

Fig. 67. Mt. Athos. Lavra cod. A7, f. 13v, Matthew and accompanying figure.

Fig. 66. Tbilisi. MSS Institute of the Academy of Sciences, MS No. A 484, f. 14v, Matthew and Christ.

Fig. 69. New York. Pierpont Morgan Library M748, f. 8v, Matthew and accompanying figure.

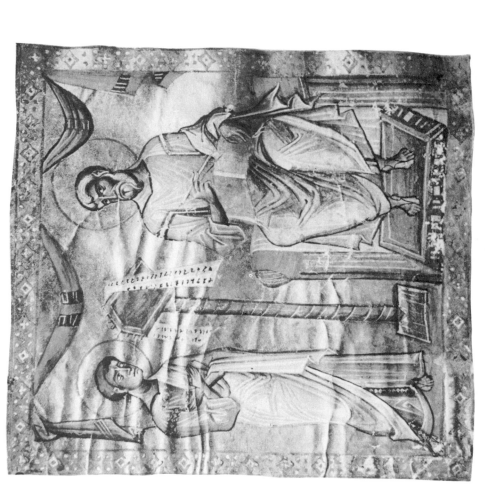

Fig. 68. Mt. Athos. Koutloumousiou cod. 61, f. 50v, Matthew and accompanying figure.

Fig. 71. Naples. Bibl. Naz. Suppl. gr. 6, f. 316v, John and Prochoros.

Fig. 70. Rome. Vat. Copt. 9, f. 388v, John and the Virgin Mary.

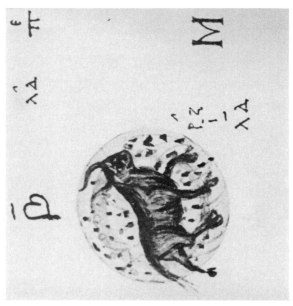

Fig. 73. Mt. Athos. Stavronikita cod. 43, f. 48v, Symbol of Matthew.

Fig. 74. Mt. Athos. Stavronikita cod. 43, f. 187v, Symbol of Luke.

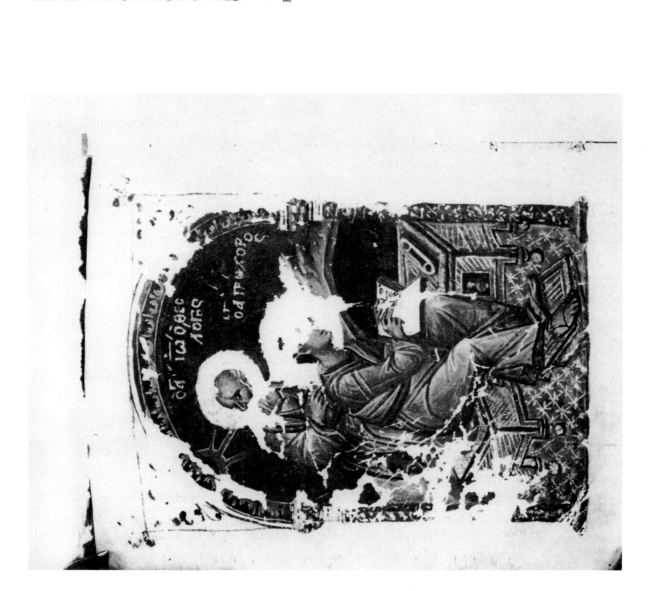

Fig. 72. Athens. Nat. Lib. cod. 151, f. 233v, John and Prochoros.

Fig. 76. Vienna, Nat. Lib. Suppl. gr. 91, f. 301r.

Fig. 75. Mt. Athos. Stavronikita cod. 43, f. 111v, Symbol of Mark.

Index

LIST OF MANUSCRIPTS